POINT OF ADORATION

POINT OF ADORATION

THE STORY OF THE SHRINE OF BAHÁ'U'LLÁH 1873–1892

By
Michael V. Day

BAHÁ'Í PUBLISHING
EVANSTON, ILLINOIS

Bahá'í Publishing
1233 Central St., Evanston, Illinois 60201

Printed in the United States of America on acid-free paper ∞

26 25 24 23 4 3 2 1

Cover design by Carlos Esparza
Book design by Patrick Falso
Photograph on front cover of Shrine of Bahá'u'lláh © Farzam Sabetian, https://www.luminouspot.com/

ISBN 978-1-61851-229-1

Library of Congress Control Number: 2023016604

"When ye desire to perform this [obligatory] prayer,
turn ye towards the Court of My Most Holy Presence,
this Hallowed Spot that God hath made the Center
round which circle the Concourse on High,
and which He hath decreed to be the Point of Adoration
for the denizens of the Cities of Eternity . . ."

—Bahá'u'lláh

Contents

Acknowledgments

After informing the Universal House of Justice of my intention to write a history of the Shrine of Bahá'u'lláh, I received guidance from the Supreme Body as well as this most welcome and needed reassurance: *"Rest assured of the prayers of the House of Justice at the Sacred Threshold that the Ancient Beauty may guide and confirm your devoted efforts in service to His Cause."*

I also appreciated the permission given to me by the Universal House of Justice to stay in the Holy Land for extra days to do research after attending the event commemorating the bicentenary of the birth of the Báb. My gratitude also resides in the fact that requests to the Universal House of Justice relating to my research resulted in valuable information coming to me via the Research Department staff.

In 2015, I asked the late Mr. Alí Nakhjavání questions relating to the history of the shrine. He answered in his usual loving, comprehensive, and swift manner. May his luminous soul be ever blessed by the Ancient Beauty. Writing about such a sacred subject is daunting. I thank my colleague Fuad Izadinia for his unwavering, wise, and prompt support and advice. I also appreciate the assistance given by his brother, the esteemed scholar Mr. Faruq Izadinia. Dr. Marjorie Tidman and Mr. Fuad Izadinia read my manuscript and gave advice before submission to the publisher. I appreciate their precious and selfless service to my work. Although due to protocols I could not cross-examine Bahá'í World Centre staff about what they had learned about the Shrine of Bahá'u'lláh during their service, I did appreciate receiving emotional and spiritual support for my project from Dr. Rostam Beheshti and Mr. Kamran Yazdani.

While visiting the Mansion and surrounds, my wife, Chris, and I were lovingly accompanied by the custodian, Mr. Farshid Sana'i. Gardens historian Andrew Blake provided me with a key map and valuable information, continuing the generous assistance that he has given me over the years. During my research I called upon the distinguished author Baharieh Ma'ani for information. I received just what I needed and more. While researching the life of Edward Granville Browne, I called upon the assistance of retired lecturer in Persian History at Oxford University, Dr. John Gurney. His insight from a researcher's point of view and from outside the Bahá'í community was of immense help to me in straightening out my understanding of the intriguing character who was drawn into the presence of Bahá'u'lláh.

Precious information about one of Bahá'u'lláh's doctors, Dr. Khálid Jarráḥ, came to me from one of his descendants, Abdul Jarrah, who by happy coincidence happened to be in the same community as me. I am very grateful to Muna Waters of Tasmania for her translations into English of tributes in Arabic to Bahá'u'lláh. Her beautiful work makes a considerable contribution to our understanding of the high regard in which the Manifestation was held by many outside the Bahá'í community of that time.

The artistry of William McBride has once again graced my work. His maps are beautiful as well as being clear and informative. From the United States Bahá'í National Office, Archivist Edward Sevcik and graphic artist Richard Doering assisted me in my requests for photographs. I appreciate the warm welcome and ongoing encouragement by Nat Yogachandra, the General Manager of the US Bahá'í Publishing Trust. I hope that publishing in the United States will also help to bring extra attention in North America to my trilogy about the Shrine of the Báb, which was expertly published (2017–2019) by the team at George Ronald. I have been very happy working with the editor of this volume, Bahhaj Taherzadeh, and with Christopher Martin his colleague. I am grateful to Carlos Esparza for his beautiful cover design and to Patrick Falso for his excellent book design.

I am also grateful to Jonah Winters of the Bahá'í Library Online for his priceless website, and to all those who have helped him. Nasser Kaviani, a friend of more than four decades, has been an ardent promoter of my books, for which I thank him. Among others who supported me in this project were: Daniel Caillaud, the late Dr. Edward Broomhall, Dr. Boris Handal, Josephine Hill, Kathryn Jewett Hogenson, Dr. Foad Khademi, Dr. Janet Khan, Farideh and Dr. Michael Knopf, Naysan Naraqi, Dr. Steven Phelps, Sir Bruce Saunders, Lady Keithie Saunders, J. Peter Smith, Paul Toloui-Wallace, Sonjel Vreeland, Wendy Wisniewski. I also thank my late parents, Noel and Win Day, for my upbringing.

Thank you, too, to the Gold Coast Bahá'í Seniors group, who invited me to present to them on an aspect of this project and who gave me such emotional and positive feedback, and to Sitarih Ala'i for her hospitality for that meeting and others. This book was written in testing times. I will be forever grateful for the care my dear friend Ruhy Soraya gave to me as I walked through the fire.

Once again, my wife, Dr. Chris Day, to whom I am so grateful, supported me financially during the years when I was deep in the middle of piles of books and papers, let alone websites and emails. During this time, we experienced the gift of grandchildren, Max and Brodie. Both of us had first visited the Shrine of Bahá'u'lláh as pilgrims in 1980 and then many times while serving at the Bahá'í World Center (2003–2006). When we returned for a short visit after thirteen years away, the experience was just as fresh, just as inspiring. My prayerbook stayed on my lap as I bathed in the peace.

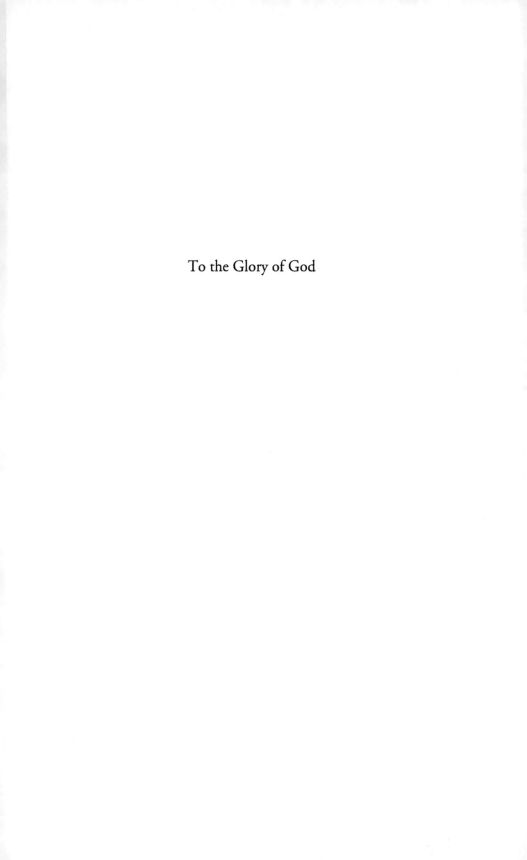

To the Glory of God

Prologue

BAHÁ'U'LLÁH, THE GLORY OF GOD, 1817–1892[1]

In 1992, the centenary year of the ascension of Bahá'u'lláh and the inauguration of His shrine, the Universal House of Justice distributed a brief introduction to His life and work. The first page of that publication includes a concise answer to a question that is often asked: "Who is Bahá'u'lláh?"[2]

> . . . Bahá'u'lláh claimed to be no less than the Messenger of God to the age of human maturity, the Bearer of a Divine Revelation that fulfills the promises made in earlier religions, and that will generate the spiritual nerves and sinews for the unification of the peoples of the world.[3]

Further into the publication, the text explains the role of the Messenger of God, Who is known as a Manifestation of God, one Who "manifests" the attributes of God but is not God. Referring to God, Bahá'u'lláh writes: "From time immemorial He, the Divine Being, hath been veiled in the ineffable sanctity of His exalted Self, and will everlasting continue to be wrapt in the impenetrable mystery of His unknowable Essence."[4]

Describing His own role and that of the other Founders of the world's great religions, Bahá'u'lláh says:

> The door of the knowledge of the Ancient of Days being thus closed in the face of all beings, He, the Source of infinite grace . . . hath caused those luminous Gems of Holiness to appear out of the realm of the spirit, in the noble form of the human temple, and be made manifest unto all men, that they may impart unto the world the mysteries of the unchangeable Being and tell of the subtleties of His imperishable Essence.[5]

The 1992 publication says Bahá'u'lláh asserts that "the human personality which the Manifestation of God shares with the rest of the race is differentiated from others in a way that fits it to serve as the channel or vehicle for the Revelation of God. Apparently contradictory references to this dual station, attributed, for example, to Christ, have been among the many sources of religious confusion and dissension throughout history."[6]

The publication goes on to quote Bahá'u'lláh on the subject, including this excerpt:

> These Manifestations of God have each a twofold station. One is the station of pure abstraction and essential unity. In this respect, if thou callest them all by one name, and dost ascribe to them the same attributes, thou hast not erred from the truth. . . .
>
> The other station is the station of distinction, and pertaineth to the world of creation, and to the limitations thereof. In this respect, each Manifestation of God hath a distinct individuality, a definitely prescribed mission, each one of them is known by a different name, is characterized by a special attribute, fulfils a definite mission.[7]

NEVER-ENDING DISCOVERIES

The common experience of those who study Bahá'u'lláh's life and writings is that there are never-ending discoveries to be made about Him, but no finality, no feeling that our minds have totally encompassed Him, His role, His insights, His teachings. The eminent

Bahá'í writer Marzieh Gail (1908–93) described this experience with an analogy: "Above all peaks, there is another peak."[8]

She observed with awe: "Most books bring you closer to the author. But when you study the work of Bahá'u'lláh, He eludes you." Her experience is confirmation of the analysis made by Shoghi Effendi,[9] who wrote that an exact and thorough comprehension of His "stupendous Revelation" was "beyond the reach and ken of our finite minds." He wrote in 1934 that Bahá'u'lláh is: "transcendental in His majesty, serene, awe-inspiring, unapproachably glorious."[10] Ten years later, He reinforced that statement when he wrote of "the august figure of Bahá'u'lláh, preeminent in holiness, awesome in the majesty of His strength and power, unapproachable in the transcendent brightness of His glory."[11]

Rather than a discouragement, this is an incentive to ponder His writings, to study His life (including His ascension), and to visit His shrine so that we can have that sweet, inspiring enjoyment of continually developing our understandings of Bahá'u'lláh.[12]

In His authoritative work, *Some Answered Questions,* 'Abdu'l-Bahá—the eldest son of Bahá'u'lláh, and the one appointed by Him to succeed Him as head of the Bahá'í Faith and as the interpreter of His word—describes the time when Bahá'u'lláh arrived in the land that was to witness His greatest work, His ascension, and the establishment of His shrine, His burial place:

> When Bahá'u'lláh arrived at this prison in the Holy Land, discerning souls were awakened to the fact that the prophecies which God had voiced through the tongue of His Prophets two or three thousand years before had been realized and that His promises had been fulfilled, for He had revealed unto certain Prophets and announced unto the Holy Land that the Lord of Hosts would be manifested therein.[13]

PART 1

THE ROAD TO BAHJÍ

1

Attaining the Sacred Threshold

Drawn as if by a magnet, modern-day pilgrims proceed slowly along the path toward the sanctuary that surrounds the Shrine of Bahá'u'lláh. Just minutes ago, they were conversing in the comforting, well-lit precinct of the Visitors Center at Bahjí. Now they are quiet, embraced by darkness. It is the early hours of the morning, ahead of the commemoration at 3:00 am of the ascension of Bahá'u'lláh, which occurred on 29 May 1892. The dark shapes of trees line the pathway like silent, spiritual sentinels.

The pilgrims adopt appropriate postures of reverence as they move along. Underfoot, the shuffling pebbles seem to click a rhythmic welcome. The night insects sound their anthems. Eventually, the illuminated Mansion of Bahjí appears in all its grandeur, reminding mere mortals that a Manifestation of God once lived here. The Collins gate, the entry to the holy precincts, is open, encouraging attentive ones to notice the fine filigree features of the arch towering above. In an instant, eyes swivel to the dignified yet humble shrine ahead and to their right. This is the sacred spot to which their hearts, minds, and souls have turned every day in their far-off countries as they recited their daily obligatory prayers. There is a collective intake of breath, and an occasional tear.

To the immediate left of the shrine, a glass clerestory under a high, tiled roof signals the presence of a large well-lit room below, the outer shrine. A tent-shaped portico, the entrance, moves into focus. The familiar calligraphic symbol of the Greatest Name above it is centered in a golden star, but its nineteen points are too far away to count. This is not the occasion to approach. The pilgrims turn right and take their seats in front of the tall candle-like cypress pines that suggest part of a circle some 200 meters or more from the shrine. Exquisite chanting and prayers begin the simple program that concludes with a silent circumambulation of the shrine. The pilgrims then return to Haifa as the first rays of the sun herald a new dawn. They are perhaps not as fortunate as those in earlier years who spent the rest of the night in the mansion.[1]

On the next afternoon, the pilgrims return with the mission to pray at the threshold of the shrine. This time the colors of late spring are on display—emerald green lawns and the reddest of flowers. The full glory of the trees seems to attract the birds, and the air is full of their music. As the pilgrims approach, some glance at the shoulder-high sculptures on pedestals that flank the pathway from the gate to the portico. One stone cherub has a finger to the lips as if issuing a gentle reminder to shush. A smiling guide, standing beside a low gilded gate, gestures to a collection of prayer books and a place to discard footwear. With lightened feet the pilgrims move slowly toward the steps, some noticing the peacock sculptures. The lamps and a chandelier above remind them of the golden glory of the night before.

The big golden-brown wooden door, inlaid with ornate rosettes, opens with an easy push, allowing the pilgrims to progress along carpets of a woven flower design. Light from the windows high above gives a shine to the surprisingly delicate green fronds of an indoor garden. The first pilgrim pauses, and then turns right. There, only a few meters ahead, is the object of the quest, the destination dreamed of—the inner shrine. With rising emotion, one after the other, the pilgrims advance, step by slow step, along the sacred corridor that was graced often by the feet of 'Abdu'l-Bahá and Shoghi Effendi.

In a deeply personal moment, each pilgrim halts at the doorway, which is robed with a golden curtain and veiled with a transparent screen that allows a view into the sacred sanctuary. The eyes take in ornaments, flowers, and a special carpet above the resting place. Then they kneel with brow lowered in humble adoration on the carpeted threshold, bedecked with petals, all aware of the nearby presence of the sacred remains of God's Manifestation for this day. Some no doubt recall the words once uttered by Bahá'u'lláh: "Praise be to God that thou hast attained!"[2] Many will have read the following guidance given by 'Abdu'l-Bahá: "Render thanks unto God that thou didst come to the Blessed Spot, didst lay thy head upon the Threshold of the Sacred Shrine, and didst make pilgrimage to the hallowed sanctuary round which circle in adoration the intimates of the spiritual realm."[3]

As many pilgrims would know, the Shrine of Bahá'u'lláh was established on the very day of His ascension. But what of the spiritual foundations for this shrine? On their pilgrimage, these Bahá'ís will visit the location where spiritual foundations were laid. It happens on their visit to the House of 'Abbúd, located near the sea wall in the port city of Acre[4] (known to Bahá'ís as 'Akká) not far from Bahjí. The pilgrims enter the house, cross a reception area, climb the flights of stairs to the upper story and then enter a room at the rear. In that spartan room, one of the most historic and important events in the history of the Bahá'í Faith took place—the revelation of Bahá'u'lláh's most important book, the Kitáb-i-Aqdas, the Book of Laws. Among other outcomes of that event, the arrival of that book, was its provision of spiritual foundations for the establishment and role of the Shrine of Bahá'u'lláh. The Revelation of the Kitáb-i-Aqdas can also be viewed as the start of the process of two decades of vigorous and profound activity by the Manifestation that was to reach its climax in His ascension and His dramatic funeral.

That story will now be told.

Bahjí in current times.

2

Scripture of Supreme Importance to the Shrine

It was in a small, barely furnished room in the bleak stone city of 'Akká that the spiritual foundations were laid for the Shrine of Bahá'u'lláh. In 1873,[1] in that upstairs room, at the back of a two-story building now known as the House of 'Abbúd, Bahá'u'lláh completed the revelation of the Kitáb-i-Aqdas, "the Most Holy Book," the crown jewel in the scriptural treasury of the Bahá'í Faith.[2]

One historian described the location as "a small room unfit to be a dwelling . . . devoid of all the luxuries of life and not even properly furnished."[3] The room offered no view of the sea just a few hundred meters away, nor was there any greenery in sight. Instead, it overlooked a square that was often noisy.[4] The contrast between the physical environment and the beautiful and world-shaking emanations from Bahá'u'lláh could hardly have been starker.

It had been in September 1871 that Bahá'u'lláh and His family moved into their new home, which was owned by an affluent merchant, 'Údí Khammár—one of the patrons of a Greek Orthodox Church in 'Akká. There were about 1,775 Greek Orthodox parishioners in the mostly Muslim city at the time.[5] 'Údí Khammár had leased to 'Abdu'l-Bahá the house, which was at the rear of, and directly connected to, the House of 'Abbúd, owned by another Greek Orthodox merchant, Ilyás 'Abbúd. Enjoying a good income from grains and other foodstuffs, 'Údí Khammár could afford to move out to his recently obtained and renovated mansion in the countryside, a couple of kilometers from the city walls—a building now known to the world as the Mansion of Bahjí.

Back in 'Akká, the conditions in the leased house were almost unbearably cramped for the thirteen people in the family group, who for a while had to cram into one room. Even when slightly more space became available, there was not enough room for a married couple to live in privacy. What made things even more unpleasant was that a few months after they moved in, their neighbor at the front of the building, Ilyás 'Abbúd, put up a barrier because he feared that the Bahá'ís might trespass.

To make matters worse, Bahá'u'lláh's enemies and former supporters were continuing their iniquitous attacks upon Him. The authorities were hostile, and some Bahá'ís did not follow Bahá'u'lláh's directions. Illustrating those attacks, more than a year earlier in the House of 'Údí Khammár, Bahá'u'lláh revealed a great Tablet of lament, now recited regularly and with fervor by Bahá'ís worldwide. It was revealed in exquisite rhyming Arabic,[6] and is known to the Persians as Lawḥ-i-Qad-Iḥtaráqa'l-Mukhliṣún, and to English speakers as the Fire Tablet.[7]

The Tablet proclaims that "Bahá is drowning in a sea of tribulation," and that "the branches of the Divine Lote-Tree[8] lie broken by the onrushing gales of destiny." Toward the end of the Fire Tablet Bahá'u'lláh reveals how God refers to His Messenger as the "Wronged One of the worlds," and comforts Him with a range of reassurances.[9] He responds: ". . . now is the face of Bahá flaming with the heat of tribulation and with the fire of Thy shining word, and He hath risen up in faithfulness at the place of sacrifice, looking toward Thy pleasure, O Ordainer of the worlds."[10] Not long afterwards, He revealed the mighty Kitáb-i-Aqdas.

There has been no description of the process yet found so the question has yet to be answered as to whether Bahá'u'lláh paced the floor and whether He spoke at considerable volume as was His practice at times when revealing scripture. The room was small and family were usually nearby, so were there any constraints on the method of revelation? We can be confident that an amanuensis was there taking down His words. Elusive as are some of the details of the revelation process, what is clearly evident is that Bahá'u'lláh enunciated verses destined to heighten and guide the spiritual experiences of millions of His followers in the years and centuries to come. Shoghi Effendi was to describe the Kitáb-i-Aqdas as a book that "may well be regarded as the brightest emanation of the mind of Bahá'u'lláh, as the Mother Book of His Dispensation, and the Charter of His New World Order."[11]

The Universal House of Justice, in its introduction to the English translation of the Kitáb-i-Aqdas, notes that Bahá'u'lláh had "superb mastery" of Arabic (in which the book was revealed),[12] and that "the style employed is of an exalted and emotive character, immensely compelling particularly to those familiar with the great literary tradition out of which it arose."[13] The Universal House of Justice has written: "[Of] the more than one hundred volumes comprising the sacred Writings of Bahá'u'lláh, the Kitáb-i-Aqdas is of supreme importance."[14]

As we plunge into this volume, we find verses that signal key ingredients in the foundation and function of the Shrine of Bahá'u'lláh.[15]

3

Guidelines for the Shrine

It is obvious that the head of the Faith immediately after the ascension of Bahá'u'lláh would be the one who was to establish the shrine. In the Kitáb-i-Aqdas, Bahá'u'lláh does not specifically refer to 'Abdu'l-Bahá by name when announcing His successor, but it was clear that it would be a member of Bahá'u'lláh's family. To the faithful Bahá'ís it seemed obvious that it would be 'Abdu'l-Bahá, often referred to as the Master.

These are the relevant verses from the Kitáb-i-Aqdas:

> O people of the world! When the Mystic Dove will have winged its flight from its Sanctuary of Praise and sought its far-off goal, its hidden habitation, refer ye whatsoever ye understand not in the Book to Him Who hath branched from this mighty Stock . . .[1]

> When the ocean of My presence hath ebbed and the Book of My Revelation is ended, turn your faces towards Him Whom God hath purposed, Who hath branched from this Ancient Root.[2]

The successor's identity as 'Abdu'l-Bahá was confirmed nearly two decades later after Bahá'u'lláh's ascension in 1892, when the

Kitáb-i-'Ahd—Bahá'u'lláh's Will and Testament—was read out to family and followers.[3]

The Kitáb-i-Aqdas also provides guidance by implication on who will be responsible for the shrine down the ages. As Shoghi Effendi writes, the Kitáb-i-Aqdas "anticipates by implication the institution of Guardianship," and it "formally ordains the institution of the 'House of Justice,'"[4] which is now known as the Universal House of Justice. As the Head of the Faith, the Guardian would have full responsibility for the shrine during his ministry (1921–57), as has the Universal House of Justice since its inception in 1963.

QIBLIH

There are no specific prescriptions in the Kitáb-i-Aqdas for the geographical location of the Qiblih, the turning point for obligatory prayer. But the principle of its location is clear from this verse, which quotes the Báb:

> O people of the Bayán! Fear ye the Most Merciful and consider what He hath revealed in another passage. He said: "The Qiblih is indeed He Whom God will make manifest; whenever He moveth, it moveth, until He shall come to rest." Thus was it set down by the Supreme Ordainer when He desired to make mention of this Most Great Beauty.[5]

Bahá'u'lláh also specifically ordains His resting place as the Qiblih after His passing:[6]

> When ye desire to perform this prayer, turn ye towards the Court of My Most Holy Presence, this Hallowed Spot that God hath made the Centre round which circle the Concourse on high, and which He hath decreed to be the Point of Adoration for the denizens of the Cities of Eternity, and the Source of Command unto all that are in heaven and on earth; and when the Sun of Truth and Utterance shall set, turn your faces

> towards the Spot that We have ordained for you. He, verily, is Almighty and Omniscient.[7]

Bahá'u'lláh had thereby fixed the Qiblih as His own shrine. For the next 1,000 years at least, His followers would turn toward it while reciting their daily obligatory prayers.

Although provisions of the Kitáb-i-Aqdas were not made known to the Bahá'ís until sometime after its revelation, the Bahá'ís were aware of the Qiblih. Knowing the teaching of the Báb that the Qiblih was the Manifestation Himself when He was alive, the Bahá'ís were likely to have turned toward Him in prayer when they knew where He was, sometimes in their immediate vicinity, sometimes far away. Naturally, this would depend upon the circumstances and whether or not it was safe or fitting. One of the instructions of Bahá'u'lláh was to be wise in carrying out the laws of the Báb or, later, Himself.[8]

The question may arise today as to why there should be a Qiblih, although it is not an unusual provision in religion.[9] In Judaism, the followers turn to the Temple site in Jerusalem, and the Christians have the concept of "ad orientem," with their altars often facing the east, to Jerusalem. The Prophet Muḥammad changed the Qiblih from Jerusalem to Mecca. As we have seen, the Báb ordained it to be the location of the Manifestation. In a letter written on his behalf, Shoghi Effendi explains by analogy: "[J]ust as the plant stretches out to the sunlight—from which it receives life and growth—so we turn our hearts to the Manifestation of God, Bahá'u'lláh, when we pray; . . . we turn our faces . . . to where His dust lies on this earth as a symbol of the inner act."[10]

This demonstrates that Bahá'ís are focusing on the spirit, the soul, the message of the Manifestation, and not the physical body itself. Bahá'ís do not regard these remains or articles associated with Him, such as His clothing, as magic talismans or fetish objects as found in some traditions of other belief systems. However, due respect is shown to the sacred remains because they once were the vessel for the Manifestation of God.[11]

'Abdu'l-Bahá explains: "Holy places are undoubtedly centers of the outpouring of Divine Grace, because on entering the illumined sites associated with martyrs and holy souls, and by observing reverence, both physical and spiritual, one's heart is moved with great tenderness."[12]

PLACES OF PILGRIMAGE

Another profoundly important provision of the Kitáb-i-Aqdas is the naming of the two places of pilgrimage, neither of which is the Shrine of Bahá'u'lláh. The relevant verse is: "The Lord hath ordained that those of you who are able shall make pilgrimage to the sacred House, and from this He hath exempted women as a mercy on His part . . ."[13]

In the selection of "Questions and Answers," which constitutes an appendix to the Kitáb-i-Aqdas, Bahá'u'lláh states: "It is an obligation to make pilgrimage to one of the two sacred Houses; but as to which, it is for the pilgrim to decide."[14] In answer to another question, He says: "By pilgrimage to the sacred House, which is enjoined upon men, is intended both the Most Great House in Baghdád and the House of the Primal Point in Shíráz; pilgrimage to either of these Houses sufficeth. They may thus make pilgrimage to whichever lieth nearer to the place where they reside."[15]

RITES OF PILGRIMAGE

In note 54, which follows the text of the Kitáb-i-Aqdas, it says: "In two separate Tablets, known as Súriy-Ḥajj . . . Bahá'u'lláh has prescribed specific rites for each of these pilgrimages. In this sense, the performance of a pilgrimage is more than simply visiting these two Houses."[16] Those Tablets were revealed while Bahá'u'lláh was in Adrianople in about March 1867.[17] Addressed to the poet and author Nabíl-i-A'ẓam, the Tablets name the House of the Báb and the House of Bahá'u'lláh as the pilgrimage sites.

Bahá'u'lláh directed Nabíl to carry out those pilgrimages, and to recite on His behalf the two recently revealed Tablets of the Pilgrimage, and also to perform, in His stead, the rites prescribed in them when visiting both houses.[18] This Nabíl did sometime between

September 1867 and August 1868.[19] Shoghi Effendi said this act "marks the inception of one of the holiest observances, which in a later period, the Kitáb-i-Aqdas, was to formally establish."[20]

The rites for the House of the Báb are outlined here:

1. On deciding to go, purify oneself spiritually.
2. When first sighting Shíráz, dismount and recite the prayer specified for addressing that city.
3. Raise one's hands and recite a prayer of thanksgiving.
4. Move on to within one thousand paces of Shíráz. Stop, wash, trim hair and nails, and put on one's best clothes. [In the Questions and Answers appended to the Kitáb-i-Aqdas, Bahá'u'lláh says: "the injunction on pilgrims to the Sacred House to shave the head hath been lifted."]
5. Recite two specified prayers.
6. Walk with due humility to within twenty paces of the city gate, repeating a prayer announcing to God one's presence.
7. Pray and gaze at those things that the Manifestation Himself has looked upon.
8. Prostrate oneself and kiss the ground. Rise and repeat nineteen times each "Alláh-u-Abhá" and "Alláh-u-Akbar."
9. Walk with humility to the House of the Báb.
10. Stop and recite a prayer praising the station of the House of the Báb.
11. Prostrate oneself and recite a prayer seeking acceptance.
12. Stand facing the right side of the House of the Báb and recite a prayer.
13. Circumambulate the House of the Báb seven times.
14. Stop and recite another prayer.
15. Finish. Out of respect, one should not enter the House of the Báb.[21]

Nabíl-i-A'ẓam seems to be the only one in that era to have carried out this rite for the House of the Báb. In addition to Nabíl, it appears that there was a second person who, with Bahá'u'lláh's leave, performed the rites of the pilgrimage to His house in Baghdád.[22] His name was Shakykh Muḥammad Damarchí. The story goes that after he became a follower of Bahá'u'lláh in Baghdád, Shakykh Damarchí went to visit Bahá'u'lláh in 'Akká. He was one of the few who managed to pass through the rows of soldiers without anyone stopping him. After attaining Bahá'u'lláh's presence, he received His blessings and was directed by Him to go back to Baghdád and perform the rites of pilgrimage as revealed. This he did. While he was performing the rites, people stoned him, but without any hesitation, he finished the rites associated with the pilgrimage.[23]

The rites for the pilgrimage to the House in Baghdád where Bahá'u'lláh resided are outlined here:[24]

1. On entering Baghdád, keep praising God until one reaches the river.
2. Change into one's best clothes and carry out ablutions.
3. Praise God while crossing the bridge.
4. When one reaches the other side, recite a specified prayer.
5. Circumambulate the House of Bahá'u'lláh seven times.
6. Kiss the door of the House of Bahá'u'lláh.
7. Ask forgiveness seventy times and recite a prayer for forgiveness.
8. Walk quietly to the door, praying to God, then recite a prayer testifying to the station of the House of Bahá'u'lláh.
9. Recite three specified prayers while standing, and then prostrated, and then kneeling at the door.
10. Walk respectfully into the court of the House of Bahá'u'lláh and recite two prayers while facing the place Bahá'u'lláh usually sat.
11. Wait silently. If one does not perceive "God's call," then repeat the rite. ('Abdu'l-Bahá said this final instruction refers to perceiving God in one's heart and is not to be taken literally).[25]

A beautiful Tablet of Visitation, shorter than the one addressed to Nabíl, was addressed to Shakykh Muḥammad Damarchí. It begins:

> When thou art departed out of the court of My presence, O Muḥammad, direct thy steps towards My House (Baghdád House), and visit it on behalf of thy Lord. When thou reachest its door, stand thou before it and say: Whither is the Ancient Beauty gone, O most great House of God, He through Whom God hath made thee the cynosure of an adoring world, and proclaimed thee to be the sign of His remembrance unto all who are in the heavens and all who are on the earth?[26]

Another sentence is: "Thou art still the symbol of the names and attributes of the Almighty, the Point towards which the eyes of the Lord of earth and heaven are directed."

Due to current circumstances, these pilgrimages are not now carried out. The rites will apply when pilgrimages to those sites can be safely resumed. The law of pilgrimage as revealed in the Kitáb-i-Aqdas was supplemented by the directions of the one He appointed in the Kitáb-i-Aqdas as His successor, His eldest son, 'Abdul-Bahá.[27]

DESIGNATION OF THE SHRINE OF BAHÁ'U'LLÁH

Some time after the passing of Bahá'u'lláh—the date is not yet known—'Abdu'l-Bahá designated the Shrine of Bahá'u'lláh at Bahjí, known as "the Most Holy Shrine," as a place of obligatory visitation (zíyárat) for men with the means to do so.[28] In a note to the Kitáb-i-Aqdas, it says that 'Abdu'l-Bahá indicates that the "Most Holy Shrine, the Blessed House in Baghdád and the venerated House of the Báb in Shíráz" are "consecrated to pilgrimage," and that it is "obligatory" to visit these places "if one can afford to do so if no obstacle stands in one's way."[29] The note says that no rites have been prescribed for pilgrimage to the Most Holy Shrine, the Shrine of Bahá'u'lláh. In note 55, it says that Bahá'u'lláh, like the Báb, exempts women from His pilgrimage requirements (the Báb said the exemption was to spare them the rigors of travel). The note also says that "the Universal House of Justice has clarified that this exemption is not a prohibition, and that women are free to perform the pilgrimage."[30]

'Abdu'l-Bahá describes the Shrine of Bahá'u'lláh as "the luminous Shrine," "the place around which circumambulate the Concourse on High"—one more than those circumambulating the Shrine of the Báb, because the Báb will be there too.[31] The Master prescribed no formal rites for pilgrims. The standard but not obligatory practice is to kneel, lowering one's forehead to the threshold at the entrance to the inner shrine.

HIS FUTURE ASCENSION

In the Kitáb-i-Aqdas, Bahá'u'lláh did not predict the time of His passing, but He did refer to that event several times, counseling the Bahá'ís to overcome and not to be paralyzed by grief but rather to confidently move the Cause forward. These are the encouraging verses on that point:

> Be not dismayed, O peoples of the world, when the daystar of My beauty is set, and the heaven of My tabernacle is concealed from your eyes. Arise to further My Cause, and to exalt My Word amongst men. We are with you at all times, and shall strengthen you through the power of truth.[32]

> Say: Let not your hearts be perturbed, O people, when the glory of My Presence is withdrawn, and the ocean of My utterance is stilled. In My presence amongst you there is a wisdom, and in My absence there is yet another, inscrutable to all but God, the Incomparable, the All-Knowing. Verily, We behold you from Our realm of glory, and will aid whosoever will arise for the triumph of Our Cause with the hosts of the Concourse on high and a company of Our favored angels.[33]

Bahá'u'lláh was to make a prophesy about His ascension in a serenely beautiful Tablet He revealed in March 1873 in the House of 'Údí Khammár.

4

Two Special Weeks

In March 1873, there were two special weeks that became part of the story of the Shrine of Bahá'u'lláh. The first was marked by an event in the mystical realm, the second by one very much of the physical world.

PROPHECY OF THE ASCENSION

In the first week of March 1873, during the period before the revelation of the Kitáb-i-Aqdas was complete, Bahá'u'lláh revealed one of the most beautiful of His Tablets. On the eve of the holy day commemorating the birth of the Báb, Bahá'u'lláh dictated in Arabic the Lawḥ-i-Ru'yá ("Tablet of the Vision").[1] In that Tablet, Bahá'u'lláh recounted His vision so that the intended recipient could obtain a glimpse of the "spiritual world of lights" while still in this world. The Master wrote:

> Ponder in your hearts that which He hath foretold in His Tablet of the Divine Vision that hath been spread throughout the world. Therein He saith: "Thereupon she wailed and exclaimed: 'May the world and all that is therein be a ransom for Thy woes. O Sovereign of heaven and earth! Wherefore hast Thou left Thyself in the hands of the dwellers of this prison-city

> of 'Akká? Hasten Thou to other dominions, to Thy retreats above, whereon the eyes of the people of names have never fallen.' We smiled and spake not. Reflect upon these most exalted words, and comprehend the purpose of this hidden and sacred mystery."[2]

Shoghi Effendi writes that the one referred to in the Tablet who had bidden Him hasten to His other dominions, was the "Luminous Maid,"[3] "clad in white."[4]

WEDDING OF THE MASTER

The second event occurred in the week following the revelation of the Tablet of the Vision. It was the wedding of 'Abdu'l-Bahá, Who married Munírih Khánum on 8 March 1873. The wedding may not have taken place had the first marital plans for each of the couple eventuated.

In 1868, Sháh-Sulṭán Khánum,[5] a half-sister of Bahá'u'lláh, a follower of Mírzá Yaḥyá, along with another relative had prevented a wedding between 'Abdu'l-Bahá and His cousin, Shahrbánú, which had been arranged according to custom when both were children. ('Abdu'l-Bahá was ten years old.) Bahá'u'lláh had made plans for Shahrbánú to travel from Ṭihrán to Adrianople for the wedding when the Master was in His early twenties. But Bahá'u'lláh's half-sister instead pressured her to marry the son of the prime minister, to whom the bride was not attracted.[6] This led to an unhappy marriage. Shahrbánú called her younger brother and asked him to say "amen" when she was reciting her prayers. She pleaded with God to speed her toward her death, the younger brother fulfilling her request by saying "amen." After a year of great misery, she passed way through shame and grief, the cause of death being cited publicly as tuberculosis.[7]

A strange episode had also unfolded for Munírih Khánum. She had married a cousin, but after the ceremony the groom sank into a mood in which he did not communicate with his bride. The marriage remained unconsummated, and he passed away six months after the wedding. In her autobiography, Munírih Khánum wrote that unquestionably there was a wisdom behind it. In reality, she wrote, her "chaste and pure cousin . . . carried me to the ideal beloved, and joined this stream of water to the most great sea."[8]

Although the Master was in no hurry to marry, Bahá'u'lláh clearly saw the time was right, and in fact it was said that He had dreamed of Munírih Khánum as a bride for the Master.[9] In order for her to meet 'Abdu'l-Bahá, Bahá'u'lláh summoned her to 'Akká from her home in Iṣfahán, the former grand capital of Persia, a city of high culture, and the scene of many historic events in the history of the Bábí and Bahá'í religions. After she arrived in 'Akká she met 'Abdu'l-Bahá, and after they got to know each other they agreed to marry. However, the wedding was not able to go ahead because of the lack of room for a married couple in the House of 'Údí Khammár, which was known as "the little house."[10]

Eventually the neighbor, Ilyás 'Abbúd—by now friendly to the Bahá'ís—asked about the delay of the wedding and when told the reason by Bahá'u'lláh,[11] said he was ill and wanted to leave the city, so he agreed to lease his house to 'Abdu'l-Bahá, Who made such arrangements on behalf of His Father.[12] A doorway was built through the common wall between his house and the house of 'Údí Khammár,[13] joining two upper courts and adding a room from his house to the house of Bahá'u'lláh. He also furnished the room, telling Bahá'u'lláh he had prepared it for 'Abdu'l-Bahá and His bride.[14] This allowed Bahá'u'lláh to move into the front room of the building, which had a clerestory with its windows flooding the room with light. The walls were stenciled. Windows looked out to a verandah and onward to the blue Mediterranean Sea. From the time He moved into that room, Bahá'u'lláh would stroll on the verandah in the morning and the late afternoon.

With the date set, the Master's fiancé came under the loving wing of her future mother-in-law, Ásíyih Khánum,[15] and her future sister-in-law, the twenty-seven-year-old Bahíyyih Khánum.[16] The wedding ahead was to be one of the happiest events in the life of Ásíyih Khánum. Bahíyyih Khánum shared similar sentiments.[17] Mother and daughter made Munírih Khánum a dainty wedding gown out of white batiste, a cotton fabric with a beautiful sheen. The grateful bride-to-be thought it "more precious than all the silks and brocades of paradise."[18] To complete the simple yet stunning ensemble, she wore a white headdress that floated over her double plaits, a hairstyle she preferred to a more elaborate one suggested by one of the three daughters of Ilyás 'Abbúd, all of whom attended the wedding.[19] 'Abdu'l-Bahá's bride was truly radiant, perhaps one of the reasons Bahá'u'lláh had earlier changed her name from Fáṭimih Nahrí to "Munírih," meaning "luminous."

At 9:00 pm on that wedding night,[20] Munírih Khánum, carrying no doubt a bouquet of the aromatic flowers of spring and accompanied by Bahíyyih Khánum, the Greatest Holy Leaf, attained the presence of Bahá'u'lláh. She received His blessing, and later was to recount in her autobiography[21] what He said to her:

> "You are welcome! You are welcome! O thou my Blessed Leaf and Maid Servant! We have chosen thee and accepted thee to be the companion of the Greatest Branch and to serve him. This is from My Bounty, to which there is no equal; the treasures of the earth and heaven cannot be compared with it."
>
> Her recollections continued: "After speaking in this manner, and showering His Mercy upon me, he referred to Baghdád, Adrianople and the Most Great Prison, saying that many girls had hoped for this great bounty, but they were not accepted. 'Thou must be very thankful for thou has attained to this most great favor and bestowal.'"

Then, after moving into the wedding room with the seven guests, she awaited the arrival of 'Abdu'l-Bahá.

He appeared at 10:00 pm, cutting an impressive figure. Aged twenty-eight, 'Abdu'l-Bahá was slim yet strongly built. His handsome face was adorned with the winning combination of blue-grey eyes and jet-black hair and beard. Dressed impeccably in a flowing white robe, He moved with His typical grace, charm, and good humor.[22] Munírih Khánum agreed to requests to depart from the usual custom of bridal silence. She burst forth with her lovely voice, chanting the Tablet Bahá'u'lláh had revealed for the couple. In English the words of that Tablet are impressive enough, but in Persian they are profound poetry:

> When the gates of the sacred garden are set open, and the holy youth issues forth, verily he hath come with a Message of great import.
> Glad tidings! Glad tidings!
> This is that holy youth who hath come, bringing the Message of great joy.[23]

Then Bahá'u'lláh Himself chanted prayers. The couple recited their vows.

After a simple supper, the guests left the room, going down the stairs and into the night. One of them, the wife of Ilyás 'Abbúd, would often say to Munírih Khánum in later years how the sweetness of her chanting was still sounding in her ears. The room provided and furnished by Ilyás 'Abbúd, was for the Master and Munírih.[24] It was probably later that they moved into the room at the rear where Bahá'u'lláh had revealed the Kitáb-i-Aqdas.[25]

Everything 'Abdu'l-Bahá did was an implicit example for Bahá'ís then and into the future. The wedding was a combination of simplicity, spirituality, and love. The bride was to recall: "At the wedding there was no cake, only cups of tea; there were no decorations, and no choir, but the blessing of Jamál-i-Mubárak ["the Blessed Beauty," a title of Bahá'u'lláh]; the glory and beauty of love and happiness were beyond and above all luxury and ceremony and circumstance. Oh the spiritual happiness which enfolded us! It cannot be described in earthly words. . . . I was the wife of my Beloved. How wonderful and noble He was in His beauty. I adored Him. I recognized His greatness, and thanked God for bringing me to Him."[26]

This wedding between 'Abdu'l-Bahá and Munírih Khánum proved to be an integral part of the story of the Shrine of Bahá'u'lláh because their union would lead to the birth, twenty-four years later, of their grandson, Shoghi Effendi. As the Head of the Faith from 1921 to 1957, Shoghi Effendi restored and embellished the shrine and its surrounds, and renovated and decorated the Mansion of Bahjí.[27]

Although still a prisoner in 'Akká, life for Bahá'u'lláh now entered a new phase.

Bahá'u'lláh revealed the Kitáb-i-Aqdas in this room.

Shuttered windows (top left) of the room in which the Kitáb-i-Aqdas was revealed.

'Abdu'l-Bahá, approximately twenty-four years old at the time this photograph was taken in Adrianople, was known to the generality of the people of 'Akká as 'Abbás Effendi.

Munírih Khánum.

5

The World of the Soul

Four years is a long time to live mainly in one room, no matter how pleasant the space, especially when one considers the confinement endured by Bahá'u'lláh for the five previous years in the rear room He occupied.[1] As Shoghi Effendi was to write later, Bahá'u'lláh's "sole exercise had been to pace, in monotonous repetition, the floor of His bed-chamber."[2] However, sometime after the wedding of the Master, the authorities in 'Akká, with only a few exceptions, became friendlier to the Bahá'ís.

Bahá'u'lláh was able to leave the building and visit His brother's house in 'Akká as well as go to the dwellings of some other Bahá'ís in that city. He would also walk through the dank alleys across the city to the Khán-i-'Avámíd, the caravanserai, and the Faith's first pilgrimage house.[3] He would meet with local Bahá'ís, some of whom lived there, and occasionally welcome the increasing number of pilgrims. The Master was often there too, having a room there that He used, for example, when meeting pilgrims.

In the afternoon, Bahá'u'lláh often moved outside His room for a stroll along the verandah. In addition to pilgrims, there were about 100 Bahá'ís resident in 'Akká. Many of the male Bahá'ís would make sure to finish work early in the afternoon so they could gather in the street below the verandah hoping for—and often obtaining—a glimpse of the Manifestation, some remaining until two or three hours after sunset. Some would circumambulate the house as much as it was possible to do so. One Bahá'í took it upon himself to clean and sweep the area to ensure it was clean. The Master said of this man: "Through his constant efforts, the square in front of Bahá'u'lláh's house was at all times swept, sprinkled and immaculate. Bahá'u'lláh would often glance at that plot of ground, and then He would smile and say: 'Muḥammad-Hádíy [-i-Ṣaḥḥáf] has turned the square in front of this prison into the bridal-bower of a palace. He has brought pleasure to all the neighbors and earned their thanks.'"[4]

When Bahá'u'lláh appeared on the verandah, the Bahá'ís would gaze up at Him in awe and expectation. They knew that it had become His practice to invite some of the believers up to His room or to a space near the rear of the same floor. Let the eyewitness, Mírzá Ḥaydar-'Alí describe the amazing scenes:

> Many a time through His bounty and loving-kindness, He would, with His blessed hand, signal to some to come up to His presence. . . . The unity which existed among the believers was such that they were as one body; each one was ready to sacrifice his life for the other. And when one individual or a group was summoned in this way, the joy which flooded their hearts was indescribable. The person would run inside with such speed that even the door and the walls vibrated with excitement. He would be so thrilled at that moment that he could not recognize anybody, and if someone talked to him, he could not hear it. He would be on his way to meet his Lord, to reach the paradise of Divine Presence which is much more glorious than paradise itself, a paradise which cannot be seen or felt or heard by those who have not experienced it.[5]
>
> And, after being dismissed from Bahá'u'lláh's presence, the individual was so carried away that it would take him some time to regain consciousness, when he would be able to recognize his friends and talk to them. Only one out of many could perhaps

> recount, in a very inadequate way, the words that he had heard in His presence. But no one was ever able to describe the spiritual experiences of his meeting with his Lord.[6]

The pilgrims[7] who attained the presence of Bahá'u'lláh at that time were forerunners of the tens of thousands of modern-day pilgrims who visit that house and other holy places, the highlight being prostration at the threshold of His shrine at Bahjí.[8]

Following the completion of the Kitáb-i-Aqdas a few months after the wedding of the Master and Munírih Khánum, it became increasingly evident that change was in the air. As historian Adib Taherzadeh writes: "The mysterious forces which the revelation of this Book released in the world may be said to have been a major factor in turning the tide of the fortunes of the Faith and its Author in 'Akká."[9] Relations with the authorities greatly improved, with most successive governors of 'Akká developing a favorable view of Him, and even acting on His advice.

One Governor, Aḥmad Big Tawfíq, who greatly respected Bahá'u'lláh, asked Him if he could render Him a service. Bahá'u'lláh suggested he restore the aqueduct, which for thirty years had fallen into disuse. This was done, and waters soon flowed from the springs of Kabri into the city.[10] The senior Islamic cleric, the Muftí, Shaykh 'Alíy-i-Mírí became so attracted to the Manifestation that he once intimated to the Master that every time he stood up to pray, the majestic figure of Bahá'u'lláh appeared before him. He also used to visit the Master to learn from Him.[11]

It was in this time of gradual change that Bahá'u'lláh revealed a mighty Tablet, the Lawḥ-i-Ḥikmat, known in English as "The Tablet of Wisdom." In this Tablet He refers to the great Greek philosophers, with Socrates most especially praised.[12] The Tablet is stunning in its explanation of the coexistence of creation and eternity. In fact, the provisions of this Tablet are relevant to some of the most profound questions being asked today in science and religion as to the origin of the universe. It also "contained some of His noblest counsels and exhortations concerning individual conduct."[13] During this time Bahá'u'lláh may also have revealed subsidiary ordinances to supplement the provisions of the Kitáb-i-Aqdas.[14]

In 1875, the Master leased the garden of Na'mayn,[15] which was about one kilometer from the city walls. He renamed it Riḍván, a tribute to the place in Baghdád where Bahá'u'lláh declared His mission.[16] Over the next two years—before His Father visited it—the Master developed it from a distance. He organized fertile soil to be brought in from nearby areas. With His encouragement, pilgrims carried plants—such as a white rose, which was Bahá'u'lláh's favorite—all the way from Persia. As we shall see later, in future years Bahá'u'lláh was to enjoy the garden as a retreat from His otherwise busy life. He exalted in the beauty of the trees and plants, the variety of fragrances, the delicious fruit such as mulberries, the birdsong, and the pleasant sounds of a gurgling fountain.

But that was in the future. One day in 1877, Bahá'u'lláh, still confined to 'Akká, happened to mention that He had not gazed on lush green vegetation for nine years, remarking that the country is the world of the soul, and the city the world of bodies. Hearing of that yearning, 'Abdu'l-Bahá made plans after He heard some intriguing news at 'Akká's principal mosque, that of al-Jazzar,[17] which He often visited and where He had His own room for prayer and meditation and counseling clergy and secular notables. He found out from the Muftí and other Muslim friends that the rules restricting Bahá'u'lláh and Himself to 'Akká would not be enforced.

So it was on one bright spring day in 1877, that 'Abdu'l-Bahá, accompanied by three fellow prisoners,[18] strode confidently through the city gates past the guards—who made no effort to stop Him—and went on to Bahjí, where they delighted in the sight of a newly planted orchard of apricot and peach trees with their exquisite blossoms. The four men, for so long confined behind the stone ramparts of 'Akká, walked and walked, reveling in the green countryside, soaking up the beauty of the Sharon tulips, the scarlet and yellow buttercups, and crown anemones.[19]

'Abdu'l-Bahá repeated that daring move the next day, but the risk was somewhat lessened because that time He was accompanied by some friends and city officials. The Master had decided to fully test the assurance that the strict restrictions would not be enforced. He first obtained permission from a Christian landowner, Jirjís al-Jamál, to hold a picnic under his grove of about eighteen pine trees on his property. It was next to the grounds of the Mansion of Bahjí, the palace that 'Abdu'l-Bahá's own landlord, 'Údí <u>Kh</u>ammár, had renovated and where he lived in luxury and threw lavish parties. 'Abdu'l-Bahá then invited officials and other notables. They agreed to attend. With that event, the Master said, "the doors of majesty and true sovereignty were flung wide open."[20]

'Abdu'l-Bahá then inquired about a place in the countryside to rent for Bahá'u'lláh. He heard of one owned by the elderly Muḥammad Pá<u>sh</u>á Ṣafwat, who was opposed to the Bahá'ís. It was what is now called the Mansion of Mazra'ih (meaning "the farm"), and is about two kilometers to the west of the coastal city of Nahariya. Before Muḥammad Ṣafwat obtained it, the building was the summer home of his uncle, the then governor 'Abdu'lláh Pá<u>sh</u>á,[21] who also owned the house in 'Akká where 'Abdul-Bahá was later to live, and where Shoghi Effendi would be born. The mansion in question had been built in the eighteenth century, a date indicated by the existing original wall around the courtyard. There are two giant cypresses near the eastern corner. A modern measurement of these showed them to be about three hundred years old, so the assumption is that the mansion is about that old.[22]

The building is at a place called Alexandrona, as the village of Mazra'ih was apparently called in the pre-Ottoman era. In those days the mansion was owned by Yosef Ma'wí and then by Abdu'l-Qádir Al-Samawí.[23] After them, the building came into the hands of the governor 'Álí Pá<u>sh</u>á, the father of 'Abdu'lláh Pá<u>sh</u>á, and was almost certainly used as a watchtower, having two rooms downstairs and the one upstairs later occupied by Bahá'u'lláh.[24] Close by the mansion was accommodation, perhaps an inn (<u>kh</u>án) or living quarters for workers who toiled in the cotton and grain fields.

The Master visited the elderly Muḥammad Ṣafwat in 'Akká and pointed out that the mansion was empty. The owner said: "I am an invalid and cannot leave the city. If I go there it is lonely and I am cut off from my friends." The Master then put a lease proposal to him, successfully negotiated the low rental of five pounds a year,[25] and paid him for five years. ʻAbdu'l-Bahá organized the papering and furnishing of all the rooms and had a bath built for Bahá'u'lláh (the bath remains there on the second floor to this day).[26] He also arranged for the gardens to be tidied up. Then He had carpenters build a horse carriage with a cover for the purpose of transporting His Father to the mansion.

He went to Bahá'u'lláh and asked Him to agree to leave, delivering the following description of the place which has surely not been bettered in the many decades since.

> A good mansion is made ready for you outside of Acre. It is wonderfully situated and very charming. From one side the lovely mountains and undulating valleys are seen; from another side there are large orange and mandarin orchards; the oranges, like unto red lanterns, shine and glow through the green boughs; from another side, verdant gardens and prairies full of narcissus and tulips are seen; the Mediterranean glistens in the distance; a stream of cool water flows in the center; in brief it is an ideal place. I supplicate to you to leave the town and live there.[27]

Nobody was more eloquent than the Master, nobody was loved more by Bahá'u'lláh. Yet His pitch was not successful. ʻAbdu'l-Bahá tells the story:

> One day I went to the Holy Presence of the Blessed Beauty and said: "the palace at Mazraʻih is ready for You, and a carriage to drive You there."
>
> He refused to go, saying: "I am a prisoner." Later I requested Him again, but got the same answer. I went so far as to ask Him a third time, but He still said "No!" and I did not dare to insist further.

> There was, however, in 'Akká a certain Muḥammadan Shaykh,[28] a well-known man with considerable influence who loved Bahá'u'lláh and was greatly favored by Him. I called this Shaykh and explained the position to him. I said, "You are daring. Go tonight to His Holy Presence, fall on your knees before Him, take hold of His hands and do not let go until He promises to leave the city!"
>
> He was an Arab. . . . He went directly to Bahá'u'lláh and sat down close to His knees. He took hold of the hands of the Blessed Beauty and kissed them and asked: "Why do you not leave the city?" He said: "I am a prisoner."
>
> The Shaykh replied: "God forbid! Who has the power to make you a prisoner? You have kept yourself in prison. It was your own will to be imprisoned, and now I beg you to come out and go to the palace. It is beautiful and verdant. The trees are lovely, and the oranges like balls of fire!"
>
> As often as the Blessed Beauty said: "I am a prisoner, it cannot be," the Shaykh took His hands and kissed them. For a whole hour he kept on pleading. At last Bahá'u'lláh said, "Khaylí khub (very good)" and the Shaykh's patience and persistence were rewarded."[29]

The next day, in June 1877, Bahá'u'lláh boarded the carriage, which was newly built, likely by carriage-maker carpenters in the German Templer community in Haifa.[30] Until that time, carriages had not been seen in 'Akká or its vicinity. Then the Master alighted from the carriage, and in a symbol of His utter respect for the Manifestation of God, walked all the way to Mazra'ih while His father enjoyed His first experience of gazing at greenery in nearly a decade. 'Abdu'l-Bahá said the whole countryside was bedecked with flowers: "The plain of Acre was dancing with joy, and the mountain, the valleys and the gardens were intoxicated with the wine of happiness and were crying out, "O rapture! O bliss!" 'Abdu'l-Bahá concisely reported the reaction of Bahá'u'lláh to the mansion: "The Blessed Perfection was most pleased with the place."[31]

This momentous event of Bahá'u'lláh's departure was to lead to a fruitful fifteen-year period up to His ascension in which He was to enjoy gardens and the countryside, and at the same time reveal one profound and vital Tablet after another. For Bahá'u'lláh it was an intensely enjoyable experience to live amidst a garden property with views out to the sea one way and the hills of Galilee to the other. Near the cypress trees there was an exquisite outdoor spot for Him to rest and view the garden—it was an open area with a colorful marble floor, and it remains there to this day. An external wall had carvings, including one of a sailing ship, that dated back a century.[32]

Nearby was the aqueduct (the route since planted with flowers) that passed along the east side of the building through the property, carrying pure water for some twelve kilometers from the hills of Kabrí to 'Akká.[33] On the mansion property there was a pool (which is still there), which stored water from the aqueduct. About 200 meters toward 'Akká, there was another pool, ten times larger than the one at the mansion itself. Water from it, as well as from the pool near the mansion, was used to irrigate large fields of wheat and cotton owned by successive governors.

The entry door and two windows that were there in Bahá'u'lláh's time also remain. On the ground floor there were two rooms, one called "the Tablet room," where Bahá'u'lláh revealed scripture, such as the Lawḥ-i-Burhán (Tablet of the Proof) in which He condemns persecutors He named as the Wolf and the She-Serpent.[34] Its floor of small gravels and lime mortar remains intact today. The other room was for His amanuensis, Mírzá Áqá Ján (today it is used by the custodian of the property). The staircase of twenty-nine stone steps used by Bahá'u'lláh to ascend to His own upstairs room was originally completely exposed to the weather. From that floor, the Manifestation enjoyed lovely views across to the eastern hills of Galilee and could also gaze in the other direction for views of the sea.[35] His room was beautiful, with traditional Ottoman-era floral paintings on the walls.[36]

The building was not big enough for Bahá'u'lláh's extended family to live there. His amanuensis, Mírzá Áqá Ján, and His doorkeeper,

Muḥammad Khán, were there with Him, but the Master and Munírih Khánum remained in 'Akká, as did Navváb and Bahíyyih Khánum. Bahá'u'lláh's second wife, Fáṭimih Khánum, titled Mahd-i-'Ulyá, and probably three of her four children went with Him,[37] as did His third wife, Gawhar Khánum,[38] and her daughter, Furúghíyyih, who was about four years old in 1877. 'Abdu'l-Bahá was a regular visitor to the mansion, and Bahíyyih Khánum came there a couple of times. Bahá'u'lláh often visited 'Akká to see His wife, Ásíyih Khánum, and family members, and to receive pilgrims.[39]

This new phase in Bahá'u'lláh's life is described by Adib Taherzadeh:

> It was not only the fresh air of the countryside at Mazra'ih and the open fields around it which enhanced the circumstances in which He lived. The major factor which brought about a new phase in His ministry was the unveiling of His greatness, His power and His authority to friends and foe alike. . . .

Mr. Taherzadeh continues:

> The believers who came on pilgrimage at this time were also rejoicing in Bahá'u'lláh's freedom. There were many who attained His presence in this Mansion, in an atmosphere far different from that of former times in Adrianople or 'Akká. There was an air of freedom, of victory and ascendancy of the Cause which exhilarated every believing heart.[40]

The friends organized feasts at the mansion and in the countryside for Bahá'u'lláh to attend. Boxes of sweets by expert Persian pastry cooks[41] were handed around. Juice from the oranges mixed with the delicious juice from crushed pomegranates refreshed everybody. And there was plenty of clean, nice-tasting water available from the aqueduct that passed through the property.

Mr. Taherzadeh's own father, Ḥájí Muḥammad Ṭáhir-i-Málmírí, attained Bahá'u'lláh's presence at this time. When asked to describe his impressions of the Manifestation he recited a Persian poem, here translated into English:

And wonder at the vision I have dreamed,
A secret by my muted tongue concealed;
Beauty that is beyond the poet's word
By an unhearing world remains unheard.[42]

The pilgrims knew of the importance of being in the presence of Bahá'u'lláh. The Báb Himself spoke about the bounty of visiting "Him Whom God shall make manifest":

> There is no paradise more wondrous for any soul than to be exposed to God's Manifestation in His Day, to hear His verses and believe in them, to attain His presence, which is naught but the presence of God, to sail upon the sea of the heavenly kingdom of His good-pleasure, and to partake of the choice fruits of the paradise of His divine Oneness.[43]

One of the pilgrims who attempted to visit Bahá'u'lláh and to partake of the fruits of paradise was Mullá Mihdíy-i-'Aṭrí, whose descendants were to include three Hands of the Cause, the most recent being Dr. 'Alí Muḥammad Varqá (1912–2007), who was the last Hand of the Cause to pass away.[44] Mullá Mihdíy-i-'Aṭrí had left Persia with his two sons—Varqá and Mírzá Ḥusayn[45]—climbing mountains and pushing their way through difficult deserts of fine sand on their pilgrimage to Bahá'u'lláh.

'Abdu'l-Bahá was to write a heart-rending description of the outcome of this journey:

> He [Mullá Mihdíy-i-'Aṭrí] set out on foot for the house of Bahá'u'lláh. Because he lacked proper shoes for the journey, his feet were bruised and torn; his sickness worsened; he could hardly move, but still he went on; somehow he reached the village of Mazra'ih and here, close by the Mansion, he died.

> His heart found his Well-Beloved One, when he could bear the separation no more. Let lovers be warned by his story; let them know how he gambled away his life in his yearning after the Light of the World. May God give him to drink of a brimming cup in the everlasting gardens; in the Supreme Assemblage, may God shed upon his face rays of light. Upon him be the glory of the Lord.[46]

The Master built "his sanctified tomb" about half a kilometer away in Mazra'ih.

According to Ḥájí Muḥammad Ṭáhir-i-Málmírí, "Whenever the Blessed Beauty passed by his grave on His way to 'Akká or Mazra'ih, He would pause there, put His blessed foot on the grave and stop beside it for a few moments."[47] Bahá'u'lláh revealed verses for Mullá Mihdíy-i-'Aṭrí, and a Tablet of Visitation for His grave, a great honor. In later years, the village cemetery was built around the grave, which was treated with respect by the villagers as the resting place of a holy man.

Respect for Bahá'u'lláh was also now shown at the highest level. The "Angel of Carmel," Ḥájí Mírzá Ḥaydar-'Alí, related the story of a visit to 'Akká by Bahá'u'lláh to celebrate a Riḍván feast:

> A new pasha had arrived in 'Akká as the head of the Custom House. On that day he was sitting in a coffeehouse with many of his officers and other dignitaries of the town. Bahá'u'lláh was on His way to His brother's house. As He passed the coffeehouse, the pasha and all his retinue stood up and bowed before Him. As He passed by, He bestowed His loving benediction upon them. Then the pasha, bewildered, approached his friends and asked, "Is this the Holy Spirit or the King of Kings? Who is He?"
>
> "He is the father of 'Abbas Effendi," was the unanimous reply.[48]

After a couple of years, the Master saw it was essential to find a larger dwelling for Bahá'u'lláh and His extended family, as well as for pilgrims to attain His presence. The opportunity to move to such a place arose out of a sad and frightening event, a pandemic of bubonic plague.

6

The Lofty Mansion

For almost a decade before Bahá'u'lláh moved in, the Mansion of Bahjí was the venue for summer parties and dinners hosted by 'Údí Khammár and his family. Fountains played and strings of oil lamps and candelabra illuminated the marble-floored interior hall ("liwan") upstairs and the balcony that reached around three sides of the mansion.[1] In 1868, 'Údí Khammár had bought the building and surrounding land from Jirjis (otherwise written as Jurjus/Georges) Al-Jamál and Iskandar (Alexander) Al-Jamál. Those brothers retained ownership of nearby land on which sat a grove of magnificent pine trees and the olive plantation, which still exists.[2]

The original owner of the land to the south was Sulaymán Páshá, who planted a beautiful garden called Bahji (delight) there for his daughter, Fáṭimih. The property passed to Álí Páshá and then his son 'Abdu'lláh Páshá, the governor of 'Akká, who built a mansion for his harem. In 1821 he built the first story of the future Mansion of Bahjí, probably for his mother,[3] just to the north on land that his father had owned. The governor later lost everything, when in 1831 Ibráhím Páshá of Egypt used the southern mansion as his headquarters while besieging 'Akká.[4]

A map by a British naval officer in 1863 includes a square indicating what we now know as the first floor of the Mansion of Bahji, and is labelled with the name "Bukjeh," identifying the area. The path of an aqueduct bringing water from Kabri is shown going between the gardens and the one-story mansion and then to a tank in gardens belonging to the mansion to the south (filling a pool there to water the orchards and garden) and on to 'Akká. The map shows that to the west was the road to Tyre.[5]

But nearly five decades after it was first built, when the one-story mansion came into the hands of 'Údí Khammár—who bought it from the then owners, the Jamál family[6]—it was in a state of disrepair. He had to start from scratch with an upper floor.[7] The renovations were costly. At the time of purchase by 'Údí Khammár, its illustrious future tenant, Bahá'u'lláh, had been confined in the prison barracks in 'Akká in appalling conditions. Insulating rubble from the roof space area of the barracks was falling through the broken ceiling so the floors were often muddy. Disease threatened, and stench was ever present. After a while, under the direction of 'Abdu'l-Bahá, the place became more livable. In 1870, Mírzá Mihdí, a son of Bahá'u'lláh and the younger brother of 'Abdu'l-Bahá, had a fatal fall from the roof of the barracks building, and expressed as his last wish that the believers be admitted to see their Lord, Bahá'u'lláh.[8]

That same year, the restoration and expansion was complete,[9] and 'Údí Khammár and his family moved into their big country house. The Bahjí compound was ideal for family and friends who wanted to spend their summers in the countryside. 'Údí Khammár was a merchant (his name means wine merchant or keeper of the wine shop),[10] so the best of food was plentiful. Clean water was readily available from the aqueduct that ran alongside the compound. There was plenty of room for families and friends to stay. 'Údí Khammár's son-in-law, Iskandar Hawwa—married to the merchant's daughter Hani[11]—had built a colony of one-story houses set back from the east and west sides of the wall that surrounded a garden adjacent to the mansion. Nassif Hawwa Khammár built a large apartment house beside the northern side of the wall that surrounded the mansion.[12] One of those houses, the building in the northwest corner, was to attain great historical and spiritual significance when it became the site of the Shrine of Bahá'u'lláh.[13]

Such were 'Údí Khammár's hopes for his mansion that he had an inscription in Arabic, the author of which is unknown, placed above the door to the stairway where it remains to this day. Translated from the Arabic, it reads: *"Greetings and salutation rest upon this Mansion which increaseth in splendour through the passage of time. Manifold wonders and marvels are found therein, and pens are baffled in attempting to describe them."*

Certainly, for the first nine years there were good times in the mansion. But then disaster suddenly struck in the form of a pandemic. Infected fleas on rats, which had probably arrived on ships moored at 'Akká, were spreading bubonic plague in the area surrounding that city, including Bahjí.[14] It was the third recorded great pandemic of this disease in the area. The plague was a very distressing illness, marked by swollen and painful glands, vomiting, and extreme pain as the victim's skin decomposed. For those infected, death was virtually inevitable.[15] The cause of the plague was not discovered until 1898. Effective treatment arrived two years later.[16]

'Údí Khammár contracted the disease and died. He was buried in a windowless room, the front of which is the wall to the east of the main gate. To this day, his grave—not visited by pilgrims—is located in the northwest corner of that room, the entry to which is a green door in the southern side of the wall that surrounds the mansion. The grave is approximately one and a half meters tall, and has an Arabic inscription in the stone top that reads, translated into English:

This 'Údi Al-Khammár hath returned to the All-Merciful,
seeking the abode of the righteous.
Having raised mansions and buildings, and acquired
wealth and prestige that will be his lasting memorial,
He said, memorize, nay record for posterity, that pearl of utterance:
"This nether world is not a permanent abode."[17]

The family of ʻÚdí Khammár deserted the mansion and the outbuildings. ʻAbdu'l-Bahá saw the opportunity and rented the mansion from the late merchant's son Andravis[18] for the reasonable sum of £150 a year.[19] By the time of the ascension of Bahá'u'lláh, ʻAbdu'l-Bahá owned two-thirds of the mansion, the remaining third owned by a disloyal half-brother, Badíʻu'lláh.[20]

After the mansion and other houses were likely sanitized, the compound was ready for Bahá'u'lláh and His family to move in. Bahá'u'lláh described His new home as the scene of His transcendent glory and asserted that "the lofty Mansion" was specially built to serve as the Seat of God in His Day, although ʻÚdí Khammár was not aware of that.[21] It was the place, Bahá'u'lláh said, which "God hath ordained as the most sublime vision of mankind."[22]

As for ʻÚdí Khammár, his mansion was—as his epitaph pointed out—his lasting memorial. In fact, the Manifestation was later to say that the recently deceased sultan[23] had gone to the fires of hell, while the one who built the mansion was now under the canopy of God's mercy and favors.[24]

JOURNEY TO THE MANSION

In ʻAkká, on a night in September 1879, two Bahá'ís peered through the glass windows of their upstairs rooms near the White Market (Souq-i-yad)[25] down to the alley below. They beheld a glorious sight. Bahá'u'lláh was departing from the House of ʻAbbúd on His historic journey to the Mansion of Bahjí. He had moved from the Mansion of Mazraʻih back into ʻAkká for a short period before He left for His new home permanently. This journey was destined to take Him to a place and time where He would reveal many highly significant Tablets. In addition, He would be active in directing the activities of His Cause, including in Central, South, and Southeast Asia, and would proclaim His teachings to the West via an English visitor.[26] That period in the life of the Manifestation would come to its dramatic conclusion nearly thirteen years later, with the ascension of Bahá'u'lláh, and the establishment of His shrine, the Point of Adoration.

The two Bahá'ís watching from their upstairs rooms of the Khán-i-'Avámíd in 'Akká in 1879 were poet and author Nabíl-i-A'ẓam, aged forty-eight, and a Bahá'í teacher and writer, twenty-seven-year-old Ḥájí Muḥammad Ṭáhir-i-Málmírí,[27] who was to spend nine months on pilgrimage in 'Akká and its surrounds. The following is a likely scenario, based on a report from Ḥájí Muḥammad, and deduced from the customs of Bahá'u'lláh, the Bahá'ís, and the wider community.

For a minute or so the two men watched in awe at the lamp-lit majestic appearance of the Manifestation, seated in a carved and decorated saddle on Lightning ("Barq"), His white mount. Bahá'u'lláh, sixty-one years old, was wearing elegant long cotton robes and an embroidered traditional hat—a towering táj. With His handsome, light olive-skinned face framed by luxuriant black hair and beard, He conveyed the image of royalty. Following Him on his mount was His secretary, Mírzá Áqá Ján, also in his finest robes and táj. 'Abdu'l-Bahá, thirty-five years old, is not mentioned in the eyewitness account but it is likely that He strode along next to Bahá'u'lláh, just as He did when the Manifestation first rode in a carriage from 'Akká to the Mansion of Mazra'ih.

It was dark, being two hours after sunset, but the occasional oil lamp on the alley walls of 'Akká threw a warm glow over the solemn procession. Curious locals took advantage of the rare opportunity to view the one they called "the Persian God." The two Bahá'ís who were watching soon scampered down the stone stairs to follow a respectful fifty steps (about forty meters) behind the procession. "Lightning" could live up to his name when it came to speed, but this was a time for a dignified steady pace as the procession exited the great land gate in the city walls. Bahá'u'lláh tugged the reins to turn toward the Mansion of Bahjí 4,600 feet (1.4 kms) away along an often sandy path. We know the distance because 'Abdu'l-Bahá referred to it years later when describing His journeys by foot to the shrine.[28]

Half an hour later, the large three-wicked oil lamp in the massive two-story mansion came into view. This was the first time Bahá'u'lláh had seen His new home. He rode in from the south, so the outlying building to the northwest that was one day to house His shrine would not have been visible. Soon, attendants helped Bahá'u'lláh dismount at a raised step a few meters east of the main gate. "Lighting" and the other mount were led away to the stables. Bahá'u'lláh acknowledged the greetings by family members, who had moved into the mansion and nearby house some days before. Holding oil lamps, attendants escorted Bahá'u'lláh and the Master through the gate, and then along the eastern side of the mansion until They reached the door to the steep interior stairs. They went up to the next floor and then through a short corridor, along the carpet on the side of the liwan—a marble-floored hall —and entered Bahá'u'lláh's room in the southeast of the upper story. His chamber was of good size. That night only the flickering lamps in the few nearby dwellings would have been visible through His windows or from the balcony. In the clear unpolluted skies, the stars and planets appeared brighter than they do today.

Next to His room was that of Bahá'u'lláh's second wife Mahd-i-'Ulyá (Fáṭimih Khánum). His third wife, Gawhar Khánum, may have had a room on that floor as well. The rest of the rooms were reserved for the male members of the immediate family. The downstairs served as the andarúní, the quarters for women and children. Those in the extended family who were not allocated rooms in the mansion occupied the houses outside the walls of the mansion.

'Abdu'l-Bahá did not move into the mansion. With His wife, Munírih Khánum, and his second child, Ḍíyá'íyyih,[29] He remained living in the House of 'Abbúd in 'Akká. That enabled the Master to maintain His important role as spokesperson and administrator of the Bahá'í community, befriending the succession of governors, public servants, the Muftí, and other notables. He could also meet the incoming pilgrims and prepare them to attain the presence of Bahá'u'lláh. There were some at Bahjí who were not happy with the special regard Bahá'u'lláh showed to 'Abdu'l-Bahá. Their disaffected and rebellious behavior,[30] which was to erupt after the ascension of the Manifestation, was such that Bahá'u'lláh said that pilgrims, rather than being exposed to their tainted human thoughts and deeds, could visit the Master in 'Akká, listen to Him, meet steadfast believers, and return home.[31] Of course, pilgrims were intent on an audience, however brief, with Bahá'u'lláh too.

Also remaining in that House of 'Abbúd was Bahá'u'lláh's highly esteemed first wife, Navváb, the Exalted Leaf,[32] who helped with Ḍíyá'íyyih and, from the next year on, with the twins, Ṭúbá and Rúḥá. Navváb, Bahá'u'lláh's "perpetual consort,"[33] would reunite with Bahá'u'lláh during the winter when He left Bahjí to stay in 'Akká, and also during His occasional visits to the city at other times of the year. From this point in time, we may be able to discern the wisdom of that arrangement. Navváb would be away from the other wives, who were likely to be competing for favors for their children. Bahá'u'lláh could visit Navváb in 'Akká, and keep these future rebels under His watch. One of those wives was to support her son in disputing the Will and Testament of Bahá'u'lláh, thereby breaking the Covenant.

A postscript to the story of Bahá'u'lláh's historic journey to the mansion came in the memoirs of Ḥájí Muḥammad Ṭáhir-i-Málmírí. He recalled that when he and his companion, Nabíl, arrived at the mansion on that autumn evening—quite a few minutes after Bahá'u'lláh—they could hear the soft murmurs and breathing of crowds of people packing the footpaths along the four sides of the mansion. They were amazed because they knew nobody else had come out from 'Akká. They came to believe they had witnessed the souls of all the Prophets and Messengers and the Concourse on High. The two stunned believers moved back thirty meters, circumambulated through muddy wheatfields, prostrated themselves in front of the gate, and headed back in the pouring rain to 'Akká. They managed to enter the city just as the guards were about to close the gate.

The first response of Nabíl was to memorialize the experience by composing poems. His young friend refilled the samovar to ensure the inspiration kept flowing. The poems, transcribed onto parchment and sent to Bahá'u'lláh the next day, contained allusions to Bahá'í historical events, as well as an account of the previous night. In response, Bahá'u'lláh revealed a Tablet that accepted their pilgrimage to the mansion (a relief for the men because no permission had been given) and bestowed the title "Bulbul" (Nightingale) upon Nabíl, and "Bahháj" (the Blissful) upon his companion.

In publishing an account of this experience, historian Adib Taherzadeh (the son of Ḥájí Muḥammad Ṭáhir-i-Málmírí),[34] makes it clear that the interpretation of what they thought they witnessed at the mansion as the presence of the "concourse on high" may be considered as personal experiences only, but not a story of confirmation for others. Nevertheless, the uplifting and poetic nature of this story emphasizes the great spiritual significance of what had happened that balmy night. Bahá'u'lláh was moving into a new and extremely fertile phase of His revelation, and the corresponding establishment of His Faith. The finale of that phase was to be His ascension and the inauguration of His glorious shrine.

THE MANSION IN DETAIL

Bahá'u'lláh's new home was an "outstanding example of Ottoman architecture."[35] Half a century later, one expert on Palestinian architecture said he considered it the most beautiful building in the land.[36] The mansion was not white with blue shutters as it appears today, but more likely to be of a pale green or yellow like other mansions in the Holy Land.[37] The upper story was designed for "comfortable and gracious living."[38] After climbing the stairs, one enters by a short corridor, as Ugo Giachery describes, "a large hall paved with marble and flooded with light penetrating from a series of large windows opening into the roof, which is supported by eight marble columns in the manner of an Islamic courtyard." It is, as Dr. Giachery wrote, of a majestic size and luminosity. Bedrooms open off the hall. In the southeast corner (walking down the hall and to the left) is the chamber of Bahá'u'lláh. A large room, it has big windows, one side looking toward the plain and the other to the terrace, from which Mt. Carmel can be seen. High upon the wall are two circular windows. A door from His room leads out to a covered terrace where a screen (now of framed plate-glass panes in color), is protection against the sun from the south during the hot summer months. There is a marble fountain, which spouted fresh water in the time of Bahá'u'lláh.

Another room on the opposite corner is the same size, opens onto the terrace, and is close to the fountain. It was later Shoghi Effendi's chamber. The upstairs balcony, with its slim columns and arches, runs along all but the eastern exterior. Frescoes of various scenes and objects decorate the wall of the mansion. Underneath that Terrace on the north, west, and south sides is a graceful arcade with massive arches. They help give the mansion a massive and impressive appearance. The ground floor rooms, used as rooms for the women and children, are spacious with high ceilings, all opening onto the colonnade. The entrance to the stairway is on the eastern side at the northern end.

A tall stone block wall surrounds the entire mansion, with a garden between it and the building itself. The main entrance was a gate through the southern wall. The gate that now exists to the northern end of the western side of the wall that encloses the mansion property was probably built by 'Údí Khammár for easy access to the outbuildings. The kitchens were likely to have been in separate buildings just outside the wall, for two main reasons. Coal and wood were used for the stoves and ovens, thereby creating smoke, so kitchens were best situated at a distance from the residential rooms. The kitchens were also the place of almost constant activity, having to cater for so many people, so were noisy and not suited to be in the mansion. On adjoining land owned by the Jamál brothers was a grove of towering pine trees,[39] under which Bahá'ís would walk and sit. It was the only outdoor place near the mansion that provided shade during the hot, dry summers.[40]

In Bahá'u'lláh's time, the Bahjí compound was a hive of activity.

Bahá'u'lláh liked to stroll on the balcony of the House of 'Abbúd.

The Mansion of Mazra'ih.

Bahá'u'lláh's stairs at Mazra'ih.

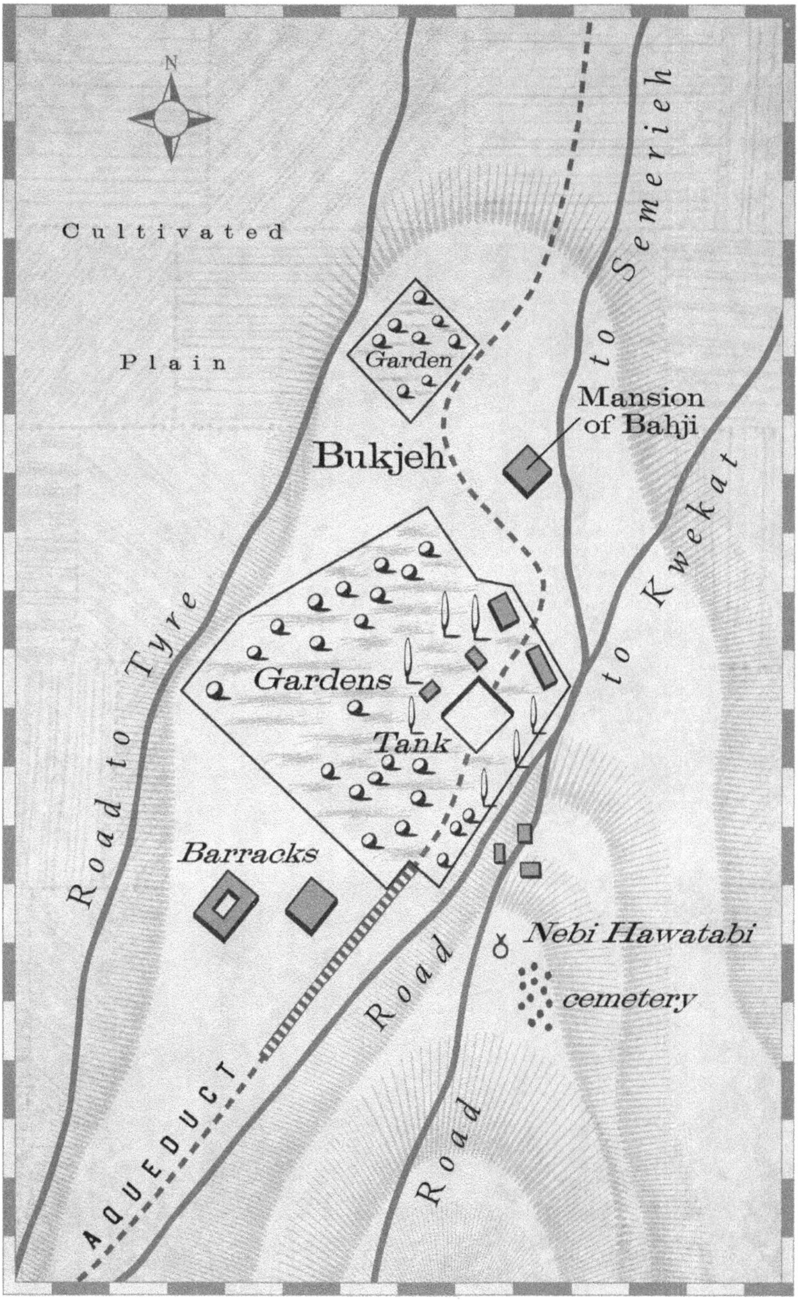

Illustration of Bahjí published in 1863 by British naval officer Lieut. F. G. D. Bedford RN.

REDRAFTED BY WILLIAM MCGUIRE IN 2023

The grave of ʻÚdí <u>Kh</u>ammár is behind this door.

1950s Bahjí, largely as it was in 1892.

COPYRIGHT © BAHÁ'Í INTERNATIONAL COMMUNITY

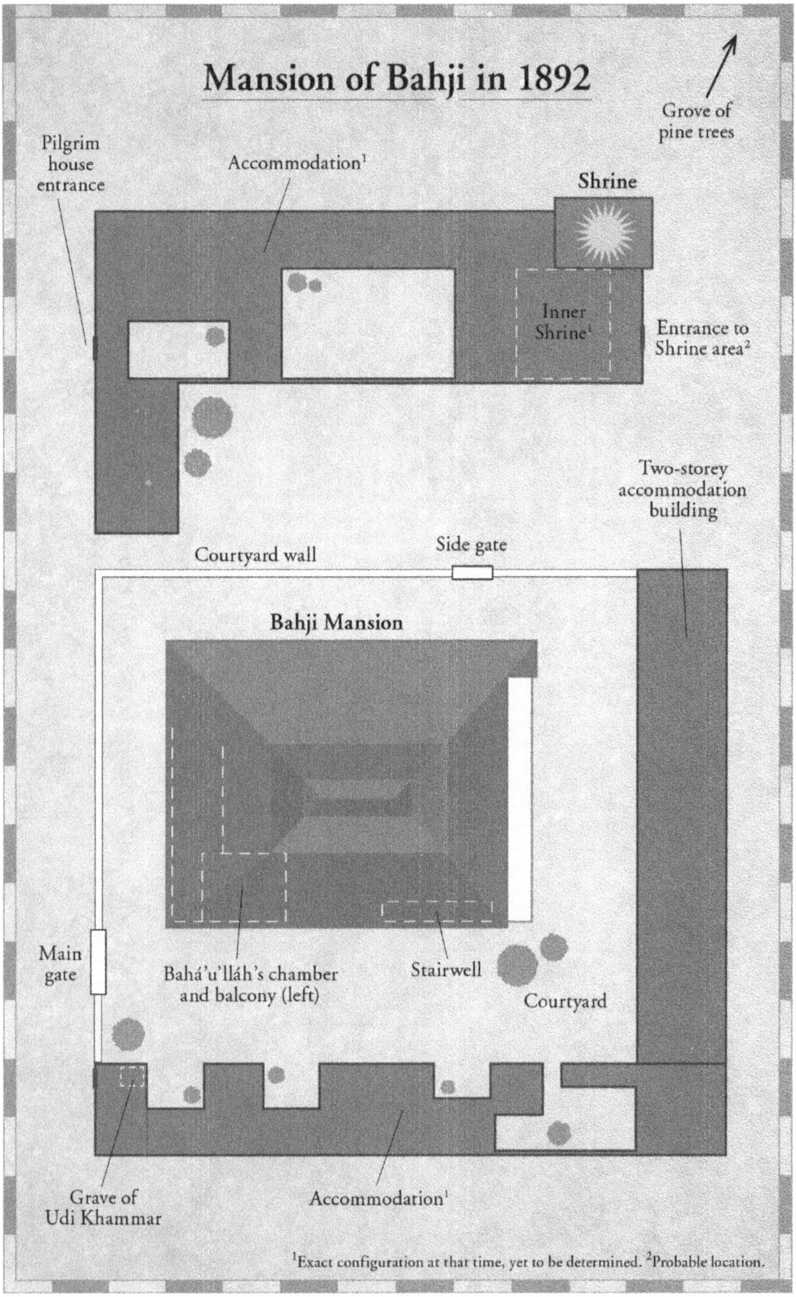

The Bahjí Compound.

ILLUSTRATION BY WILLIAM MCGUIRE IN 2023

The house in which Bahá'u'lláh stayed during His visits to the Riḍván Garden.

7

Lively Scenes

For a rounded perspective on Bahá'u'lláh's life leading up to His ascension, it is important to contemplate the context in which He conducted His activities.

EVERYDAY LIFE

The Bahjí compound, including the mansion and the outbuildings—the houses on both sides of the mansion, the apartment building just to the north of the mansion (demolished in the 1950s), and others—was quite different from the reverential place that pilgrims now experience. The Manifestation's chamber was a quiet retreat on an upstairs corner as it remains today, but the ground floor was a hive of activity. In fact, the whole compound was a thriving, sometimes noisy place with families—children, teenagers, adults—pursuing their own activities. Pilgrims came and went in increasing numbers.

The following description is based on some confirmed details as well as understandings of how life was lived in those days in that part of the world. The descriptions are based on likely scenarios and customs. There are few accounts provided from that time. The women in the kitchens would have been busy, not only preparing meals but also receiving supplies that came on carts pulled by mules from the markets of 'Akká. Servants carried dishes on trays upstairs and set them out on carpets. Bahá'u'lláh usually ate with family members at Bahjí but would eat by Himself when away.[1] Bathroom facilities, including the provision of hot water, would have been available for them on their floor. The conditions would be regarded as somewhat basic today. Other bathrooms were situated away from the mansion. Other members of the family took their meals on the ground floor of the mansion or in the nearby houses. Bahá'u'lláh would occasionally join them.

WHO WAS THERE?

The core group living at Bahjí in the years 1879–92 was comprised of Bahá'u'lláh and most of His extended family. However, as we have seen, 'Abdu'l-Bahá and His wife, Munírih Khánum, and their children lived in 'Akká, as did Bahá'u'lláh's first wife, Ásíyih Khánum (Navváb), who was to pass away in 1886. Some Bahá'ís lived in the compound for a long time, others just for a few months. After examining mentions in various source materials,[2] we can obtain what is likely to be a reasonably accurate though not comprehensive list of the residents, always bearing in mind that women and girls were not mentioned anywhere near to the extent men and boys were identified.[3] If men referred to their wives, they traditionally called them "the mother of the children" rather than by name.[4] In fact, those wives and children were often not referred to in historical accounts. So, although we have a list of thirty, there is bound to have been more. Among the estimated fifty or so people who lived at Bahjí while Bahá'u'lláh was there, were some close relatives of the Manifestation.

A. His second and third wives, Mahd-i-'Ulyá (Fáṭimih Khánum) and Gawhar Khánum.
B. A son of Bahá'u'lláh and Mahd-i-'Ulyá, Muḥammad-'Alí and his wife, Ṣamadíyyih Khánum[5] (the daughter of Áqáy-i-Kalím), and four children.
C. Two brothers of Muḥammad-'Alí, Mírzá Badí'u'lláh and Mírzá Ḍíyá'u'lláh (and his wife Soraya (Thurayyá), and their sister Ṣamadíyyih Khánum.[6]

D. The daughter of Bahá'u'lláh and Gawhar Khánum, Furúghíyyih Khánum, her husband Siyyid 'Alí Afnán, and her father-in-law, Ḥájí Mírzá Siyyid Hasan-i-Afnán-i-Kabír, the Great Afnán.

WIVES

A letter written on behalf of the Universal House of Justice in 1995, to an individual believer, states:

> Regarding the wives of Bahá'u'lláh, extracts from letters written on behalf of the beloved Guardian set this subject in context. They indicate that Bahá'u'lláh was "acting according to the laws of Islam, which had not yet been superseded," and that He was following "the customs of the people of His own land."[7]

Under Muslim law, it was permitted to have up to four wives,[8] and it was usual in Persian society at the time for a prominent man to have at least two wives. Before the promulgation of the laws of the Kitáb-i-Aqdas, the Islamic code was followed.[9] The Bahá'í law is that monogamy alone is permissible.

The Báb had two wives, and Bahá'u'lláh three. It would have been unusual if such a prominent person as Bahá'u'lláh had only one wife. In Persian society, and in Muslim society as a whole, marriages were arranged for a variety of reasons, including forming alliances with others to have a wide extended family, and to give security to a woman who might be widowed or without protection by a family.[10] Bahá'u'lláh's first wife was Ásíyih Khánum (also known as Navváb and Most Exalted Leaf), whom he married in about 1835. They had seven children, three surviving into adulthood: 'Abdu'l-Bahá; Bahíyyih Khánum, the Greatest Holy Leaf; and Mírzá Mihdí, the Purest Branch, who died by accident in 1870. Bahá'u'lláh's second wife, Fáṭimih Khánum (titled Mahd-i-'Ulyá), had married an elderly mullá in 1842 but he died in 1843. They had no children. Bahá'u'lláh married her either in Núr or in Ṭihrán, probably after He left the Síyáh-Chál in 1852.[11]

A specialist historian on the topic of the lives of women closely related to the Báb and Bahá'u'lláh has written, ". . . the circumstances leading to the marriage are unclear. The popular belief is that since Fáṭimih Khánum had been widowed at the age of 15 or 16 and tradition required a male member of the family, well placed and able, provide her with security and protection. Her mother had set her hopes on Bahá'u'lláh and made entreaties to Him in this regard."[12] They had six children, three sons and two daughters. One of the daughters died in infancy. After the ascension of Bahá'u'lláh, Fáṭimih Khánum and her five children broke the Covenant.

Bahá'u'lláh married Gawhar Khánum, possibly in 'Akká in the early 1870s.[13] She was born in about 1847 and had come to the Holy Land with her brother, who died shortly after his arrival. Bahá'u'lláh and Gawhar Khánum had one child—a daughter, Furúghíyyih. When the daughter married, she and her husband lived in the house that now includes the inner and outer parts of the Shrine of Bahá'u'lláh. After the ascension of Bahá'u'lláh, Gawhar Khánum and her daughter broke the Covenant.

WOMEN'S ROLE

The society in the Holy Land was heavily influenced by the Ottomans. There were cultural prohibitions against upper class women interacting with men outside their families. Bahá'í women living in the Bahjí compound, although often wearing scarves—especially when men were around—according to Turkish custom, did not wear the chador, a Persian custom. They would have been active in their home, looking after the children, cooking, cleaning, weaving, and sewing. They likely milked the sheep and goats, providing milk, yoghurt, and cheese, and probably gathered and pressed the olives from nearby trees under an arrangement with the then owners.

MEN'S JOBS

The jobs for the men likely included shearing and slaughtering the sheep and dressing the meat for kababs. Some probably went fishing in the nearby sea. Others plied their trade as blacksmiths—there was a blacksmith shop at Bahjí—and as carpenters and bricklayers. Some were weavers of straw mats, just as the Master had been for some time in 'Akká.[14] Those skilled at calligraphy had plenty of work to do on Bahá'u'lláh's manuscripts and Tablets. Couriers took messages to 'Akká, including to the Telegraph office there.

FOOD

Most inhabitants were either from Persia or of Persian heritage so the food would mainly be Persian cuisine, though not lavish, and often simple. We know that Bahá'u'lláh Himself lived in utmost simplicity.[15] It is probable that dishes such as ghormeh sabzi or ash-e jo were eaten. On Feast days there would be delicious morasa polo, tahdig, roast lamb, chicken, and bread. The styles of kabab, when meat was available, would likely have included kabab torsh (a favorite in Bahá'u'lláh's home province of Mázindarán), kabab Barg (thin chunks on metal stakes) or kabab Ḥusayní (smaller pieces of meat on thin wooden stakes).[16]

For breakfast there was freshly baked bread as well as white cheese plus sweetened black tea. Homemade butter and all kinds of jams, as well as honey, would be provided from time to time. Nuts, especially pistachio and almond, were there as well. Seasonal fruits or dried fruits such as dates and raisins were often available, mostly for children. An occasional hard-boiled egg or fried eggs would also be a part of the diet. Persian teas, often with the pleasant cardamom flavor and scent, were popular, and the samovar—a large container of water heated via a tube in the middle—was always ready to deliver via tap into a teapot with tea leaves inside. Tea was by far the most popular beverage among Persians, although the occasional coffee may have been included. In the Ba<u>gh</u>dád days, Bahá'u'lláh frequented coffee houses. Fresh water was available from the aqueduct that passed alongside the property.[17]

Years spent in regions of the Ottoman Empire meant that residents would be aware of, and probably occasionally enjoyed, Turkish food, with its own style of kababs, as well as yaprak dolma, eggplant dishes, and the traditional Turkish pastry, gozleme. Arab cuisine, such as falafel and shawarma also probably made their way on the menus of the Bahá'í community. Bahá'u'lláh liked to distribute sweets like baklava, as He did special Persian delights prepared by two Bahá'ís, Áqá Mírzá Maḥmúd of Káshán and Áqá Riḍáy-i-Qannád of Shíráz, from their confectionary shop.[18] He is recorded as giving out sweets to children and asking that they be given dessert.[19]

CHILDREN'S CLASSES

A room was set aside on the ground floor of the mansion for tutoring the children.[20] The pupils would learn to read, write, and speak Persian at the level of a highly educated person. That would be in addition to gaining competence in Arabic and Turkish, the languages of the area. Naturally, spiritual topics were high on the agenda. The teachers were at various times Mírzá Yúsuf Khán-i-Vujdání and Áqá Siyyid Asadu'lláh-i-Qumí. The great Mishkín-Qalam taught calligraphy. Among the pupils were the "Branches" (the male children of Fáṭimih Khánum and Gawhar Khánum) plus Ḥájí Mírzá Ḥabíbu'lláh-i-Afnán and his brothers, Ḥájí Mírzá Buzurg and Ḥájí Mírzá Ḍíyá.[21]

ANIMALS

Outside the walls of the mansion were stables for donkeys, mules, and horses.[22] We know that at least in later years valuable horses were kept inside at night. There was a barnyard at Bahjí that had chickens and almost certainly ducks and geese.[23] Children would supervise the grazing of those animals, as still seen in some countries today. There were pens to enclose goats and sheep. Bahá'u'lláh had His own personal flock of sheep and herd of goats, and others would have had their own too. Towards the end of His life, He would drink the milk of the goats. Ḥájí Ḥusayn was the shepherd, and it was he who milked the goats.

It could have been that Bahjí had its own pigeon coops, such as were found in rural compounds in Persia. If so, they would have housed beautiful Persian high-flying Tumbler pigeons (called Ṭihrání in Persia), which, once released, would have been soon high out-of-sight on their missions, often carrying messages. Nightingales would sing after dark. During the day, many other birds, such as the Eurasian hoopoe and blue-winged kingfisher, would be sighted in or near the compound.[24] Pet parrots were popular, so some would probably chatter in the three dominant languages spoken in the compound: Persian, Arabic, and Turkish. Dogs were not usual as pets among Persians, but they were handy sentinels. The jackal, with its distinctive howl, and mongoose were two animals that would roam on the borders of the property. As for creatures to watch out for, there were scorpions, snakes, and mosquitoes.

EVENINGS

At night, it is likely, given our knowledge of the culture of the Persian expatriates at the time, that those residents of the compound with melodious voices would uplift and entertain with their chanting of scriptures revealed by Bahá'u'lláh or verses by the great Persian poets, such as Ḥáfiẓ and Rúmí. Storytellers captivated their audiences by recounting favorite traditional stories or tales they had written themselves. If there were music—and there may not have been—the musicians would have played traditional Persian instruments, such as the santour and tonbak. The residents also would have been influenced by Turkish entertainment, which had borrowed a lot from Eastern Europe and so had some liberal, Christian influences from Bulgaria, Rumania, and Greece. Because there was no electricity, most of the lighting came from candles and oil lamps as well as fire pits. Bedtime was earlier than it became decades later when electric lights arrived.

Mis͟hkín-Qalam.
PROVIDED BY THE US BAHÁ'Í NATIONAL ARCHIVES

8

Bahá'u'lláh at Bahjí

Pilgrims coming and going from 'Akká went to the pilgrim house on the southern side of the compound to the west of the main entrance to the mansion. Before they set out for the mansion, the Master ensured that those whose clothes had been damaged on the way to the Holy Land were fitted out in clean and neat garb.[1] When the appointed time arrived for the pilgrims, guides escorted them through the main gate and then to Bahá'u'lláh's chamber where they would attain His presence, remaining for various lengths of time.

The Englishman, Edward Granville Browne, a guest at Bahjí in 1890, noted that "not a day passes but numerous Bábís [his term for Bahá'ís] of all classes are permitted to wait upon him."[2] Bahá'u'lláh placed great emphasis on punctuality and efficiency. He would reserve different times of the day to get things done—appointments were made, and meetings could be short and sweet.[3] Who did the pilgrims see before them? Here is a composite description by historian Fáḍil-i-Mázindarání, who made a summary from descriptions by others who were in the presence of Bahá'u'lláh:

> Bahá'u'lláh's matchless beauty, his heart-enthralling, sky-blue shining eyes [His eyes are more usually described as dark rather than blue][4] which saw and took note of the visible and the

> hidden, his high forehead and long eyebrows, his long black hair and beard, his imposing presence and great majesty were what most visitors and travellers, whether friend or stranger, commented upon.
>
> He wore firmly placed upon his head, a light brown táj of the type used by Ṣúfís, somewhat taller than usual and of great beauty, embroidered with coloured threads round the base of which was tied a small white turban, and also loosely fitting clothes of white or a grey colour, with a cloak (*abá*) over his shoulders.[5]
>
> The majority of pilgrims however were, on account of being overwhelmed by the awe and ecstasy that they felt in His presence, unable to contemplate His face and robes.
>
> Bahá'u'lláh was of average build, neither tall nor short, neither corpulent, nor thin. His appearance was of the utmost nobility, authority and might, his limbs of perfect proportions and beauty. He was indeed the very example and proof of the statement that God is "the Best of Creators."[6]

This description does not mention the fine beauty of His hands. The hands of Shoghi Effendi were said to be similar to those of Bahá'u'lláh. That is not the only physical similarity. It is generally accepted that Shoghi Effendi was not as tall as the Master, and was probably of similar height to his great-grandfather when an adult.[7]

After the experience of being in His presence, the pilgrims—overwhelmed, inspired, and emotional—would return to the pilgrim house and, before heading back to 'Akká, would exchange their experiences over tea provided from a bubbling samovar.

'AKKÁ AND HAIFA

During the winter, Bahá'u'lláh would return to live in 'Akká, where it was easier to keep warm, and then move back to the Mansion of Bahjí in spring. In other seasons, He also liked to go into 'Akká from time to time, often to visit His wife, Navváb, His son 'Abdu'l-Bahá, His daughter Bahíyyih Khánum, and His grandchildren. He also liked to see His brothers Mírzá Músá Kalím and Mírzá Muḥammad-Qulí there, and to see Bahá'í families living in the Suq al-Abyaḍ, and in the Jewish quarter. He also would see the friends in the Khán-i-Afranj and the Khán-i-'Avámíd. He stayed in other houses too.[8] He once visited the site of the ancient city of 'Akká. He also enjoyed going out to the Druze villages of Abú-Sinán and Yirkih, where He was paid the greatest respect.

During three of the four visits He made to Haifa,[9] where He was seen occasionally walking on the streets and acknowledging greetings by the German Templers, Bahá'u'lláh pitched His tent where number 10 Haparsim Street is now, and also at the base of Mount Carmel. He also stayed at the Templer Inn and houses in the Templer Colony.[10] His final visit, described in a subsequent chapter, became famous for His revelation of the Tablet of Carmel, the spiritual underpinning of the Shrine of the Báb and the Bahá'í World Center. At that time, Bahá'u'lláh also visited the Stella Maris (Star of the Sea) Catholic monastery on Mount Camel.

GARDENS

To the delight of the Bahá'ís, Bahá'u'lláh would often venture out with the friends from the compound to local beauty spots for picnics, which were characterized by chanting, relaxing, and enjoying kababs as well as sweetmeats like baklava. His favorite destination was the Garden of Riḍván, named after the place of His declaration in Baghdád in 1863. He called this place just outside 'Akká "that most sanctified, that most sublime, that blest, and most exalted Spot."[11]

Adjacent were the Gardens of Firdaws and 'Alí-Ashraf.[12] The Firdaws Garden[13] was purchased along with the Garden of Riḍván in 1881,[14] four years after Bahá'u'lláh first visited. He once pitched His tent in that garden.[15] The 'Alí-Ashraf Garden had been bought by the wealthy Mullá Abú-Ṭálib, the father of two masons who were builders of the Shrine of the Báb. Abú-Ṭálib left the garden to his son, 'Alí-Ashraf, who later donated it to the Faith.[16] Bahá'u'lláh bestowed on the Garden of Riḍván the names "New Jerusalem" and "Our Verdant Isle."[17] He often sat cross-legged on wide benches with carved backrests under the shade of mulberry trees. At first it seems He would spend the warm nights sleeping on the benches under a mosquito net, but would later sleep in a bedroom that was built for Him in a small house,[18] which remains there to this day. He often spent days or weeks sleeping there.[19]

Bahá'u'lláh recounts a number of vivid mystical revelations associated with the place, such as the scene described in the following passage: "Every tree uttered a word, and every leaf sang a melody. The trees proclaimed: 'Behold the evidence of God's Mercy, and twin streams recited in the eloquent tongue,[20] the sacred verse 'From us all things were made alive.'"[21] In the Lawḥ-i-Ṭarázát (Tablet of Ornaments), He states that one day He was enjoying the stream and sunlit trees in "Our Green Island" when He turned to the right and "beheld what the pen is powerless to describe." Then, turning to the left, He "gazed upon one of the Beauties of the Most sublime Paradise, standing on a pillar of light," who proclaimed to be the "manifestation of trustworthiness" and asserted: "I am the supreme instrument for the prosperity of the world, and the horizon of assurance unto all beings."[22]

One of His granddaughters, Ṭúbá Khánum, left behind some reminiscences of Bahá'u'lláh and the Garden of Riḍván from a child's perspective:

> We children looked upon Bahá'u'lláh as another loving Father; to Him we carried all our little difficulties and troubles. He took an interest in everything which concerned us.
>
> He used to send a servant to Beirut every year to buy stuff for our clothes. Bahá'u'lláh would then call for us to choose which we liked best for our frocks. My mother, my aunt, and the children would make this cotton material into garments.
>
> He was always punctual, and loved daintiness and order. He was very particular and refined in His personal arrangements, and liked to see everybody well groomed, and as neatly dressed as possible. Above all things, cleanliness was desirable to Him.

"Why not put on your prettiest frocks?" He would say to us. All our holidays, all our treats and our happiness came from Him in those days; when boxes of sweets were brought to Him He would set some aside for us.

"Put that box of sweets over there, or Áqá (the Master) will give it away to the people," He would say in fun.

"Let the dear children come in, and have some dessert," He often said, when we were being sent off to bed—my Father and my mother not wishing that we should disturb Him—but He always welcomed us with loving words.

How we adored Him!

"Now children, to-morrow you shall come with Me for a picnic to the Riḍván," He would say, and our night was so full of joy we could scarcely sleep."[23]

NAHR

Other destinations included Nahr (meaning "small river" (present-day Nahariya) where there were gardens and orchards irrigated by the local springs. At one such place, Bahá'u'lláh began the revelation of His last great work, Epistle to the Son of the Wolf.[24] He enjoyed the Garden of 'Afífí, a beautiful spot near the springs of Kabrí.[25] There was also the Bustán-i-Kabír at Mazra'ih.

THE CRIMSON SPOT

Bahá'u'lláh liked to pitch His tent on the hill overlooking Bahjí, which was called the Buq'atu'l-Ḥamrá' (the Crimson Spot) when it was covered with red flowers such as poppies and anemones. It was a favorite place of the Master's too.[26]

JUNAYN GARDENS

Bahá'u'lláh also occasionally visited the Junayn Gardens, a small farmhouse and orchard north of Bahjí. Land associated with those gardens was donated by the Jarráh family to the Faith. Ṭarázu'lláh Samandarí, later appointed a Hand of the Cause of God, recalled:

> . . . Toward morning [of Naw-Rúz] we were told that Bahá'u'lláh would be visiting Junaynih that day, and that He had summoned all the settlers and pilgrims to that spot. They provided us with conveyances and brought us there. It is quite a long way from Haifa to Junaynih, and in those days people went by carriage. Junaynih is near the Mansion of Mazra'ih; not far from there, in fact, quite near.
>
> We came to Junaynih, where we found Bahá'u'lláh. So there, too, I entered His presence. About thirty of us, perhaps, were guests at luncheon; among the poets were, it seems to me, Jináb-i-'Andalíb, Ustád Muḥammad-'Alí [Salmání] was there and Nabíl-i-A'ẓam. The last-named and 'Andalíb sang verses that day, from an ode. Lunch had been made ready for us.
>
> They had prepared a lamb for our luncheon; cooked it in the stove; and brought it on a large tray, which they placed on the table in Bahá'u'lláh's room. I was at that moment standing near Him, with my arms folded across my chest. He touched the lamb with His finger and said, "Take it away."
>
> They took it out to the outer room where they had laid the luncheon cloth on the floor. We had bread too, with the lamb. We all ate luncheon there. Following the meal, it seems to me there was also a revelation of verses. I listened a little from outside the door; I heard a little. Then, that afternoon, Bahá'u'lláh was to return to the Mansion of Bahjí. There was a white donkey which, I know, Ḥájí Gh͟ulám-'Alí Kás͟hání had brought to Bahá'u'lláh at that time. The Blessed Beauty mounted, and a servant held an umbrella over Him, for a light rain was falling. I also accompanied Him. On His right hand [side], the servant held up the umbrella, while I was on His left. And thus we came from Junaynih to the Mansion of Bahjí.[27]

Edward Granville Browne of Cambridge University also saw Bahá'u'lláh in the Junayn Garden sometime during his five-day visit to Bahjí from April 15 to April 20, 1890.[28]

THE MASTER

Bahá'u'lláh revealed a special Tablet in 1879 on the occasion of the visit of 'Abdu'l-Bahá to Beirut.[29] Can there be any more eloquent a tribute from a father to a son, a Manifestation of God to His successor?

> Praise be to Him Who hath honored the Land of Bá through the presence of Him round Whom all names revolve. All the atoms of the earth have announced unto all created things that from behind the gate of the Prison-city there hath appeared and above its horizon there hath shone forth the Orb of the beauty of the great, the Most Mighty Branch of God—His ancient and immutable Mystery—proceeding on its way to another land. Sorrow, thereby, hath enveloped this Prison-city, whilst another land rejoiceth. . . .
>
> Blessed, doubly blessed, is the ground which His footsteps have trodden, the eye that hath been cheered by the beauty of His countenance, the ear that hath been honored by hearkening to His call, the heart that hath tasted the sweetness of His love, the breast that hath dilated through His remembrance, the pen that hath voiced His praise, the scroll that hath borne the testimony of His writings. We beseech God—blessed and exalted be He—that He may honor us with meeting Him soon. He is, in truth, the All-Hearing, the All-Powerful, He Who is ready to answer.[30]

OASIS OF CALM

In His chamber in the southeast corner of the Mansion, Bahá'u'lláh would reveal His Tablets, meet pilgrims, and occasionally meet others from overseas. 'Abdu'l-Bahá describes the scene, His words translated by Shoghi Effendi:

> Bahá'u'lláh was nominally a prisoner (for the drastic firmán of Sulṭán 'Abdu'l-'Azíz were never repealed), yet in reality He showed forth such nobility and dignity in His life and bearing

> that He was reverenced by all, and the Rulers of Palestine envied His influence and power.
>
> Governors and Mutaṣarrifs,[31] generals and local officials, would humbly request the honor of attaining His presence—a request to which He seldom acceded.[32]

Ḥájí Mírzá Ḥaydar-'Alí quoted Bahá'u'lláh about the change in His policy from Adrianople, where He met many people. Not so in Bahjí:

> We seldom receive visitors who are not believers. The burden of all these affairs have fallen upon the shoulders of the Master. To provide Us with some peace and comfort, He had made Himself Our shield, and thus He sees to Our affairs both with the government and with the people. . . . He is so devoted to His services and so intensely preoccupied that sometimes weeks pass by and He cannot come here to visit Us. While We consort with friends and reveal Tablets, He is immersed in the toils and troubles of the world.[33]

'Abdu'l-Bahá recounts the following:

> On one occasion a Governor of the city implored this favor [of an audience] on the ground of his being ordered by higher authorities to visit, with a certain general, the Blessed Perfection. The request being granted, the general, who was a very corpulent individual, a European [likely to have been General Gordon of Khartoum][34] was so impressed by the majestic presence of Bahá'u'lláh that he remained kneeling on the ground near the door.
>
> Such was the diffidence of both visitors that it was only after repeated invitations from Bahá'u'lláh that they were induced to smoke the nargileh (hubble-bubble pipe) offered to them. Even then they only touched it with their lips, and then, putting it aside, folded their arms and sat in an attitude of such humility and respect as to astonish all those who were present.

> The loving reverence of friends, the consideration and respect that were shown by all officials and notables, the inflow of pilgrims and seekers after truth, the spirit of devotion and service that was manifest all around, the majestic and kingly countenance of the Blessed Perfection, the effectiveness of His command, the number of His zealous devotees—all bore witness to the fact that Bahá'u'lláh was in reality no prisoner, but a King of Kings.
>
> Two despotic sovereigns were against Him, two powerful autocratic rulers, yet, even when confined in their own prisons, He addressed them in very austere terms, like a king addressing his subjects. Afterwards, in spite of severe firmáns, He lived at Bahjí like a prince. Often He would say: "Verily, verily, the most wretched prison has been converted into a Paradise of Eden."[35]

The term "living like a prince" should not be confused with living in luxury, as pointed out by author John Esslemont, who was posthumously elevated to the rank of Hand of the Cause.

> Having in His earlier years of hardship shown how to glorify God in a state of poverty and ignominy, Bahá'u'lláh in His later years at Bahjí showed how to glorify God in a state of honor and affluence. The offering of hundreds of thousands of devoted followers placed at His disposal large funds which He was called upon to administer. Although His life at Bahjí has been described as truly regal, in the highest sense of the word, yet it must not be imagined that it was characterized by material splendor or extravagance. The Blessed Perfection and His family lived in very simple and modest fashion, and expenditure on selfish luxury was a thing unknown in that household.[36]

'Abdu'l-Bahá would not arrange audiences with Bahá'u'lláh for politicians seeking their own advancement. However, some genuine social reformers did establish contact, and Bahá'u'lláh directed 'Abdu'l-Bahá to write a treatise on the subject of social and economic development. The resulting work, written in 1875 and published in 1882, was addressed to the rulers and people of Persia, and was widely circulated in the region. An English translation was first published in 1957 under the title *The Secret of Divine Civilization*.[37]

* * *

Bahá'u'lláh's location at the mansion meant that not only could He have privacy and quiet, but He was in a convenient spot when news came that 'Abdu'l-Bahá was approaching. Bahá'u'lláh would go out onto the balcony outside His room and wait with loving anticipation the arrival of His beloved son, Who was walking to show respect.

Like the Báb, Bahá'u'lláh was meticulous about cleanliness of both body and clothing. His personal barber was Salmání,[38] a brilliant poet [see chapter 9], whose memoirs offer us a glimpse of some relatively private details concerning the everyday life of the Manifestation. Salmání goes into some detail regarding how he refined his craft as a barber in Baghdád by watching a head-shaver shaving Bahá'u'lláh. No doubt, Salmání adopted the same standards of care later in Bahjí. [The methods are reminiscent of current techniques in the bathhouses of Istanbul.]

Salmání describes the treatment further:

> Water was then brought, and I soaped Bahá'u'lláh's hair two or three times—the various soaps were from Aleppo—and then He withdrew to the place where henna would be applied and the body rubbed with a rough bath mitt.
>
> I then brought Him His own bath towel, and once He was dry He stretched out so that I could apply henna to His beard, after which He seated Himself and I used the henna on His hair. He then lay down again (and I placed a pillow under His head) so that I could rub Him with the mitt—and two or three

times I kissed His feet. He rose again and seated Himself, and I took the mitt to the backs of His hands and arms.

Very soon, He directed me to fetch the rinse water. I rinsed off the henna, added the dark dye, and finally soaped and rinsed Him off and He departed. I was in a state of utter bliss.

The Master and the Branches and Áqáy-i-Kalím used to frequent the same bathhouse. I worked there two or three months and every ten days or less they would come in.[39]

PART 2

GUESTS OF BAHÁ'U'LLÁH

9

Three Poets

In His mystical works, the Seven Valleys and the Four Valleys, Bahá'u'lláh quoted from the thirteenth century poet Rúmí[1] as well as from other well-known mystic poets such as 'Aṭṭár, Saná'í, and Sa'dí.[2] He also quoted from Rúmí in one potent paragraph in His major theological work, the Kitáb-i-Íqán.[3] No wonder, then, that while at Bahjí, Bahá'u'lláh welcomed into His presence three poets so talented in both Persian and Arabic poetry that their fame had spread to the wider community of Persia.[4]

Their pen names were Nabíl ("Noble"), 'Andalíb ("Nightingale"), and Salmání (just part of his name). Their poetry alone qualifies them to take their place in the pantheon of Bahá'í heroes, but they provided other significant contributions as well. Two wrote down what they experienced at the time of the ascension of Bahá'u'lláh and during the inauguration of His shrine. The third gave us insight into how a prayer for artistic inspiration was rewarded.

Among Persians, poets have been celebrities for millennia, the best retaining their fame despite many centuries having passed since they put pen to paper. Their contribution to the literary heritage of humankind includes often—but not always—employing images of human love to refer to spiritual ecstasy with a clarity of expression that arrows deep into the heart as it entrances the mind. Here is an example of a poem by Ḥáfiẓ:

WHY NOT BE POLITE

Everyone
Is God speaking.
Why not be polite and
Listen to
Him?[5]

In addition to Ḥáfiẓ of the fourteenth century and Rúmí of the thirteenth century and other great poets such as their predecessors Firdawsí,[6] 'Aṭṭár, and Saná'í, there are three more whose names are emblazoned in the annals of the Persian poets who have burst through the borders of their homeland and bestowed their genius upon all humanity.

NABÍL (1830–1892)

A shepherd in his youth, Muḥammad-i-Zarandí, later named Nabíl, used to recite under the stars the passages from the holy Qur'án that he had memorized. From occupying one of the most humble roles in the stratified Persian society, Nabíl rose to became not only a master of both poetry and prose, but one so beloved he was at times "almost daily . . . admitted to the presence of the Manifestation."[7] Bahá'u'lláh Himself bestowed upon this poet and historian the Arabic name "Nabíl-i-A'ẓam," meaning "the Greatest Nobleman."[8]

Nabíl has several direct connections to the story of the Shrine of Bahá'u'lláh. Because he was present at the interment of the sacred remains of Bahá'u'lláh, he was among the first to pray at that shrine, and he also left a legacy to every individual pilgrim who attains the sacred threshold. At the invitation of 'Abdu'l-Bahá, Nabíl selected from the writings of Bahá'u'lláh the content of the Tablet of Visitation that pilgrims now recite at the shrine.[9] In fact, Nabíl can be regarded as the first Bahá'í pilgrim. At the direction of Bahá'u'lláh, he undertook two pilgrimages—acts that mark, according to Shoghi Effendi, "the inception of one of the holiest observances [pilgrimage], which in a later period, the Kitáb-i-Aqdas was to formally establish."[10] The Manifestation instructed Nabíl to go in His stead to the pilgrimage sites for the Bahá'í Faith as later revealed in the Kitáb-i-Aqdas: the House of the Báb in Shíráz and the House of Bahá'u'lláh in Baghdád. Bahá'u'lláh directed Nabíl to recite on His behalf "the two newly revealed Tablets of the Pilgrimage, and perform, in His stead, the rites prescribed in them."[11]

As an historian, Nabíl also provided posterity an eyewitness description of the days leading up to and including the ascension of Bahá'u'lláh and the interment of His sacred remains. That priceless contribution to humanity is in addition to his book *Matláli'-i-Anwár,*[12] which details the history of the Bábí and Bahá'í Faiths up to 1890. The first part of that work, which takes the reader up to 1852, was translated into English and entitled *The Dawn-Breakers* by Shoghi Effendi,[13] who referred to Nabíl as the "immortal chronicler" of those days, who "may well rank as [Bahá'u'lláh's] Poet-Laureate."

In a stirring and appropriately poetic obituary 'Abdu'l-Bahá wrote that Nabíl had heard "from the lips of the Manifestation . . . marvelous things. He was shown the lights of Paradise. He won his dearest wish. . . . "[14] The Master said: "He was a gifted poet, and his tongue most eloquent; a man of mettle, and on fire with passionate love."[15] "Day and night he sang the praises of the one Beloved of both worlds and of those about His threshold, writing verses in the pentameter and hexameter forms, composing lyrics and long odes."[16]

Edward Granville Browne, a British academic and talented linguist in Persian and Arabic, praised Nabíl's poem "Bahá, Bahá" as being "a very fine address to Bahá'u'lláh." 'Abdu'l-Bahá said Nabíl had written that poem in a state of (spiritual) ecstasy. Poetry is notoriously difficult to translate in a way that conveys its beauty as well as meaning, but Browne did it well as this excerpt shows (note the reference to polo in the last line here):

Bahá, Bahá

Though the Night of Parting endless seems as thy night-black hair,
Bahá, Bahá,
Yet we meet at last, and the gloom is past in thy lightning's glare,
Bahá, Bahá!
To my heart from thee was a signal shown that I to all men should make known
That they, as the ball to the goal doth fly, should to thee repair,
Bahá, Bahá![17]

In the second half of the poem there are these fine lines, which capture an aim of Bahá'u'lláh—the happiness of the nations:

The World hath attained to Heaven's worth, and a Paradise is the face of the earth
Since at length, thereon a breeze hath blown from thy nature rare,
Bahá, Bahá!

Skilled at telling the stories of others, Nabíl led an adventurous life worthy of a book of its own. In a Tablet Bahá'u'lláh addressed to him, Nabíl was directed to take the Faith to the East and West.[18] Nabíl first met 'Abdu'l-Bahá when the Master was a young boy. He witnessed the events in the Garden of Riḍván when Bahá'u'lláh declared His Mission in 1863. He went on multiple teaching missions to Persia (he taught the Faith to the Bahá'í hero Badí') and influenced the Báb's widow to recognize the station of Bahá'u'lláh as the Promised One.[19]

Nabíl was jailed for his faith in Persia and in Egypt, where he was seeking the release of imprisoned Bahá'ís. In the Holy Land, he made his home for a while in Safed (Tsfat), a beautiful hill town still favored by mystics, and later he lived in a cave on Mount Carmel.[20] Upon the direction of Bahá'u'lláh, he transcribed the text of the Badí' Calendar and instructed the Bahá'ís in its details.[21]

Nabíl, in what seems to have been a state of deep depression, drowned on 3 September 1892, a little more than three months after the ascension of His beloved Bahá'u'lláh. 'Abdu'l-Bahá wrote: "And at the end, when the Daystar of the world [Bahá'u'lláh] had set, he could endure no more, and flung himself into the sea. The waters of sacrifice closed over him; he was drowned, and he came, at last, to the Most High." The Master, Who referred to him as "the great Nabil," concluded His tribute with a supplication for abundant blessings and tender mercies to be bestowed upon him.[22]

'ANDALÍB (C. 1853–1920)

The Bahá'í poet 'Andalíb ("Nightingale") stayed at Bahjí for the two months prior to the ascension of Bahá'u'lláh and for four months afterwards. He witnessed the last illness of Bahá'u'lláh, and was said to have been complimented by the Manifestation with these words: "The loving devotion of 'Andalíb has touched me very much. . . ."[23] The poet was present at Bahá'u'lláh's funeral and at Bahjí during the mourning period that followed. He was one of the first Bahá'ís to have the privilege of setting foot in the holy Shrine of Bahá'u'lláh. In poetry and prose, 'Andalíb wrote about those historic events he witnessed, especially the deep grief of the Bahá'ís and the generality of the population in the area. In this, 'Andalíb provided a service to successive generations by helping describe the greatness of Bahá'u'lláh, as well as depicting how much He was loved during His lifetime on this earth.

Born Áqá Mírzá A<u>sh</u>raf-'Alí Láhíján, 'Andalíb's great gift was noticed by a teacher, who then bestowed upon him an appropriate pen name, 'Andalíb, thereby comparing the sweetness of his verses to the sound of the nightingale, the great songster of the natural world.[24] The admiration that the Manifestation of God and the Center of the Covenant had for 'Andalíb is demonstrated in numbers alone. The poet received twenty-one Tablets from Bahá'u'lláh and fifty-six from 'Abdu'l-Bahá.

Fluent in Persian and Arabic, 'Andalíb had many artistic skills apart from creating poetry. He was highly skilled in illuminating manuscripts, for example, as well as in making beautiful papier-mâché pencases. Today there are thousands upon thousands of people of Persian heritage who recall that when they were children, they drifted off to sleep as their mothers sang the hypnotic melody that accompanies a sweet lullaby written by 'Andalíb. The poet wrote those verses for Shoghi Effendi when the future Guardian was but a baby in his cradle. Here is the first verse, translated into English, with a soothing repetition at the end of some lines:

He is God!
O thou the luminous moon — go to sleep my love
Oh thou the flowing soul — go to sleep my love
Thou art the balm of the soul — go to sleep my love
Oh thou sweet tongued — go to sleep my love.[25]

'Andalíb came from the city of Láhíján, a place renowned for silk and tea, set in luxuriant green vegetation on the northern slopes of the Alborz mountains and close to the Caspian Sea. It was a perfect spot for a great poet to arise. Of a mystical disposition, 'Andalíb became interested in Shaykhism, an incubator of many of the followers of the Báb. He became a Bábí after hearing of the new faith via travel teachers. He was later to be put in chains and thrown into prison in Rasht for two years because of his beliefs.

'Andalíb soon pledged his allegiance to Bahá'u'lláh and became a master teacher of His Faith. One of those who became a Bahá'í through him was his friend, Náẓimu'l-Ḥukama, who became the father of a future Hand of the Cause, Shu'á'u'lláh 'Alá'í, and the ancestor of a family, many of whose members are well known for their service to the Faith to this day. 'Andalíb was a superb teacher of the Faith. This assessment is not based on hearsay. We know it to be true via the verbatim reports by the young English academic, Edward Granville Browne, who encountered 'Andalíb in Yazd in 1888. From Cambridge University, Browne, aged twenty-six, was totally fluent in Persian and had an outstanding memory. He could recall long conversions word for word, and to the benefit of history, he wrote down what 'Andalíb told him about the Bahá'í Faith.

The way 'Andalíb told Browne about the Faith is similar to how Bahá'ís often explain the teachings to seekers today. 'Andalíb had quickly grasped not only an understanding of the essence of the Faith but how to explain it, using appropriate analogies for those before him. In his highly readable masterpiece *A Year Among the Persians,* Browne recounts his first meeting with ʻAndalíb, describing him as "a man of about thirty-five years of age, whose eloquence filled me with admiration." He further described him as "one of the most distinguished of the poets who have concentrated their talents to the glory of the new Theophany."[26]

Browne recorded ʻAndalíb dismissing the evidential power of descriptions of miracles as a proof of the station of a Manifestation of God: "No, it is the Divine Word which is the token and sign of a prophet, the convincing proof to all men and all ages, the everlasting miracle," ʻAndalíb said. He added that the essential characteristic of the Divine Word is its "penetrative power" (nofuz); it is not spoken in vain, it compels, it constrains, it creates, it rules, it works in men's hearts, it lives and it dies not."[27]

After a discussion with the young Englishman about the spiritual role of the Manifestation, ʻAndalíb took him by the hand and urged him to go to ʻAkká and see "Beha" (Bahá'u'lláh) for himself. "How noble a work might be yours," he said, "if you could become assured for the truth of his claim in spreading the good news through your country!"[28] Browne did receive the privilege of attaining the presence of Bahá'u'lláh, and his words continue to "spread the good news" not only in his own country but worldwide.[29]

On another occasion, Browne conversed with ʻAndalíb, who read him some of his own poems and also wrote down "one of the beautiful odes attributed to the Bábí heroine and martyr Qurratu'l-ʻAyn [Ṭáhirih]."[30] "He talked a great deal about the identity of all the prophets, whom he regarded as successive Manifestations or Incarnations of the Divine Will or Universal Reason," Browne said. When ʻAndalíb was telling Browne about the Faith, the Englishman continued translating and writing in his notebook the words he used, including a verse from Rúmí that makes the point he was advancing:

It needs an eye which is king-discerning
To recognize the King in whatever garb.[31]

After his first visit to the Holy Land in the last weeks of the life of Bahá'u'lláh, 'Andalíb returned to his wife and children in Persia. Years later, he returned to the Holy Land where, in 1909, in the presence of 'Abdu'l-Bahá, he recited some impromptu poetry on the occasion of the opening of the Pilgrim House.[32] Upon returning again to Persia, he endured the early death of his wife, and then took on the care of his four daughters and two sons. He passed away in 1920 aged about sixty-seven.[33]

So highly regarded was this nightingale of the Bahá'í Faith that 'Abdu'l-Bahá wrote a potent Tablet of Visitation to be read at his grave.

SALMÁNÍ (1835–C. 1910)

Before looking at the details of the life of Ustád Muḥammad-'Alíy-i-Salmání, it is both useful and enjoyable to encounter a description of him as the personality he truly was. It comes from the distinguished historian and authority on Bahá'í poetry, the late Dr. Amín Banání:

> This ebullient spirit, unschooled in formal learning and impassioned with the love of Bahá'u'lláh, could overcome the inhibitions of the old and grasp the exultation of the new. . . . He was a personality of vivid colors; a man of humble origins, unlettered, quick-witted, full of bravado and abundant humor (and not a little mischief) with a truly lyrical gift for poetry.[34]

Ustád Muḥammad-'Alíy-i-Salmání, who had become Bahá'u'lláh's barber and bath attendant in Baghdád, accompanied the Manifestation to Adrianople (Edirne) and later met up with Him again in 'Akká. His life had its share of dramatic incidents, such as having had his ear cut off during the 1852 persecutions of Bábís in Persia; his deportation from Adrianople to Persia and his escape from imprisonment there; and then more imprisonment—this time in 'Akká—for going against Bahá'u'lláh's explicit command and joining with others in attacking enemies of the Faith.[35]

While in Adrianople, Bahá'u'lláh had asked Salmání what he wanted in life, and the answer came back that he would like to be a poet like Sa'dí—quite an ambition for an illiterate man. Bahá'u'lláh instructed him to study poetry. The results were dramatic. As Dr. Banání pointed out: "His lyrical gift, which was moved to flow in rapturous outpourings by his love for Bahá'u'lláh, sets Salmání above legions of other, more learned and literate Bahá'í poets. Much of his poetry bears the mark of genuine passion and emotional immediacy."

In the tradition of Persia, his love images are in fact a tribute to the Manifestation. In translation to English by Marzieh Gail, the verses bear witness to the insight of Dr. Banání. For example, this stanza:

Thou stealest from the sugar all its sweet,
And from the rose its red,
With every smile of Thine,
And very blandishment.

And then there are verses like this where the meaning does not require a metaphor:

O Thou Messiah, raising up dead hearts!
With Thy breath, like a scented breeze
Raise up this corpse to Thee.
Thou art love's flutist,
I am but the flute:
What dost Thou play in me?
What song is this that to the world's edge brings
Poor helpless me?"
O Candle of desire!
Moth-like I'm shedding fire
From my wings.[36]

After the ascension of Bahá'u'lláh, he was a true servant of 'Abdu'l-Bahá, and often recited his poems for Him. In 1907, Salmání and his wife left for 'Ishqábád, where they passed away and were buried.[37]

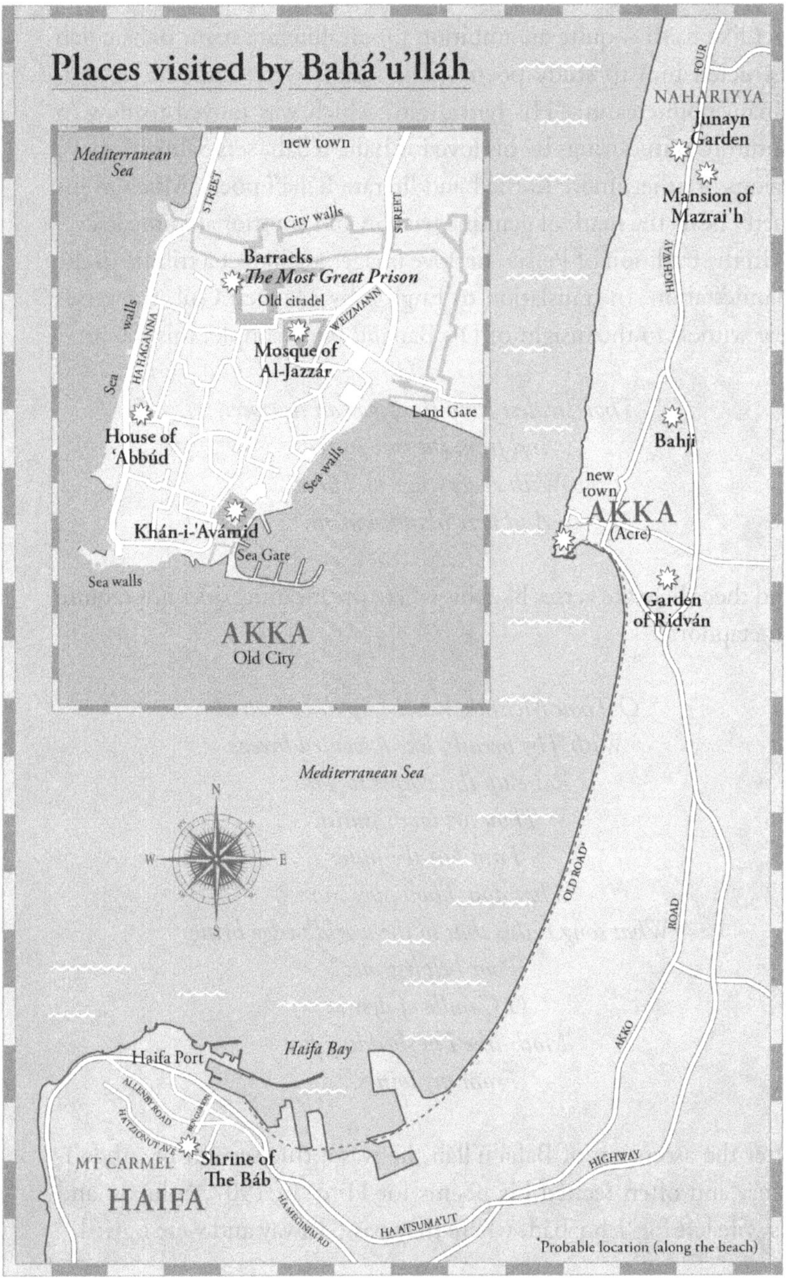

Places visited by Bahá'u'lláh
Mediterranean Sea
new town
STREET
City walls
STREET
Barracks
The Most Great Prison
Old citadel
WEIZMANN
Mosque of
Al-Jazzár
walls
HA HAGANNA
Sea
Land Gate
House of
'Abbúd
Sea walls
Khán-i-'Avámid
Sea Gate
Sea walls
AKKA
Old City
FOUR
NAHARIYYA
Junayn
Garden
Mansion of
Mazrai'h
HIGHWAY
Bahjí
new
town
AKKA
(Acre)
Garden
of Riḍván
Mediterranean Sea
N
W
E
S
OLD ROAD*
ROAD
AKKO
Haifa Port
Haifa Bay
ALLENBY ROAD
HATZIONUT AVE
MT CARMEL
Shrine of
The Báb
HAIFA
HA MEGINIM RD
HA ATSUMA'UT
HIGHWAY
*Probable location (along the beach)

The 'Akká-Haifa area.

MAP BY WILLIAM MCGUIRE

Nabíl-i-A'ẓam.

'Andalíb.

10

A Curious Visitor

"Whomsoever Thou willest Thou causest to draw nigh unto the Most Great Ocean, and on whomsoever Thou desirest Thou conferrest the honor of recognizing Thy Most Ancient Name."

—Bahá'u'lláh[1]

By 1890, the Faith of Bahá'u'lláh had made astounding inroads into lands far away from the Mansion of Bahjí. With Bahá'u'lláh's encouragement, either directly or indirectly, Bahá'í teachers had taken the Faith to many parts of Persia, Iraq, and India,[2] introducing the teachings to many people, and deepening the knowledge of the existing believers. During His ministry, twelve other countries were also opened to the Faith,[3] including Turkey, Georgia, Egypt, Sudan, Pakistan, and Burma (today's Myanmar). There were even individual Bahá'ís in the distant Dutch East Indies (now Indonesia) and in China.[4]

About two decades previously in Adrianople and 'Akká, Bahá'u'lláh had proclaimed His teachings to the kings and rulers of the world, to the religious leaders, and to humanity as a whole, but His messages were largely ignored.[5] It was in April 1890 that an event took place that would prove to be the springboard for the first public proclamations of the Bahá'í teachings in Great Britain and in the United States of America. This was important to the future expansion of the Bahá'í Faith. By the last decade of the nineteenth century, one quarter of the total population of the world lived in the British Empire, which controlled close to a quarter of the planet's land surface.[6] The United States was destined to be Britain's successor as the major world power.

In Bahá'u'lláh's gracious chamber in the Mansion of Bahjí, He granted four audiences to Edward Granville Browne, a twenty-eight-year-old English academic and medical doctor from Cambridge University, one of the greatest institutions of higher learning in the world.[7] Remarkably fluent in Persian,[8] Turkish, and Arabic,[9] personable and gregarious, Edward Granville Browne was a genius with a highly unusual gift, as described by his eminent colleague, Professor Sir E. Denison Ross. "E. G. B.'s memory was astonishing, and he not only understood what was said to him, but usually remembered conversations verbatim,"[10] Professor Ross recalled in a memoir of his friend. Browne's fluency in Persian and his uncanny memory were to serve him well when he met Bahá'u'lláh.[11]

Some two years earlier, in 1887–88, Browne had spent a year in Persia, eventually meeting Bahá'ís. and being impressed by them. He engaged in deep discussions on spiritual topics with knowledgeable believers, such as Ḥájí Mírzá Ḥaydar-'Alí, who Browne refers to in his book, *A Year Among the Persians,* as Haji Mirza Hasan for his protection, and who was later given the title "the Angel of Carmel" by 'Abdu'l-Bahá.[12] Another was Ḥájí Mírzá Ḥusayn-i-Kh̲arṭúmí (called Mirza Hasan in the book).[13]

In the same book, which is a masterfully written travelogue, Browne describes how he went against the advice of one of the Persian Bahá'ís, the poet 'Andalíb, who said: "I advise you to give up the idea of going to Kirman altogether . . . you will get no good by it, and you see the difficulties that it involves. Go to Acre instead; that will be easily done on your homeward journey and therefrom far greater blessing and advantages are likely to result."[14] Disregarding that wise advice, Browne travelled to Kirman, where he spent time with followers of Mírzá Yaḥyá (1831–1912), reinforcing his view that Bahá'u'lláh's half-brother was the legitimate head of the community founded by the

Báb. Browne was a compulsive supporter of somebody he considered the underdog, and was sympathetic toward Yaḥyá and his followers despite being given strong evidence of the falsehood of their claims.[15]

Although the mysticism of the Persian poets appealed to him, he was not on a spiritual quest when investigating the Bábí and Bahá'í Faiths.[16] He wrote that his interest in the Bábí Faith was "quite apart from its success or failure. I think it throws much light on the history of religions, and it is a manifestation of a heroic spirit rare enough in these days."[17] As Professor Ross recalled: "I never heard him discuss either Religion or Art."[18] Browne had been introduced to the Bábí Faith, not via spiritual search, but rather due to a book by a French orientalist he happened upon in the Cambridge library. He borrowed the book and was thrilled by the accounts of the heroics of the followers of the Báb.[19] As an academic by profession and inclination, he enjoyed collecting and translating manuscripts and rare books. Later he became a keen supporter of political reform in Persia.

In 1889, back at Cambridge, Browne wrote the first account in English of the history and doctrines of the Bábí movement in a paper in the Journal of the Royal Asiatic Society. In March 1890, Browne visited Mírzá Yaḥyá in Cyprus for two weeks before he spent a week at Bahjí. The Englishman spent a long time with Bahá'u'lláh's treacherous half-brother but did not seem to gather any information from him worth telling, but nor did he correct his view of him as a Letter of the Living.[20]

Browne then obtained permission from the Bahá'ís to visit 'Akká. He obtained it with the help of Ḥájí Muḥammad Áqá (the father of the historian Hasan Balyuzi, a future Hand of the Cause) and his cousin Siyyid 'Alí Afnán, Bahá'u'lláh's son-in-law who lived in the house that two years later would become the Shrine of Bahá'u'lláh.[21] In his later report of his first morning in 'Akká in April 1890, Browne wrote that he met somebody, whom he "guessed from the first by the extraordinary deference shewn to him by all present, was none other than Behá's eldest son 'Abbás Efendí [sic]."[22]

He then provides an extraordinary account of his first impressions of the Master:

> Seldom have I seen one whose appearance impressed me more. A tall strongly-built man holding himself straight as an arrow, with white turban and raiment, long black locks reaching almost to the shoulder, broad powerful forehead indicating a strong intellect combined with an unswerving will, eyes keen as a hawk's, and strongly-marked but pleasing features—such was my first impression of 'Abbás Efendí, "the master" (*Áká*) as he *par excellence* is called by the Bábís [sic. Brown referred to Bahá'ís as Bábís].
>
> Subsequent conversation with him served only to heighten the respect with which his appearance had from the first inspired me. One more eloquent of speech, more ready of argument, more apt of illustration, more intimately acquainted with the sacred books of the Jews, the Christians, and the Muhammadans, could, I should think, scarcely be found even amongst the eloquent, ready, and subtle race to which he belongs.
>
> These qualities, combined with a bearing at once majestic and genial, made me cease to wonder at the influence and esteem which he enjoyed even beyond the circle of his father's followers. About the greatness of this man and his power no one who had seen him could entertain a doubt.[23]

Browne then describes the events that followed while waiting to go from 'Akká to Bahjí with 'Abdu'l-Bahá and one other person: "[A] weird-looking old man, who proved to be none other than the famous [calligrapher] *Mushkín-Kalam,* came and seated himself beside us. He told me that he had heard all about me from a relation of his at Isfahán, and that he had been expecting to see me at Acre ever since that time. . . ."

This indicates that reports of Browne's discussions with the Bahá'ís in Persia in 1887–88 were likely to have come to 'Abdu'l-Bahá, perhaps by that calligrapher or via Mírzá Muḥammad Áqá. The Master is likely to have briefed Bahá'u'lláh on the Englishman. Browne describes how a man brought three "fine white asses" for the three to ride to Bahjí, the mansion visible in the distance next to a stand of towering pine trees. Being April—the month considered by many the most beautiful in the Holy land—the journey would have been pleasant as they rode through a plain of fresh spring flowers including red poppies, pink cyclamens, and blue irises.

> A quarter of an hour later we alighted in front of the large mansion, . . . whereof the name, *Behjé* (Joy), is said to be a corruption (though, as the Bábís do not fail to point out, a very happy corruption) of *Bághcha* (which signifies a garden). I was almost immediately conducted into a large room on the ground-floor, where I was most cordially received by several persons whom I had not hitherto seen.
>
> Amongst these were two of Behá's [sic. As Browne refers to Bahá'u'lláh] younger sons, one of whom one was apparently about twenty-five and the other about twenty-one years of age.[24] Both were handsome and distinguished enough in appearance, and the expression of the younger was singularly sweet and winning.
>
> Besides these a very old man with light blue eyes and white beard, whose green turban proclaimed him a descendant of the Prophet,[25] advanced to welcome me, saying, "We know not how we should greet thee, whether we should salute thee with '*as-selámu 'aleykum*' or with '*Alláhu abhá*.'"[26] When I discovered that this venerable old man was not only one of the original companions of the Báb but his relative and comrade from earliest childhood, it may well be imagined with what eagerness I gazed upon him and listened to his every utterance.

That elderly man was the Great Afnán (Ḥájí Mírzá Ḥasan)—a former merchant and current astronomer—who was living in the room later to become the inner sanctuary of the Shrine of Bahá'u'lláh, and who had the great privilege of being in the presence of Bahá'u'lláh every morning and evening.[27] In later years, the Master described him as "a man amazing to behold, his face so luminous that even those who were not believers used to say that a heavenly light shone from his forehead."[28]

Browne continues his story:

So here at *Behjé* was I installed as a guest, in the very midst of all that Bábíism accounts most noble and most holy; and here did I spend five most memorable days, during which I enjoyed unparalleled and unhoped-for opportunities of holding intercourse [in the nineteenth century it meant "communication"] with those who are the very fountain-heads of that mighty and wondrous spirit which works with invisible but ever-increasing force for the transformation and quickening of a people [Persians] who slumber in a sleep like unto death.

It was in truth a strange and moving experience, but one whereof I despair of conveying any save the feeblest impression. I might, indeed, strive to describe in greater detail the faces and forms which surrounded me, the conversations to which I was privileged to listen, the solemn melodious reading of the sacred books, the general sense of harmony and content which pervaded the place, and the fragrant shady gardens whither in the afternoon we sometimes repaired; but all this was as nought in comparison with the spiritual atmosphere with which I was encompassed.

Persian Muslims will tell you often that the Bábís bewitch or drug their guests so that these, impelled by a fascination which they cannot resist, become similarly affected with what the aforesaid Muslims regard as a strange and incomprehensible madness. Idle and absurd as this belief is, it yet rests on a basis of fact stronger than that which supports the greater part of what they allege concerning this people. The spirit which pervades the Bábís is such that it can hardly fail to affect most powerfully all subjected to its influence. It may appall or attract: it cannot be ignored or disregarded. Let those who have not seen disbelieve me if they will; but, should that spirit once reveal itself to them, they will experience an emotion which they are not likely to forget.[29]

Ahead lay the momentous meeting that has continued down the years to serve as an eloquent proclamation of the teachings of Bahá'u'lláh, and at the same time provide a remarkable description of the Manifestation and the feeling of being in His presence.

11

The Manifestation Grants an Audience

It proved to be an historic occasion in the history of the Bahá'í Faith when Bahá'u'lláh drew into His presence the young Englishman, Edward Granville Browne. The report by the Cambridge academic of the audience granted him would contain a landmark description of the Manifestation and lead to the initial public proclamations of the teachings in the United Kingdom and the United States of America. Edward Granville Browne wrote an unforgettably eloquent account of his first meeting with Bahá'u'lláh on Wednesday, 16 April 1890.[1]

> Of the culminating event of this my journey some few words at least must be said. During the morning of the day after my installation at *Behjé* one of Behá's younger sons entered the room where I was sitting and beckoned to me to follow him.[2] I did so, and was conducted through passages and rooms [on the ground floor] at which I scarcely had time to glance [Browne then went up the stairs] to a spacious hall, paved, so far as I remember (for my mind was occupied with other thoughts) with a mosaic of marble. Before a curtain suspended from the wall of this great ante-chamber my conductor paused for a moment while I removed my shoes.

> Then, with a quick movement of the hand, he withdrew, and, as I passed, replaced the curtain; and I found myself in a large apartment, along the upper end of which ran a low divan, while on the side opposite to the door were placed two or three chairs. Though I dimly suspected whither I was going and whom I was to behold (for no distinct intimation had been given to me), a second or two lapsed ere, with a throb of wonder and awe, I became definitely conscious that the room was not untenanted.

Browne then bequeaths to posterity, a "unique, unparalleled pen-portrait of Bahá'u'lláh."[3]

> In the corner where the divan met the wall sat a wondrous and venerable figure, crowned with a felt head-dress of the kind called *táj* by dervishes (but of unusual height and make), round the base of which was wound a small white turban. The face of him on whom I gazed I can never forget, though I cannot describe it. Those piercing eyes seemed to read one's very soul; power and authority sat on that ample brow; while the deep lines on the forehead and face implied an age which the jet-black hair[4] and beard flowing down in indistinguishable luxuriance almost to the waist seemed to belie. No need to ask in whose presence I stood, as I bowed myself before one who is the object of a devotion and love which kings might envy and emperors sigh for in vain!

In His melodious voice, Bahá'u'lláh then addressed Edward Granville Browne in Persian. The Englishman with the magic memory later recorded what the Manifestation said, word for word and translated it all into English.

> A mild dignified voice bade me be seated, and then continued: "Praise be to God that thou hast attained! . . . Thou hast come to see a prisoner and an exile. . . . We desire but the good of the

world and the happiness of the nations; yet they deem us a stirrer up of strife and sedition worthy of bondage and banishment. . . . That all nations should become one in faith and all men as brothers; that the bonds of affection and unity between the sons of men should be strengthened; that diversity of religion should cease, and differences of race be annulled—what harm is there in this? . . . Yet so it shall be; these fruitless strifes, these ruinous wars shall pass away, and the 'Most Great Peace' shall come. . . .

Do not you in Europe need this also? Is not this that which Christ foretold? . . . Yet do we see your kings and rulers lavishing their treasures more freely on means for the destruction of the human race than on that which would conduce to the happiness of mankind. . . . These strifes and this bloodshed and discord must cease, and all men be as one kindred and one family. . . . Let not a man glory in this, that he loves his country; let him rather glory in this, that he loves his kind. . . ."

Browne wrote modestly—given his remarkable memory—that "Such, so far as I can recall them, were the words which, besides many others, I heard from Behá. Let those who read them consider well with themselves whether such doctrines merit death and bonds, and whether the world is more likely to gain or lose by their diffusion." Browne said his interview lasted about twenty minutes, during the last part of which Bahá'u'lláh read from one of His Tablets. From Browne's references, the following are the words—translated by Browne into English—the Manifestation read to him:[5]

He is God, exalted is His state, wisdom and utterance. The True One (glorious is His glory) for the shewing forth of the gems of ideals from the mine of man, hath, in every age, sent a trusted one. The primary foundation of the faith of God and the religion of God is this, that they should not make diverse sects and various paths the cause and reason of hatred. These principles and laws and firm sure roads appear from one dawning-place and shine from one dayspring, and these diversities were out of regard for the requirements of the time, season, ages, and epochs. O unitarians, make firm the girdle of endeavour, that perchance religious strife and conflict may be removed from amongst the people of the world and be annulled. For love of God and His servants engage in this great and mighty matter. Religious hatred and rancour is a world-consuming fire, and the quenching thereof most arduous, unless the hand of Divine Might give men deliverance from this unfruitful calamity. Consider a war which happeneth between two states: both sides have foregone wealth and life: how many villages were beheld as though they were not! This precept is in the position of the light in the lamp of utterance.

O people of the world, ye are all the fruit of one tree and the leaves of one branch. Walk with perfect charity, concord, affection, and agreement. I swear by the Sun of Truth, the light of agreement shall brighten and illumine the horizons. The all-knowing Truth hath been and is the witness to this saying. Endeavour to attain to this high supreme station which is the station of protection and preservation of mankind. This is the intent of the King of intentions, and this the hope of the Lord of hopes.

Browne wrote that "during the five days spent at *Behjé* [Tuesday, April 15 to Sunday, April 20], I was admitted to Behá's presence four times. These interviews always took place an hour or two before noon, and lasted from twenty minutes to half-an-hour. One of Behá's sons always accompanied me, and once Áká Mírzá Aká Ján (*Jenáb-i-Khádimu'lláh*) the amanuensis (*kátib-i-áyát*) was also present. In their general features these interviews resembled the first, of which I have attempted to give a description."

Although Browne confirms that he met with Bahá'u'lláh four times, we only know details about two of those audiences. In his notebook, Browne shares further information about his first meeting with Bahá'u'lláh, in addition to what he included in the introduction to the book *A Traveller's Narrative:*

> In morning admitted to audience with Beha. It was wonderful—only one of his sons besides myself was present. He motioned me to a seat, and began to talk—Marvellous fire and vigour—He kept beating the ground with His foot (slippered) and now and then looking out of the window. He began by saying "Alhamdu'lilah kih fa'iz shudid [Praise be to God that you have attained]." Then he said, "You have come to see a prisoner." He went on to speak of his sufferings and the letters he had written to the Kings, asking me if I had read them. He then read part of a Lawh [tablet]. . . ."[6] [See above for that extract.]

Recently, more information has come to light about that famous audience with Bahá'u'lláh. It appears in a paper by Dr. Christopher Buck and Dr. Youli Ioannesyan, based on handwritten letters by Browne to Baron V. Rosen recently discovered in the archives of the Russian Academy of Sciences.[7] In his letter to Rosen, Browne describes his audience with Bahá'u'lláh with a slightly different perspective from the one found in his introduction to his translation of *A Traveller's Narrative,* the depiction that is quoted above and now known throughout the Bahá'í world. Browne wrote:

> I sat humbly before him while he talked. His discourse was oracular but rather general in character. He spoke as "one having authority," but not exactly as I had expected—like a Master, and a Prophet—but not as an Incarnation of the Divinity.[8] He is to look at a very majestic old man—but though he must be 70 at least his long beard & hair are quite black.[9] He wears a very tall namad cap . . . with a small white turban. His manner is gracious and dignified, but somewhat restless, suggesting great stores of energy. He talked for the most part of the necessity of all nations choosing one language as a means of international communication & one writing (a sort of a sermon on the concluding text of the Most Holy Tablet) of the necessity of putting down war & international jealousy & hostility. Of doctrine so called he spoke little."[10]

In his memoirs, Bahá'u'lláh's youngest son, Mírzá Badí'u'lláh [who later broke the Covenant, then confessed, but later reneged] provided a brief description of the audience before giving a description of Browne's reaction.

> This writer [Mírzá Badí'u'lláh] and Ghuṣn-i-Áthár [Mirza Ḍíyá'u'lláh, his brother] was hosting this dear guest [Browne]. . . . He was a very learned man. He spoke eloquently well in the sweet Persian language. . . . The first time that he had the honour of attaining Bahá'u'lláh's holy Presence, although he [Browne] had a few questions, [in fact] he only asked one question about discord and disunity of all religions. Then he observed silence and the condition and manner of his behaviour changed.
>
> After he had been dismissed from His [Bahá'u'lláh's] presence, he [Browne] entered the room that we had provided for him. He was dazed [senseless] and was just moving [silently] his lips. . . . After that, he became motionless and quiescent. I asked him, "What happened to you? You became completely silent!" He replied: "After He [Bahá'u'lláh] looked at me, I saw a power and authority that changed my normal condition. I noticed such penetrating and influential power and authority in His eyes that I had never seen in any of the kings or rulers that I had ever met." I asked [him] about the reason why he was moving his lips. He said: "I repeated [to myself] the reply which He gave concerning the cause of the discord between religions in order not to forget it."

Buck and Ioannesyan explain in their paper[11] why they think Browne became "dazed." As they note, Bahá'u'lláh was known to avert His gaze from those who had attained an audience, primarily because it would overwhelm the person. Perhaps, they write, He may have looked directly at him because He had asked Browne if He had read His letters to the kings. An alternative explanation, is that Bahá'u'lláh may have looked directly at Browne when the Englishman asked Him about interreligious discord.

Later that same day, the authors note, Browne was in the presence of 'Abdu'l-Bahá, and wrote the following notes about it: "Visit from [?]Abbas Effendi, who spoke much of humanity and civilization. . . ."[12] Then Browne wrote that Bahá'u'lláh's amanuensis, Mírzá Áqá Ján, "came and talked with great eloquence." Buck and Ioannesyan, basing their view on a provisional translation of Áqá Ján's Persian, said it seemed that Bahá'u'lláh had indicated it was possible that Browne, through his future publications, had every potential of rendering a great service in providing accurate information and insights regarding the nature of the Bahá'í Faith.[13]

The only other meeting we know about is fascinating for its content, particularly regarding reference to the Universal House of Justice. It is reported in Browne's diary entry for Friday, April 17, 1890 [sic. It was actually April 18, 1890]. He wrote:

> Admittance to audience with Behá in morning for some 20 min. or ½ an hour . . .
>
> He again insisted very strongly on the necessity of unity and concord among the nations, and spoke of the Sulh-i-Akbar [later translated by Shoghi Effendi as "Lesser Peace" to distinguish it from the Most Great Peace, "al-Ṣulḥ al-A'ẓam"] which will come soon. . . .
>
> There must be one language and one writing. The former may be either one of those now existing, or one invented for the purpose by a conference of *savants* of all countries.
>
> All nations must bind themselves to combine and put down any nation which attempts to disturb the general peace.
>
> Beha also spoke of the Bayt al-'Adl [House of Justice] which, he said, is to settle all disputes. The members of this will be "inspired" (mulham). *Jihad* [holy war] is entirely forbidden in this Zuhur [manifestation].[14]
>
> Besides this, one afternoon I saw Behá walking in one of the gardens which belong to him. [Junayn Garden].[15] He was surrounded by a little group of his chief followers. How the

journey to and from the garden was accomplished I know not: probably under cover of the darkness of night.

Browne wrote in his diary that he had to leave Bahjí—despite being warmly invited to stay on—so he could arrive home before the end of his leave from Cambridge.

Bahá'u'lláh later referred to Browne in a Tablet. [Bahá'u'lláh refers to Browne as "the youth" and to Himself as "this Wronged One." The Afnán that is mentioned is His son-in-law.]

> Your letter was sent to the Supreme Threshold by Afnán on whom be My Glory. The youth mentioned therein attained Our presence. Although this Wronged One had not consorted for many years past with people from foreign lands, We received him on several occasions. Portents of sincerity could be discerned on his visage. We beseech God to aid him in such undertakings which would be conducive to the effacement of mischief and the promotion of the betterment of the world. He is the Hearing, the Prayer-Answering. Afnán will write and give you details.[16]

After returning from the Holy Land, Browne gave a lecture on the new religion at the South Place Institute in London. Historian Moojan Momen writes that this lecture on 15 February 1891 may count as the first public lecture on the Bahá'í Faith in the West.[17] Browne translated into English a manuscript of 'Abdu'l-Bahá's titled "A Traveller's Narrative,"[18] which had been handed to him in 'Akká, though he had not been told of the author's identity. The book, published in 1891, had an introduction by Browne that included his historic report of his encounter with Bahá'u'lláh.[19]

The first public quoting of the words of Bahá'u'lláh in North America came at the inaugural meeting of the Parliament of the World's Religions, held in Chicago in 1893,[20] when a United States clergyman, George A. Ford, read a paper written by Rev. Henry H.

Jessup,[21] an American Presbyterian missionary, that included extracts of the report by Browne.

The Englishman's treatment of the Bahá'í Faith and of 'Abdu'l-Bahá was to take a perplexing turn in the following decades—a distressing outcome that the Master's forbearance and love seemed to eventually counter, as a future volume will show.

More than 130 years after he penned his beautiful description of Bahá'u'lláh and accurately quoted what the Manifestation said to him, his report continues to appear in Bahá'í histories, websites, and talks, and is distributed to inquirers and others. Pilgrims arriving at the room of Bahá'u'lláh at the mansion today have the opportunity to remind themselves of what happened there, and of what was said, by reading a framed copy that Shoghi Effendi placed on the wall.

Edward Granville Browne in Persian attire.

CAMBRIDGE UNIVERSITY LIBRARY, CAMBRIDGE TRAINEE LIBRARIANS ONLINE GROUP

A táj belonging to Bahá'u'lláh.

12

Apostle of the Crimson Ark

In February 1892, three months before His ascension, Bahá'u'lláh granted a seventeen-year-old pilgrim a special one-on-one audience and there imparted a teaching that was to have a profound effect on the young man. The pilgrim was Ṭarázu'lláh Samandarí, whose first name, meaning "Ornament of God," had been bestowed upon him by Bahá'u'lláh when he was an infant. After his audience at Bahjí, his destiny was to live seventy-six more years, during which time he would devote himself with astounding effect to propagating and protecting the religion of Bahá'u'lláh. He was to become a Hand of the Cause of God in December 1951, and would not pass away until 1968 at the advanced age of ninety-four.

If the Manifestation were to select any one pilgrim to whom He would give an important instruction, could He have chosen anybody who would prove more dedicated, more dynamic, more effective or longer living than Ṭarázu'lláh Samandarí? In retrospect, like so many actions of Bahá'u'lláh, the choice seems deliberate. Could it have been one based on the Manifestation's foreknowledge? Bahá'u'lláh's message sunk deep into the consciousness of the young Bahá'í, who passed it on to eager audiences and individuals at every possible opportunity. What was that lesson, the one that appears to be the only direct spiritual instruction Mr. Samandarí remembered from

Bahá'u'lláh? It emerges in a story Mr. Samandarí often told about one particular encounter with Bahá'u'lláh.[1]

The young man had been unwell in 'Akká and for two weeks had not been able to go to Bahjí to enter the presence of Bahá'u'lláh, an experience he had eagerly anticipated since he had arrived as a pilgrim with his aunt and sister in December 1891. When Ṭarázu'lláh felt better, he went alone from 'Akká to the Mansion of Bahjí. At the bottom of the staircase to the upper floor where Bahá'u'lláh resided, he asked one of the children of the Holy Family to go to Bahá'u'lláh, Who was alone at the time. He gave the young girl a message he wanted her to pass to the Manifestation: "Say to Him, it is Ṭaráz. He has not been in Your presence for several days. May he approach You now?" She did as asked and returned with His message: "He says: "Bismu'lláh—come in the name of God." Hearing those words, his limbs began to shake, but with his characteristic energy, Ṭarázu'lláh bounded up the staircase, slowed to a reverent walk along the upper courtyard and then, trembling with excitement, entered Bahá'u'lláh's room where he encountered Him pacing the floor.

Ṭarázu'lláh continues with the story: "I bowed low, then stood with my arms folded across my chest. He came over to me, and He drew His hand across my face and head, expressing infinite grace and favour." Bahá'u'lláh remarked that Ṭarázu'lláh had complained that he had not been in His presence for two weeks, and asked: "In 'Akká, do you not seek out the presence of Sarkár-i-Áqá [the Master]?" Telling the story, Ṭarázu'lláh said that until that day, he had never unsealed his lips in the holy presence of the Manifestation. He continues: "Now I answered: 'I attended upon Him day and night, may I be Thy sacrifice.' [Bahá'u'lláh] smiled: 'Then why do you complain . . . that you have not been in My presence?'"

He was clearly implying that meeting with the Master was as meeting with Himself, in effect emphasizing that 'Abdu'l-Bahá was His designated successor, the Center of His Covenant to Whom all must listen carefully and obey. Many years later, in a talk delivered to an eager and fascinated audience in the United States, Ṭarázu'lláh said: "truly it was He [Bahá'u'lláh] Who sowed the love of the Covenant in my inmost heart, and wrote it there with the words of His holy mouth." After Bahá'u'lláh assured him that he was always permitted to come to Bahjí, his real home, He gave Ṭarázu'lláh some sweets and bid him farewell, saying: "Fí Amanu'lláh—go in God's care." Ṭarázu'lláh told his audience, "I left feeling intoxicated—full of joy, ecstasy, and inspiration."

For decades, traveling throughout Persia and later other countries, Ṭarázu'lláh Samandarí raised the call of loyalty to the Covenant, as, in his eyes, Bahá'u'lláh had intended him to, and as 'Abdu'l-Bahá had explicitly directed him. Mr. Samandarí relied on his own service and did not bask in the reputation of his distinguished ancestry. His eminent father, Shaykh Muḥammad Káẓim-i-Qazvíní, had also been on pilgrimage in 1891, a little earlier than his son. Bahá'u'lláh had given the father the title Samandar (in English "Phoenix"). Ṭarázu'lláh's grandmother had been a companion of the poet Ṭáhirih, a Letter of the Living, and his mother was from a devout Bábí family.

Ṭarázu'lláh, who had studied Arabic and Persian, was a skilled calligrapher and became renowned for his prowess in that artform. His ability to read and confirm the identity of the author of Tablets was just one of the factors that made his contributions to the Faith highly valuable. The intense study it involved enabled him to speak confidently on almost any topic in his later life as a teacher and specifically as a Hand of the Cause. If the description "pocket dynamo" could be respectfully applied to any human being, then Ṭarázu'lláh Samandarí was the perfect candidate. Although small in stature, he was a whirlwind of energy. His son, Mihdi, gave a pen portrait of his father:

> Ṭaráz Effendi was an arresting figure—small, [he was under 150 cm tall, or 4 feet 11 inches] trim, upright, with quick movements—and he walked so swiftly that few could keep pace with him. His eyes were penetrating and dark; his hair neat and black (it never became white), his hands strong and sensitive and his voice clear and resonant. His rapidity of movement and mental ability remained with him to the end of his life. He personified

> courtesy, dignity and kindliness. He was a very early riser and methodical in his ways. . . . Children and youth were drawn to him. Generations of youth inspired by his encouragement and example have matured as ardent, active Bahá'ís acknowledging that it was he who set them on the path of service.[2]

Mr. Samandarí married a female namesake, Ṭaráziyyih, his cousin. She was one of the founders of a Bahá'í girls' school in Qazvín, and was its principal. 'Abdu'l-Bahá sent her a Tablet full of praise, encouragement, and promises of endless bounties for her. The Master referred to Ṭarázu'lláh in Tablets as "a luminous candle," "a cause of happiness of souls," and "a mine of joy." Shoghi Effendi, who appointed him a Hand of the Cause of God in December 1951, paid him many tributes, referring to him as a "knight of the arena of detachment," "a true Herald of the Greatest name," and "the shining lamp among Bahá'í teachings." One particularly evocative title he bestowed upon him was "an Apostle of the Crimson Ark."

When in the West and delivering his talks in Persian, Mr. Samandarí would "speak at the top of his voice, almost shouting each sentence aloud, engaging his audience to the full and attracting others outside the room to see what was going on."[3] His address about his memories of Bahá'u'lláh to the first Bahá'í Congress at the Royal Albert Hall in London in 1963 was spellbinding. In Haifa in 1968, a few days after the commemoration of the centenary of Bahá'u'lláh's arrival in the Holy Land, the Hand of the Cause of God Mr. Ṭarázu'lláh Samandarí passed away, and was interred in the Bahá'í cemetery there, next to his teaching partner, the distinguished Ḥájí Mírzá Ḥaydar-'Alí, the Angel of Carmel. In a message to the Bahá'í world about his passing, a grieving Universal House of Justice said he had been "faithful to the last breath of the instructions from his Lord, his Master, and his Guardian. . . ."[4]

Those "instructions from his Lord" were given to Ṭarázu'lláh just three months before he witnessed the final illness and funeral of the Manifestation. Mr. Samandarí was also present at the reading in the Shrine of Bahá'u'lláh of the Manifestation's Will and Testament, the document known as the Kitáb-i-'Ahd ('Ahd means "Covenant"), which clearly set out that 'Abdu'l-Bahá was now the Head of the Faith. At that time, the teenaged Ṭarázu'lláh Samandarí had no idea that he would one day be elevated to the special rank given to four eminent believers of the time. Bahá'u'lláh had appointed those four to the rank of Hand of the Cause of God. To understand the potential seen in Ṭarázu'lláh, later realized in action, we need to learn something of the background of those four deemed worthy by Bahá'u'lláh of that high station.

13

Light and Glory

Bahá'u'lláh had been laying down the administrative foundation for the development of His vision of divine civilization from the time when, in His mid-fifties, He was revealing the Kitáb-i-Aqdas. A decade later, within six years of His ascension, He took further significant steps to promote and safeguard the Faith. One of His decisions was to put into operation a clause in the Kitáb-i-Aqdas that spoke of "the learned ones in Bahá." In that Book of Laws, He had described such Bahá'ís as "the manifestations of steadfastness amidst men and the daysprings of Divine Utterance to all that dwell on earth."[1]

In 1886 and 1892, Bahá'u'lláh bestowed the rank of "Hand of the Cause of God" on four such "manifestations of steadfastness," who each received a Tablet so designating them.[2] All four had suffered greatly for their beliefs and were strikingly effective teachers and defenders of the Faith. As Bahá'u'lláh was to direct, their duty was to propagate and defend the Faith.[3] The Hands of the Cause appointed by Bahá'u'lláh held consultative meetings together, and they became known among the believers as occupying a position of spiritual leadership.[4] In fact, the consultative meetings of the Hands of the Cause "evolved into the Spiritual Assembly of Ṭihrán, the first assembly in the world."[5] Shoghi Effendi was to include all four in his list of nineteen "Apostles of Bahá'u'lláh."[6]

CREATED FOR THE PURPOSE

The first Hand of the Cause appointed was Ibn-i-Abhar (mid-nineteenth century–1917), whose role was decided before his birth. Bahá'u'lláh said in one of His Tablets that this man "was created to extol God and magnify His name, to teach His cause and to serve Him."[7] In 1886, the same year Ibn-i-Abhar attained the presence of Bahá'u'lláh, the Manifestation appointed him a Hand of the Cause of God. Five years later, the authorities arrested Ibn-i-Abhar on false charges and threw him into a dungeon in Ṭihrán. The very chains that had been used on Bahá'u'lláh in 1852, now weighed down and confined this magnificent teacher of the Faith. The fiendish torturers would haul him out to beat the soles of his feet with rods, inflicting intense pain of the type that rendered victims immobile for several days. To those who offered sympathy, the Hand of the Cause asked whether it would be fitting that Bahá'u'lláh should suffer such tribulations "while this insignificant being, who considers himself as one of His servants, be exempt from similar suffering."[8] When the Master saw a photograph of Ibn-i-Abhar in chains, He wrote: "I was so affected that all sorrow was turned into joy and radiance. . . ."[9]

In 1892 when Bahá'u'lláh ascended and His shrine was inaugurated, Ibn-i-Abhar was still imprisoned. Plunged into deep sorrow by the passing of the Manifestation, he wrote to the Master asking for help to overcome his grief. 'Abdu'l-Bahá, despite Himself being immersed in intense suffering for the same reason, wrote to the Hand of the Cause, consoling and comforting him. Ibn-i-Abhar had successfully taught the Faith in prison and even written a Bahá'í book. The initial manuscript was inscribed on wrappers of sugar, tea, and candles, and then smuggled out of the prison.[10] When the jailers freed him in 1895, it was as if they had released a coiled spring. Far from dissuaded by imprisonment from teaching the Faith, the Hand of the Cause visited 'Abdu'l-Bahá and followed His instruction to go to 'Ishqábád, and then travel extensively, teaching and protecting the Faith in Persia and the Caucasus. When he went to India in 1907, accompanied by American Bahá'ís Hooper Harris and Harlan Ober, and by Maḥmúd Zarqání and his brother, he traveled widely throughout the subcontinent, building on the achievements of teachers that Bahá'u'lláh had previously sent there.

Eleven visits to 'Abdu'l-Bahá in the Holy Land seemed to spiritually refuel this energetic teacher. His achievements included teaching the Faith to highly educated and influential people in Persia. He helped establish the Tarbiyat Bahá'í school for boys, and also served alongside his wife in promoting the education of women and girls in Persia.[11]

BLESSED IS THE SPOT

Bahá'u'lláh first used the title "Hand of the Cause" to refer to an individual with certain responsibilities in an 1887 Tablet in honor of Ibn-i-Aṣdaq (c. 1850–1928).[12] But the encounter of Ibn-i-Aṣdaq with the Manifestation had occurred much earlier, when, as an eleven-year-old boy, he had traveled to Baghdád with his father. For two years, father and son stayed in the presence of Bahá'u'lláh. The Manifestation revealed a prayer for the young boy, asking God for His bounty so that, when the boy became an adult, he would arise to serve the Cause.[13] Interestingly, although his son was appointed a Hand of the Cause by Bahá'u'lláh, the boy's father, Mullá Ṣádiq-i-Muqaddas (Ismu'lláhu'l-Aṣdaq) (c. 1800–89), was posthumously appointed a Hand of the Cause by 'Abdu'l-Bahá, Who praised him with a stunning tribute.[14]

When father and son returned to Persia, they were incarcerated for two and a quarter years in the Síyáh-Chál, the pestilential underground prison where Bahá'u'lláh received His revelation in 1852. Upon release, Ibn-i-Aṣdaq and Mullá Ṣádiq went on teaching expeditions throughout Persia. Ibn-i-Aṣdaq married the niece of Mullá Ḥusayn, the first person to whom the Báb proclaimed His mission. She unfortunately soon passed away. He then married Udhrá Khánum, a Bahá'í who was also a member of Persian royalty. Through her connections, the Hand of the Cause was able to teach the Faith to royalty and members of the Persian aristocracy.

He traveled to India, Burma, and Russian Turkestan, as well as throughout Persia, where, like the other Hands down the generations, he fulfilled his sacred assignment to teach the Bahá'ís about the Covenant. A Tablet revealed by Bahá'u'lláh in his honor includes the well-known verse: "The movement itself from place to place, undertaken for the sake of God, has always exerted and can now exert, its influence in the world."[15] In another Tablet to him, Bahá'u'lláh revealed a prayer full of lovely imagery—one which for generations has been recited, chanted, and sung in many languages by Bahá'ís throughout the world: "Blessed is the spot, and the house, and the place, and the city, and the heart, and the mountain, and the refuge, and the cave, and the valley, and the land, and the sea and the island and the meadow where mention of God hath been made, and His praise glorified."[16]

After the ascension of Bahá'u'lláh and the establishment of His shrine, Ibn-i-Aṣdaq faithfully served 'Abdul-Bahá. In 1919, together with Aḥmad Yazdání, he delivered the Master's Tablet on peace to the Central Organization for a Durable Peace, which was meeting in the Hague. He coauthored with other Hands a refutation of some erroneous statements made by Professor Edward Granville Browne about the Bahá'í Faith, and he delivered the Master's Treatise on Politics to the Sh̲áh of Persia. After the ascension of 'Abdu'l-Bahá, Ibn-i-Aṣdaq served Shoghi Effendi with continued distinction.

UNMET YET APPOINTED

The only Hand of the Cause appointed by Bahá'u'lláh who did not meet Him was a new Bahá'í named Mírzá Ḥasan-i-Adíb (1848–1919). We can only speculate that the Manifestation was able to imbibe the depths and intensity of the man's spirituality by reports of his teaching prowess, and perhaps by reading his works. Even though Mírzá Ḥasan-i-Adíb became a Bahá'í only two years before the ascension of Bahá'u'lláh, he received many Tablets from the Manifestation.

Hand of the Cause Adíb was an expert on Persian literature to the extent that he provided writings for royalty who then published them under their own names. The degree of his poetic talents can be ascertained by reading the beautiful tribute to his works paid by

'Abdu'l-Bahá, Who Himself is renowned for the breathtaking beauty of the prayers He revealed and the other works He created. Addressing this gifted Hand of the Cause, the Master wrote: "The verses of thy poem, each like unto a shining and luminous pearl, were perused. These lines were in truth of the utmost grace, lustre, and brilliance. . . . It moved me to the depths of heart and soul."[17] He also wrote books on proofs of the Faith and its history and was a superb teacher of the Faith. He taught the youth in Ṭihrán, and was also one of the founders of the famous Tarbiyat Boys' School in that city.

In 1903, Mírzá Ḥasan-i-Adíb met with great sufferings during the persecution of Bahá'ís in Iṣfahán, and endured a brief spell in jail. Later he went to India, and then went on pilgrimage and was exhilarated upon attaining the presence of the Master, Who asked him to return to India and then travel on to Burma with Sydney Sprague, a Bahá'í from the United States.[18]

LIGHT AND GLORY

One of the Hands of the Cause appointed by Bahá'u'lláh had a direct connection with both Him and the Báb. Ḥájí Á<u>kh</u>únd (1842–1910)[19] was one of the select few Bahá'ís in Persia who had responsibility for the transport and security of the sacred remains of the Báb.[20] He first met Bahá'u'lláh while on pilgrimage in 1873,[21] and for a second time in 1888 when the Manifestation appointed him as a Hand of the Cause of God.

In the Tablet of the World (Lawḥ-i-Dunyá) Bahá'u'lláh mentions Ḥájí Á<u>kh</u>únd in the opening lines, along with the name of one who was later to be named a Hand of the Cause: "Praise and thanksgiving beseem the Lord of manifest dominion Who hath adorned the mighty prison with the presence of their honors 'Alí-Akbar and Amín,[22] and hath illumined it with the light of certitude, constancy and assurance. The glory of God and the glory of all that are in the heavens and on the earth be upon them."

This mention was ahead of the exquisite and now well-known prayer for the Hands of the Cause of God:

Light and glory, greeting and praise be upon the Hands of His Cause, through whom the light of fortitude hath shone forth and the truth hath been established that the authority to choose rests with God, the Powerful, the Mighty, the Unconstrained, through whom the ocean of bounty hath surged and the fragrance of the gracious favors of God, the Lord of mankind, hath been diffused. We beseech Him—exalted is He—to shield them through the power of His hosts, to protect them through the potency of His dominion and to aid them through His indomitable strength which prevaileth over all created things. Sovereignty is God's, the Creator of the heavens and the Lord of the Kingdom of Names.[23]

In another Tablet, Bahá'u'lláh states that the Supreme Concourse [the souls of the faithful departed] weeps over Ḥájí Ákhúnd's sufferings and urges him to be joyful for having endured hardships in the path of God.[24]

Imprisoned for his faith at least five or six times,[25] the Hand of the Cause expected to suffer and did so "in a spirit of joy, of pride, of thankfulness to His Lord."[26] Jailed in all for seven years, he started a seven-month term three days after his marriage. In one episode he was confined in a narrow, dark prison cell with a chain around his neck and with stocks on his feet. So well-known did he become, that in 1882 the sháh ordered his photographer to take a photo of him seated in chains and stocks. In the following generations, the name of that sháh would be forgotten by all but historians. However, via that image and many accounts of his activities, the fame of this Hand of the Cause has spread throughout the admiring worldwide Bahá'í community.

Ḥájí Ákhúnd was again imprisoned at the time of the ascension of Bahá'u'lláh. He died in Ṭihrán in 1910 and was buried in the Shrine of Imám-Zádih Ma'ṣúm, where forty-three years earlier, the Hand had uplifted the sacred remains of the Báb and taken them to a safer place. In His beautiful written tribute to Ḥájí Ákhúnd, 'Abdu'l-Bahá said of this Hand of the Cause: "I loved him very much, for he was delightful to converse with, and as a companion second to none."[27] Ḥájí Á<u>kh</u>únd even appeared to Him in a dream that is both humorous and profoundly inspiring.[28]

The Master said this Hand of the Cause was extremely well-educated in secular philosophy and religious jurisprudence. He converted a multitude of souls to the Faith. "After the ascension of Bahá'u'lláh, Mullá 'Alí-Akbar-i-<u>Sh</u>ahmírzádí [Ḥájí Á<u>kh</u>únd] continued on, loyal to the Testament of the Light of the World, staunch in the Covenant which he served and heralded," 'Abdu'l-Bahá wrote. "He was one of the Hands of the Cause, steadfast, unshakable, not to be moved."[29]

Hand of the Cause Ṭarázu'lláh Samandarí.

Hand of the Cause Ibn-i-Abhar.

Hand of the Cause Ibn-i-Asdaq.

Hand of the Cause Mírzá Ḥasan-i-Adíb.

Hand of the Cause Ḥájí Á<u>kh</u>únd.

PART 3

HOLY WRITINGS

14

Encountering Revelation

In the last two decades of His life, Bahá'u'lláh let Bahá'ís have a glimpse of the mystical process of revelation. Often those who were present while Bahá'u'lláh was revealing Tablets said they witnessed scenes that astounded, even overwhelmed, them. Thankfully, for the generations that followed, some recorded their experiences. One who did so was seventeen-year-old Ṭarázu'lláh Samandarí,[1] who twice witnessed Bahá'u'lláh in the process of revealing sacred scripture in the Mansion of Bahjí in 1892. In one of those instances, the only other person present—taking dictation while seated—was Bahá'u'lláh's secretary, Mírzá Áqá Ján. In the other it was His son, Mírzá Badí'u'lláh.[2] Mr. Samandarí recalls:

> On these two precious occasion, as the Essence of Glory and Dignity [Bahá'u'lláh] paced the room and chanted verses, I could gaze upon Him and contemplate His luminous face, and behold the vision of the majesty of God and His divine Kingdom. This was indeed a great blessing.
>
> As He revealed the verses of God, His face was radiant. Sometimes, He would gesture with His hands while He looked through the window onto the sea. [He could see the

Mediterranean from His room] It was His custom to drink water while revealing the verses when His lips became dry.

Mírzá Áqá Ján was occupied in taking down the revealed words. The floor of the room was covered with papers from the dictation. One might guess that they amounted to about one-fifth of the Qu'rán, revealed during those few hours.

The verses were revealed sometimes in a melodious voice, and sometimes with majesty and power—depending on the context of the revealed words: For instance, when the subject was prayer, a heavenly melody was heard; while admonitions and words of warning were uttered with the power of the Lord of lords![3]

Giving a talk in Florida in 1967,[4] Mr. Samandarí said:

Bahá'u'lláh Himself tells us that day and night the verses descended like torrential rain. From this, whoever is mindful will ask: What can He mean, that the verses descended like torrential rain? This means, without thought. This means, without deliberation. This means, that first the revelation comes down—and only then is it read. This question deserves much, much, much meditation.[5]

The rule always was that when the letters came in from the friends, Khádim [Mírzá Áqá Ján] would be directed by Bahá'u'lláh to read Him the letters. Then, at Bahá'u'lláh's direction, he would make ready paper and pen, and an answer would be vouchsafed. To one after the other, upon each of those who had written, He would bestow an answer. . . .

At the highest possible speed, without any premeditation, these utterances would be revealed [by Bahá'u'lláh]. At such speed that it would be impossible to conceive any swifter, he [Khádim][6] would write them down. No one could read that "Revelation writing," with the exception of a very, very few early believers who had some familiarity with it. Perhaps they could read some of the verses so recorded—but not the whole.

> Even Mírzá Áqá Ján, the Revelation scribe himself, was sometimes unable to read this writing, and he would then take it to Bahá'u'lláh, and Bahá'u'lláh would solve the problem.

Mírzá Áqá Ján (1837–1901), both an amanuensis and servant, had little education, but for forty years he served Bahá'u'lláh.[7]

Once the text was established, often another scribe wrote it out. His name, given by Bahá'u'lláh, was Zaynu'l-Muqarrabín (1818–1903),[8] meaning, appropriately, "the ornament of them that are nigh unto God." Formerly a learned mujtahid (doctor of Islamic law), he became such an ardent follower of Bahá'u'lláh that he was named one of His Apostles. Historian Adib Taherzadeh wrote of him: "He was meticulous in transcribing the Writings of Bahá'u'lláh and took great pains to ensure that they were correctly recorded. Any Tablet in the handwriting of Zaynu'l-Muqarrabín is considered accurate. He has left to posterity, in his exquisite hand, many volumes comprising most of Bahá'u'lláh's important Tablets; today Bahá'í publications in Persian and Arabic are authenticated by comparison with these."[9]

He asked questions of Bahá'u'lláh for the supplement to the Kitáb-i-Aqdas known as Questions & Answers. Bahá'u'lláh enjoyed his sense of humor as well as that of another eminent Bahá'í who transcribed the scripture—the calligraphic genius, and also an Apostle of Bahá'u'lláh, Mishkín-Qalam (1826–1912), whose name means "musk-scented pen" or "jet-black pen."

Another who related his experiences encountering Bahá'u'lláh revealing sacred scripture was an older friend of Mr. Samandarí, Ḥájí Mírzá Ḥaydar-'Alí, then aged sixty-two, and known to history as "the Angel of Carmel."[10] In his memoirs, he leads into a description of his encounter with the revelation process by outlining what it felt like for him to be in the presence of Bahá'u'lláh:

> The spiritual transformation experienced by those who have attained the presence of Bahá'u'lláh is so far above limited experience that it cannot be described. It is that Paradise which is said never to have been seen by mortal eyes, nor experienced by

> earthly senses. The experience is like a tempestuous ocean, each wave of which brings forth pearls of beauty. Yet the waters of this ocean are so blissful that one does even want to swim, but only wishes to be drowned in its ecstasy. This unbelievable joy often comes and passes like lightning.

He moves on to describe an experience given to but a few:

> Once I requested to be in Bahá'u'lláh's room when He was revealing Tablets. This request met with His approval. As I entered His room, I heard streams of words sweeping along in a torrential flow from His lips. It seemed that the atmosphere, the floor, the walls, and every atom in the room was filled with perfume.
>
> Only those who have had this indescribable experience can ever imagine what I mean. The flow of revelation continued for about five minutes. Then Bahá'u'lláh said to me, "You have on several occasion been here when the revelation of Tablets has taken place. Should the people of the whole world wish to be present and hear the words of revelation, We would permit them. But since We have approved courtesy and ordained it upon men, We are reluctant to display this power publicly."[11]

Another eyewitness to the revelation processes was Ḥájí Mírzá Ḥabíbu'lláh-i-Afnán, who bequeathed to posterity priceless records of being in the presence of Bahá'u'lláh:

> . . . [Bahá'u'lláh's] blessed chamber [at Bahjí] was visible from our house. We saw Him several times at dawn and early morning, while He was speaking the revealed Word and Mírzá Áqá Ján was writing it down as He spoke it.
>
> Mírzá Áqá Ján used to have several [reed] pens well-cut and pointed, with ink and paper ready. The flow of verses from the heaven of Revelation was swift. It was indeed like unto a fast-billowing ocean. Mírzá Áqá Ján wrote as quickly as he

> could—so quickly that the pen at times jumped out of his hand. He would immediately take up another pen. There were times when he could not keep up and would say: "I am incapable of writing." Then the Blessed Perfection would repeat what He had spoken.[12]

Another pilgrim, 'Azízu'lláh, the son of the Hand of the Cause 'Alí-Muḥammad-i-Varqá, witnessed the process at Bahjí when he was a child on pilgrimage in 1890 or 1891. 'Azízu'lláh said that when Bahá'u'lláh wished to reveal a Tablet, He used to dismiss everybody with great haste. He recounts the following:

> One day I was in Bahá'u'lláh's Presence with the whole family and He called for the secretary to bring ink and paper quickly and in the same moment He requested us all to go. I was just a child, but seeing this haste to send everyone away, I had a great longing to be present sometime when a Tablet is revealed.
>
> I had asked from one of the members of His family to ask Bahá'u'lláh if I could come, please, to see a Tablet revealed. A few weeks later in the Garden at Bahjí, when I was playing with some children, the door of the home was opened and one member of the family called me and said that Bahá'u'lláh wished to see me. I ran to His room and entering I saw that He was chanting revealed Tablets and poems.
>
> So entering His room that day, I thought everything was the same as on other days, that Bahá'u'lláh was only chanting. I stood near the door which I had entered, and was only a few moments in the room when I began trembling in my whole body. I felt I could not stand any more on my feet. His Holiness Bahá'u'lláh turning to me said "Good-bye."
>
> As I lifted the curtain to go out, I fell on the threshold and was unconscious. They took me to the room of the wife of His Holiness Bahá'u'lláh [the room of Fáṭimih Khánum (Mahd-i-'Ulyá) was next to Bahá'u'lláh's] where they poured rose water and cold water on my face until I revived.

> The members of the Family asked me what had happened and I told them about going to Bahá'u'lláh to hear the chanting. When I was relating this, the lady who had called me first, came in, and she said to me: "You, yourself, had asked me to permit you to be present, now that was the time when a Tablet was being revealed."
>
> Then I understood why Bahá'u'lláh in haste dismissed everybody. It is because the people cannot endure it, there is such a Power in the room.

'Azízu'lláh said that his father had a similar experience during this visit to 'Akká:

> Father had been asked by someone to implore Bahá'u'lláh's help concerning a certain matter and to beg that a Tablet be sent. When my father presented this petition, Bahá'u'lláh called a secretary to bring ink and paper, and He also sent for His brother Músśá-Kalím [sic] and another one of the relatives.
>
> He put a hand on each one's shoulder and began to walk up and down revealing the Tablet. Father began to tremble and he said he couldn't say what was happening. He heard Bahá'u'lláh's voice but He could not understand His Words. Some minutes passed and He dismissed them all.
>
> Then outside they began to discuss and none of the three had understood Him, they had only felt the Power. It is certainly interesting to hear about Bahá'u'lláh from those who saw and spoke with Him. They said they could not look upon His Face, it was so glorious, the eyes so shining. There was such a vibration that everyone began to tremble and they could not understand His Words; there was such a Power there.[13]

Adib Taherzadeh has provided an account by Siyyid Asadu'lláh-i-Qumí, who attained the presence of Bahá'u'lláh in about 1886 and was allowed to stay permanently in 'Akká. He later accompanied

'Abdu'l-Bahá to Europe and America, and on these journeys often served the Master as a cook. He wrote in this account:

> I recall that as Mírzá Áqá Ján was recording the words of Bahá'u'lláh at the time of revelation, the shrill sound of his pen could be heard from a distance of about twenty paces.[14] In the history of the Faith not a great deal has been recorded about the manner in which Tablets were revealed. For this reason . . . I shall describe it. . . .
>
> Mírzá Áqá Ján had a large ink-pot the size of a small bowl. He also had available about ten to twelve pens and large sheets of paper in stacks. In those days all letters which arrived for Bahá'u'lláh were received by Mírzá Áqá Ján. He would bring these into the presence of Bahá'u'lláh and, having obtained permission, would read them. Afterwards the Blessed Beauty would direct him to take up his pen and record the Tablet which was revealed in reply. . . .
>
> Such was the speed with which he used to write the revealed Word that the ink of the first word was scarcely yet dry when the whole page was finished. It seemed as if someone had dipped a lock of hair in the ink and applied it over the whole page.
>
> None of the words was written clearly and they were illegible to all except Mírzá Áqá Ján. There were occasions when even he could not decipher the words and had to seek the help of Bahá'u'lláh. When revelation had ceased, then in accordance with Bahá'u'lláh's instruction Mírzá Áqá Ján would rewrite the Tablet in his best hand and dispatch it to its destination. . . .[15]

In His great exposition on philosophy, the Tablet of Wisdom (Lawḥ-i-Ḥikmat), Bahá'u'lláh describes what He experienced during the process of revealing:

> Thou knowest full well that We perused not the books which men possess and We acquired not the learning current amongst

> them, and yet whenever We desire to quote the sayings of the learned and of the wise, presently there will appear before the face of thy Lord in the form of a tablet all that which hath appeared in the world and is revealed in the Holy Books and Scriptures. Thus do We set down in writing that which the eye perceiveth. Verily His knowledge encompasseth the earth and the heavens.[16]

Bahá'u'lláh repeatedly emphasized that He had not studied at educational institutions or in other ways to encounter the current learning. One pilgrim described a time when the Blessed Beauty was seated on a cushion while His amanuensis, Mírzá Áqá Ján, was seated opposite, writing down what Bahá'u'lláh was revealing:

> Like a torrent the words were streaming from His blessed lips. He bade me be seated. Thrice during the revelation of the verses He requested water. On several occasions, Mírzá Áqá Ján was unable to keep up. Bahá'u'lláh would pause and ask him what point he had reached; He would then repeat the phrase, and, in exactly the same manner as before, He would continue until the Tablet was ended. During this time, the Blessed countenance was flushed, and His forehead was wet with perspiration. The Tablet came to an end. And Bahá'u'lláh turned to us and said: "You are most welcome! It gives Us joy to see you!"[17]

In the last decade of His life, Bahá'u'lláh revealed some of His mightiest Tablets.

Ḥájí Mírzá Ḥaydar-'Alí.
PROVIDED BY THE US BAHÁ'Í NATIONAL ARCHIVES

15

The Final Tablets

From when Bahá'u'lláh, aged sixty-two, moved to Bahjí in 1879 almost until He passed away at the age of seventy-four, He was mostly in excellent health. He revealed so many Tablets during this time that Shoghi Effendi describes them as "unnumbered."[1] As the author Adib Taherzadeh writes: "The prodigious outpouring of the Word of God during Bahá'u'lláh's residence in the Mansion of Bahjí staggers the imagination."[2] We can picture the completion of the revelation of His Kitáb-Aqdas in 1873 as the foundation upon which He would raise up the structural framework of His Faith. That framework can be seen in the Tablets which He revealed in the last years of His ministry, mainly in Bahjí. He also decreed that His resting place would be the Qiblih.

As Shoghi Effendi was to point out more than fifty years later, those Tablets "must rank among the choicest fruits which His mind has yielded, and mark the consummation of His forty-year-long ministry."[3] The Tablets that poured onto parchment in this amazingly fertile period of revelation detailed specifics of the principles and teachings of the Faith. Assembled together, they could well be described as the prescription for the healing of society today.[4]

Those final Tablets, as Shoghi Effendi pointed out in *God Passes By*,

- enunciated certain precepts and principles that lay at the very core of His Faith;
- reaffirmed truths He had previously proclaimed;
- elaborated and elucidated some of the laws He had already laid down;
- revealed further prophecies and warnings;
- established subsidiary ordinances designed to supplement the provisions in the Kitáb-i-Aqdas.[5]

The most vital of the principles enshrined in the final Tablets, wrote Shoghi Effendi, is that of the oneness and wholeness of the human race, which he says "may well be regarded as the hall-mark of His Revelation and the pivot of His teachings."[6]

Other principles Shoghi Effendi elected to mention from the final Tablets are:

1. Collective security, including reduction in national armaments, and "necessary and inevitable," a world gathering of leaders to establish peace among the nations.
2. Justice: upon it depends "the organization of the world and tranquility of mankind."
3. Moderation in all things; predicts civilization carried to excess "will devour the cities."
4. Consultation: this form of consensus decision-making is one of the Faith's fundamentals.
5. Knowledge: incumbent on all; lauds arts, crafts, and sciences.
6. Consorting with all in a spirit of friendliness and fellowship.
7. Necessity of adopting a universal language and script.
8. Duty of House of Justice to legislate on matters not expressly provided for in His writings.
9. Constitutional form of government in which republicanism and kingship combined is recommended.
10. Special regard to agriculture.
11. Prescribes that journalists should be "sanctified from malice, passion and prejudice, to be just and fair-minded, to be pains-

taking in their inquiries, and ascertain all the facts in every situation."

12. Infallibility of the Manifestation. (There is also guidance from the Universal House of Justice on this topic.)[7]
13. Obligation reaffirmed of believers to "behave towards the government of the country in which they reside with loyalty, honesty and truthfulness."
14. Ban re-emphasized on waging of holy war and destruction of books.
15. Special praise for people of learning and wisdom.[8]

Shoghi Effendi listed the most noteworthy of the Tablets. Here they are accompanied by a brief description by this current author.[9]

1. **Is<u>h</u>ráqát (Splendors):** Infallibility of the Manifestation; outline of some basic teachings and principles. It contains, for example, a repeat of the statement: "Ye are the fruits of one tree and the leaves of one branch."[10]
2. **Bis<u>h</u>árát (Glad Tidings):** Existing beliefs and practices of past religions.
3. **Ṭarázát (Ornaments):** Some of His choicest teachings and exhortations.
4. **Kalimát-i-Firdawsíyyih (Words of Paradise):** Some essential teachings.
5. **Lawḥ-i-Aqdas (Most Holy Tablet, Tablet to the Christians):** Proclaims message to Christians, covering His station as that of the Father.
6. **Lawḥ-i-Dunyá (Tablet of the World):** Choicest exhortations, such as to consort with followers of all religions; counsels humanity to fix thoughts on what will rehabilitate mankind; forbids contention.
7. **Lawḥ-i-Maqṣúd (Tablet of Maqṣúd (the Goal, the Desired One):** Man is supreme Talisman, rich in gems, which only education can reveal; world stability sustained by reward and punishment; refers to moderation, consultation, and compassion.

Shoghi Effendi said a review of Bahá'u'lláh's writings at this time should also include reference to:

1. **Lawḥ-i-Ḥikmat (Tablet of Wisdom):** The fundamentals of true philosophy.
2. **Tablet of Visitation** in honor of the Imám Ḥusayn.
3. **Questions and Answers**: Elucidates the laws and ordinances of the Kitáb-i-Aqdas.
4. **Lawḥ-i-Burhán (Tablet of the Proof):** Severely condemns acts perpetrated by two persecutors.[11]
5. **Lawḥ-i-Karmil (Tablet of Carmel):** See a later chapter in this volume.
6. **Epistle to Son of the Wolf**: See a later chapter in this volume.

In a later chapter of *God Passes By,* Shoghi Effendi singles out for special attention the "Book of my Covenant," (the Kitáb-i-'Ahd), Bahá'u'lláh's last Will and Testament, revealed at least one year before His passing.[12] "In the evening of His life," while surveying the entire range of the revelation, Bahá'u'lláh wrote: "We, verily have not fallen short of Our duty to exhort men, and to deliver that whereunto I was bidden by God, the Almighty, the All-Praised."[13]

One mighty Tablet revealed in His last years that specifically refers to the Shrine of the Báb can shed some light on the importance of the Shrine of Bahá'u'lláh. This is the Tablet of Carmel, to which our attention now turns.

16

The Tablet of Carmel

One summer's day in 1891, Bahá'u'lláh began His ascent up Mount Carmel from the western side. As yet there is no contemporary description of that journey, but we can be confident that He rode a donkey up the steep slope and was accompanied by 'Abdu'l-Bahá as well as by His amanuensis, Mírzá Áqá Ján.[1] Bahá'u'lláh, attired in distinctive robes and táj, had lunch as a guest of the French monks in the Stella Maris Carmelite monastery, which is located at the promontory of Mount Carmel.[2] He wrote some words in the guestbook (daftar) on the table in the visitor's room, and was extraordinarily gracious to the monks, politely declining their invitation to make Himself at home in the monastery.

Privately, He exhibited His distress at statues depicting Jesus Christ, particularly one which showed Jesus fallen on the ground, drenched in His own blood—no doubt a scene from the Stations of the Cross. In majestic tones He repeated that such a depiction was not permissible, though added that the Christians in the monastery were not aware of that prohibition.[3] He visited the Upper Cave of the prophet Elijah,[4] "whose return the Báb Himself symbolizes,"[5] which is located under an altar at the monastery.[6]

His tent was pitched a few hundred yards to the east of the monastery, not far from the current Bahá'í Temple site.[7] This in itself could be considered a fulfilment of scriptural prophecy. As 'Abdu'l-Bahá later wrote, the prophets had prophesied that the "Lord of Hosts would come and the tent of the Lord would be pitched on Mount Carmel. . . ."[8] Shoghi Effendi cited extracts from the following Biblical quotation in this connection:[9] "And it shall come to pass in the last days, that the mountain of the Lord's house shall be established in the top of the mountains, and shall be exalted above the hills; and all nations shall flow unto it."[10]

From that vantage point on Mount Carmel, Bahá'u'lláh would have been able to gaze eastward toward the site of the future Shrine of the Báb and also across to the city of 'Akká, shining white in the sun. In those unpolluted days, He could have seen the towering pines near His home, the Mansion of Bahjí. In a voice so melodious, so powerful and so loud that the monks—standing outside their monastery in reverence—were deeply impressed, Bahá'u'lláh began revealing the Tablet of Carmel (Lawḥ-i-Karmil).[11] His amanuensis took down His swiftly flowing words.

Such is the importance of this Tablet, Shoghi Effendi was later to describe it as "the Charter of the World Spiritual and Administrative Centres of the Faith on that mountain."[12] The world spiritual center is the Shrine of the Báb; the world administrative center is the Universal House of Justice.[13] The Tablet of Carmel is one of the most sublime revealed by Bahá'u'lláh, not only for its content but also for its poetic beauty. Shoghi Effendi wrote that it is "remarkable for its allusions and prophecies."[14] The text tells of a spiritual dialogue between Bahá'u'lláh and Mount Carmel in a somewhat similar style to Tablets in which He symbolically addressed other locations.

In an authoritative interpretation years later, Shoghi Effendi said the "City of God" as mentioned in the following extract refers to the Shrine of the Báb:[15] "Hasten forth and circumambulate the City of God that hath descended from heaven, the celestial Kaaba around which have circled in adoration the favored of God, the pure in heart, and the company of the most exalted angels."[16] Historian Adib Taherzadeh wrote that the revelation of this Tablet saw "forces released by Bahá'u'lláh for the implementation of the mighty enterprise involving the transfer of the remains of the Báb and the building of His Shrine."[17]

Later, in His Epistle to the Son of the Wolf, Bahá'u'lláh cited Biblical prophetic references to Zion, Jerusalem, Palestine, and 'Akká, and then said: "Carmel, in the Book of God, hath been designated as the Hill of God, and His Vineyard. It is here that, by the grace of the Lord of Revelation, the Tabernacle of Glory hath been raised. Happy are they that attain thereunto; happy they that set their faces towards it."[18]

On another occasion during that same visit,[19] Bahá'u'lláh ascended the northern face of Mount Carmel accompanied by 'Abdu'l-Bahá, and instructed the Master to arrange the transfer of the sacred remains of the Báb from their place of concealment in Persia to the Holy Land. He pointed to a spot down the slope and instructed 'Abdu'l-Bahá to purchase it and to inter the remains of the Báb in a shrine there.[20] Hand of the Cause Rúḥíyyih Khánum wrote that Shoghi Effendi said the hub of the Tablet of Carmel was the words: "ere long God will sail His Ark upon thee and will manifest the people of Bahá who have been mentioned in the Book of Names." Citing Shoghi Effendi, she said that the "Ark" was the world administrative center of the Bahá'í Faith and the "people of Bahá" were the members of the Universal House of Justice.[21]

The Tablet of Carmel does not appear to have any direct link to the future Shrine of Bahá'u'lláh, but it could be said to indicate the towering importance in the Bahá'í Faith of a Shrine of a Manifestation, its spiritual power, and the utter respect and honor with which the Bahá'ís must treat it when they visit. Although the shrines have been called "twin Shrines,"[22] their roles are not exactly similar. Rúḥíyyih Khánum wrote that the "Dust of the Báb had been chosen by Bahá'u'lláh Himself to be the Centre around which His Administrative Institutions would cluster and under Whose shadow they would function." Basing her comments on what Shoghi Effendi said, she wrote: "Bahá'u'lláh's Dust, the 'Point of Adoration' or 'Qiblih' of the faithful, was too sacred in its essence, His station too infinitely exalted, to act as the spiritual dynamo galvanizing the institutions of

His World Order."[23] No record has been found so far of any conversation that Bahá'u'lláh may have had with 'Abdu'l-Bahá about His own shrine. As revealed in the Kitáb-i-Aqdas, the location of His own shrine was to be the Qiblih of the Faith, the point to which His followers would turn as they recited their obligatory prayers. This confirmed the Báb's decree on this point.

Although still healthy, with a firm pulse and no debilitating infirmities, Bahá'u'lláh had reached the age of seventy-three, which was more than the average lifespan in an environment that had its share of health challenges and pandemics. His ascension could well have been expected. During His time at Bahjí, Bahá'u'lláh ventured no further than Haifa. The likelihood that His shrine was destined to be established in the vicinity of the Mansion of Bahjí grew ever stronger with each passing day.

17

Extraordinary Epistle

In the last year of His life, Bahá'u'lláh revealed a major work, the final of the many volumes revealed over forty years. The revelation of that work, Epistle to the Son of the Wolf, began in a beautiful garden near what is modern-day Nahariya, just to the north of 'Akká.[1] This volume, which is partly an anthology of some of Bahá'u'lláh's main teachings, is a stunning work. It contains the "re-revelation" of certain passages of scripture. As historian Adib Taherzadeh has pointed out, the quotations are almost precisely similar to the originals revealed many years previously.[2]

Yet Bahá'u'lláh could not have consulted any transcriptions of His previous works. Most of His 15,000 Tablets were not easily accessible or indexed for Him to refer to even if He were so inclined. Bahá'u'lláh was also able to quote from the writings of the Báb despite not having them at hand. He says in the Epistle that He had "not perused the Bayán, nor been acquainted with its contents."[3] He explained that when He wanted to cite the sayings of the learned and wise "there will appear before the face of Thy Lord in the form of a tablet all that which hath appeared in the world and is revealed in the Holy Books and Scriptures. Thus do we set down that which the eye perceiveth."[4]

The Epistle was a final, comprehensive statement of Bahá'u'lláh's teachings, and it adduces proofs of the validity of His Cause.[5] A handy summary of the Epistle comes from Marzieh Gail, the writer who provides an introduction to the translation by Shoghi Effendi of the Epistle from Persian and Arabic into English.[6] She notes that it gives a moral code, stresses the fear of God, discusses precepts, and answers the question "why a new religion?" It offers historical material. Bahá'u'lláh speaks of, for example:

1. His arrest in Níyávarán and of the kind of chains with which He was bound;
2. The machinations against Him by Persian officials in Constantinople;
3. The fact that Mírzá Yaḥyá was not exiled out of Persia;
4. That Mírzá Yaḥyá abandoned the writings of the Báb in Baghdád;
5. That in 1863 (this date is given in *God Passes By*) Bahá'u'lláh suggested to a Turkish official, Kamál Páshá, that his government convene a gathering to plan for a world language and script.

The revelation of the Epistle to the Son of the Wolf came about a year after Bahá'u'lláh had revealed His last Will and Testament, the Kitáb-i-'Ahd, upon which He affixed His seal before placing it in a locked box and handing it to the Master for safekeeping in 'Akká. Bahá'u'lláh addressed the Epistle to a nefarious persecutor of Bahá'ís, who was surnamed the Son of the Wolf (Ibn-i-Dhi'b). His notorious father, who was surnamed "Wolf" (Dhi'b), had also perpetrated heinous acts against the followers of Bahá'u'lláh. Bahá'u'lláh's condemnation of the iniquities of the persecutor is accompanied by statements of loving compassion and exhortations to recite a prayer—which He provides in the text—to plead for forgiveness from God.[7]

PURPOSE

But what was the main purpose of this final volume of Bahá'u'lláh, this omnibus work? Looking at the Guardian's communications to the Bahá'ís of the United States at the time he sent them his English translation of the volume,[8] it becomes clear that the purpose of the Epistle is to provide a source of knowledge that will lead the Bahá'ís to enhance their own spiritual progress and to empower their efforts in the fields of administering the Faith and teaching it to others.[9]

Bahá'u'lláh twice cites the passage in which He affirms His station as a Manifestation of God, and affirms that His revelation was not a product of any education He received: "O King! I was but a man like others, asleep upon My couch, when lo, the breezes of the All-Glorious were wafted over me and taught Me the knowledge of all that has been. This thing is not from Me, but from One Who is Almighty and All-Knowing. And He bade Me lift up My voice between earth and heaven. . . ." [10]

The Epistle also includes what was to become a widely known and well-loved passage, a guide to behavior for all Bahá'ís. It begins with an injunction, part of which could be a reminder of the first Hidden Word in Arabic:

> Be generous in prosperity, and thankful in adversity. Be worthy of the trust of thy neighbor, and look upon him with a bright and friendly face.[11]

It then moves on to a lovely litany:

> Be a treasure to the poor, an admonisher to the rich, an answerer of the cry of the needy, a preserver of the sanctity of thy pledge. Be fair in thy judgment, and guarded in thy speech. Be unjust to no man, and show all meekness to all men. Be as a lamp unto them that walk in darkness, a joy to the sorrowful, a sea for the thirsty, a haven for the distressed, an upholder and defender of the victim of oppression. Let integrity and uprightness distinguish all thine acts. Be a home for the stranger, a balm to the suffering, a tower of strength for the fugitive. Be eyes to the blind, and a guiding light unto the feet of the erring.

A series of beautiful images then mounts in intensity until it reaches a soaring climax in which Bahá'u'lláh calls upon His readers to play, with all humility, a special enlightened role in their generation:

> Be an ornament to the countenance of truth, a crown to the brow of fidelity, a pillar of the temple of righteousness, a breath of life to the body of mankind, an ensign of the hosts of justice, a luminary above the horizon of virtue, a dew to the soil of the human heart, an ark on the ocean of knowledge, a sun in the heaven of bounty, a gem on the diadem of wisdom, a shining light in the firmament of thy generation, a fruit upon the tree of humility.[12]

COMPLETION

Shoghi Effendi stated that Epistle to the Son of the Wolf is in itself a library, and that it was a book Bahá'u'lláh enjoyed composing.[13] The Guardian says that with its revelation, the "prodigious achievement as author of a hundred volumes . . . may be said to have practically terminated."[14] Bahá'u'lláh's revealed word totaled the volume of the scripture of the Manifestations of God preceding Him.[15]

About this time, He spoke of His wish to leave this world.[16]

PART 4

THE ESTABLISHMENT OF THE SHRINE

18

Final Illness

Mounted on horses, 'Abdu'l-Bahá and his sister, Bahíyyih Khánum, galloped to Bahjí after receiving the news that Bahá'u'lláh had taken ill with a fever. It was the start of the second week of May 1892. A servant had come into 'Akká from the mansion with two horses and a note from their Father letting them know that He was ill and asking them to visit.[1] 'Abdu'l-Bahá was renowned as an expert horseman, and it is likely that His sister was also a skilled rider, as such a thing was not unusual for women of her social class.[2]

There was no lead-up to the news that Baha'u'llah was sick enough to warrant a summons to the Master and His sister. Just a few days earlier, in a tent pitched next to the mansion, Bahá'u'lláh had been in typically good health as He supervised the last of three meetings on successive days to commemorate three Bahá'ís who had passed away.[3] The ride to the mansion took about twenty minutes. 'Abdu'l-Bahá and Bahíyyih Khánum dismounted, and were soon in the presence of Bahá'u'lláh, discussing His illness with Him. From that day and for the next three weeks they were to monitor His health, as His fever increased, declined, and then reappeared again. The Master's wife, Munírih Khánum, and the couple's four daughters had initially remained at home in the House of 'Abbúd, but were growing ever more anxious after hearing daily reports about Bahá'u'lláh's condition.

Over the decades Bahá'u'lláh had fended off many assaults on His physical well-being. Examples of what He had survived since the 1850s gives testimony to His physical resilience. He had suffered:

- torture involving sixty heavy strokes on the soles of His feet (the bastinado)
- a forced march in extreme heat, without a hat, wearing chains, pelted with stones
- four months imprisonment in chains and stocks in an underground dungeon, deprived of food and water for three days, intentionally poisoned
- another intentional poisoning, causing a hand tremor that lasted the rest of His life
- exposure to extreme cold during a journey from Istanbul to Adrianople
- exposure to epidemics of cholera, dysentery, bubonic plague, and malaria (with which He may have been infected)
- confined under house arrest for nine years in 'Akká, a place so averse He was to label it the "Most Great Prison"[4]
- physical weakness that He attributed to the sufferings inflicted upon Him by the people of tyranny, including the slander and mocking by disaffected relatives and former supporters which led to Him withholding further diffusion of divine fragrances[5]

When He took ill, some thought He had malaria, but there have been doubts about that diagnosis.[6] It is more likely that the accumulated stress of His experiences,[7] and particularly of being slandered continually for decades, caused Him bodily harm. It certainly reduced His ability physically to reveal verses,[8] and He had referred to such attacks more than two decades earlier. In His magnificent lament, the Fire Tablet, revealed by Him in 1871, "the Wronged One of the worlds" cries out: "This Face is hidden in the dust of slander: Where are the breezes of Thy compassion, O Mercy of the worlds?"[9]

Decades later, Shoghi Effendi, as recounted by his biographer, was to identify the sustained slander by disaffected relatives and their supporters as a cause of Bahá'u'lláh's death: "Shoghi Effendi has been talking to me [Rúḥíyyih Khánum] about his own miseries. He says those around Him killed 'Abdu'l-Bahá as they killed Bahá'u'lláh—he even says 'They will kill me too.'"[10]

The news of Bahá'u'lláh's illness would not have been very surprising to the Master. In mid-1891—while Bahá'u'lláh was on His last visit to Haifa, the occasion in which He revealed His landmark Tablet of Carmel—He had expressed His wish to leave this world. Later, after the revelation of the Epistle to the Son of the Wolf, He made a similar remark. Over the next months, the tone of His remarks made it increasingly evident that His ascension was approaching.[11]

And then, on an occasion when the Master was tidying up His father's papers scattered on a divan, Bahá'u'lláh indicated there was little use in doing so. 'Abdu'l-Bahá took this as a hint by His Father that the ascension of the Manifestation was approaching. Nevertheless, before this sudden crisis in May 1892, Bahá'u'lláh's doctors had always found Him well. He had a steady pulse, a keen sense of smell (He liked perfumes, His favorite being attar of roses), and excellent eyesight—He could read fine type without the help of glasses. He was active and flexible, not at all bent with age.[12] His overall health was good despite Him having little appetite for food during the last three years of His life.[13]

Now, though, there was real cause to worry. The fever that began on the evening of 7 May, grew worse the next day.[14] Only one Bahá'í was permitted to visit in addition to Bahá'u'lláh's personal physician, Dr. Khálid Jarráḥ. Dr. Jarráḥ was joined by a Greek doctor from 'Akká (likely either Dr. Nikolaki Bey or Dr. Petro or both).[15] The great Bahá'í poet Jináb-i-'Andalíb was at Bahjí at the time and composed an ode in which the word for a trunk of a tree is translated in English for poetic purposes using an antiquated term: "bole."

O Thou,
Doctor of the ailing soul,
Why suffer these doctors
And all they claim?

Weep now for the Branches
From this mighty Bole!
Weep now for the meekness
Of the Lord we extol!
Keep us,
These servants of Thine in our grief,
Ever true to Thy love,
Ever speaking Thy name.[16]

Although ill, Bahá'u'lláh was not incapacitated. For example, on the third day of His illness He gave a midday audience to the poet and author Nabíl, speaking to him for half an hour. That afternoon He invited to His chamber a well-known Bahá'í, Ḥájí Níyáz, newly arrived from Egypt, and others. Later, other groups of Bahá'ís also visited Him, leaving Him at sunset.

ONGOING GLOOM

Bahá'u'lláh's condition did not improve, causing ongoing gloom. Nobody was permitted to visit Him the following day. On about the sixth day of his illness, Munírih Khánum and her four daughters came out to stay at Bahjí—an indication of their mounting anxiety. On the ninth day, the Master visited the Bahá'ís in the Pilgrim House, conveying to all present the greetings and a message from Bahá'u'lláh: "All the friends must remain patient and steadfast, and arise for the promotion of the Cause of God. They should not become perturbed, because I shall always be with them, and will remember and care for them." The Bahá'ís cried out in grief because it was clear from the tone of the Master's words that the Manifestation's ascension was approaching.[17]

There was a reprieve on the tenth day. 'Abdu'l-Bahá, Who was staying on the upper floor of the mansion, went across to His Father's room and found Him to be well. It was early morning but the Master quickly went down to the Pilgrim House, woke each believer separately, invited them to start the day in prayer and thanksgiving, served them tea, and conveyed the good news. Among the pilgrims who were present was a certain Mírzá Maḥram, who traveled to the Holy Land from Iran via India.[18] Another was a new believer called Ḥájí Ḥusayn, a servant of Mullá Mihdí of Kand. Ḥájí Ḥusayn's role was also to be a shepherd, taking care of Bahá'u'lláh's flock of sheep and herd of goats. He milked the goats and took the milk to Bahá'u'lláh, Who drank it during the last days of His life.[19]

To add to everybody's joy, news came that a royal telegram had arrived in which the sultan had ordered the release of 1,000 conscripts—farmers and poor men—who had camped nearby and, having been given military uniforms, were expecting to be sent to distant posts in the Ottoman Empire. The Master contributed to the rapturous celebrations by giving food and funds to those men and their families, many of whom now attributed their good fortune to the blessings of Bahá'u'lláh. 'Abdu'l-Bahá then rode into 'Akká, where He visited every Bahá'í home and passed on greetings from Bahá'u'lláh to everybody there. It was probably at this stage that, in accordance with Persian tradition, He ordered the slaughter of two lambs, their sacrifice being a symbolic plea for the lengthening of the life of a beloved one who was ill. After the cooking, the lamb was distributed to the poor of 'Akká.[20]

The reprieve was short lasting. On the fifteenth day after sunset, just as the holy day of the Declaration of the Báb was beginning, a servant descended from the upper floor and summoned to Bahá'u'lláh's chamber nine Bahá'ís who happened to be there on the ground floor. They were pilgrims, Bahá'ís from 'Akká, and some who lived in Bahjí. They quickly climbed up the first flight of steep stairs, hurried through the great upper hall, and then slowing and with all due reverence, entered the hallowed presence of the Manifestation.

Bahá'u'lláh was on His bed in the middle of the room. White sheets and a quilt covered His mattress. He was propped up on pillows and leaning against 'Abdu'l-Bahá. On His left, one of His other sons was fanning Him, and on His right another son was doing the same.[21] Bahá'u'lláh looked frail. His voice was not as strong as usual but His words were clear. Among those also present were the young Ṭarázu'lláh Samandarí, the blind poet Mírzá Baṣṣár, and the fifty-five-year-old Siyyid Asadu'lláh Qumí.[22] As He spoke to them, some of the Bahá'ís were praying and weeping in their sorrow, circumambulating His bed, and begging to swap their lives for His so that He could spend longer on this earth.

Bahá'u'lláh then addressed them, referring to His declining health, and to His imminent departure from this life. He spoke calming words, saying how pleased He was with them for visiting every morning and evening and for their many services. He then quoted directly from the great book of laws He had revealed nineteen years previously, the Kitáb-i-Aqdas:

> Let not your hearts be perturbed, O people, when the glory of My Presence is withdrawn, and the ocean of My utterance is stilled. In My presence amongst you there is a wisdom, and in My absence there is yet another, inscrutable to all but God, the Incomparable, the All-Knowing. Verily, We behold you from Our realm of glory, and shall aid whosoever will arise for the triumph of Our Cause with the hosts of the Concourse on high and a company of Our favored angels.[23]

Bahá'u'lláh then drew on another passage from the Most Holy Book. It was another reference to His passing.

> Be not dismayed, O peoples of the world, when the day star of My beauty is set, and the heaven of My tabernacle is concealed from your eyes. Arise to further My Cause, and to exalt My Word amongst men. We are with you at all times, and shall strengthen you through the power of truth. We are truly almighty. Whoso hath recognized Me, will arise and serve Me with such determination that the powers of earth and heaven shall be unable to defeat his purpose.[24]

It was probably at this stage that Bahá'u'lláh assured His family that a special Tablet (His Will and Testament) had been entrusted to 'Abdu'l-Bahá, and that He had clearly directed their steps in the service of the Cause.[25]

As Mr. Samandarí later recalled,: "Bahá'u'lláh spoke further of the importance of unity, love and friendship and urged us to avoid disunity, discord and schism."[26] A distraught 'Andalíb shed tears as he cried out "Yá Bahá! Yá Bahá!"[27] Bahá'u'lláh then dismissed those present saying "Go in God's care." The Bahá'ís prostrated themselves at His feet, and, in obedience to a direction from 'Abdu'l-Bahá, circumambulated Bahá'u'lláh's bed and left the room.

At about that time, Bahá'u'lláh summoned the women and children of His family, and told them that in His will was guidance for the future. He reassured them that 'Abdu'l-Bahá would arrange matters for the family, the Bahá'ís, and the Cause. His condition gradually worsened. He asked that doctors be called in. They felt His pulse and listened to His heart, with its steady regular beat—nothing wrong there. But there was another symptom, one that in the often disease-ravaged Holy Land at that time could be ominous. Bahá'u'lláh was running a fever again.

19

The Supreme Affliction

In the early hours of Sunday morning, 29 May 1892,[1] Bahá'u'lláh's illness was moving toward its terrible climax. He was in His room at the southeast corner of the upper floor of the mansion.[2] With Him was 'Abdu'l-Bahá, aged forty-eight, Who had been staying in a room on the western side of the mansion's upper floor. Bahá'u'lláh's other sons—Mírzá Muḥammad-'Alí, Mírzá Badí'u'lláh, and Mírzá Ḍíyá'u'lláh[3]—were there too, as likely were Bahá'u'lláh's two wives, Mahd-i-'Ulyá (Fáṭimih <u>Kh</u>ánum) and Gawhar <u>Kh</u>ánum,[4] both of whom also lived on the top floor.[5] His daughters, the Greatest Holy Leaf and Ṣamadíyyih, would also probably have been present.[6]

Attending the Manifestation was Bahá'u'lláh's personal physician, Dr. <u>Kh</u>álid Jarráḥ, a Bahá'í. Other doctors such as the Greeks Dr. Nikolaki Bey and Dr. Petro may have been present too.[7] According to a report from his descendants, Dr. Jarráḥ was measuring Bahá'u'lláh's pulse but when he proposed to change the medicine being used, Bahá'u'lláh dissuaded him from doing so with an eye gesture. Bahá'u'lláh may also have verbally told him not to change the medicine.[8]

THE ASCENSION

In his book *God Passes By,* Shoghi Effendi reports the last moments on earth of the Manifestation, his source no doubt being 'Abdu'l-Bahá: "His fever returned in a more acute form than before, His general condition grew steadily worse, complications ensued which at last culminated in His ascension, at the hour of dawn, on the 2nd of Dhi'l-Qa'dih 1309 A.H. (May 29, 1892), eight hours after sunset, in the 75th year of His age."[9]

Placing the ascension in a spiritual context, the Guardian cites the Tablet of the Vision, which Bahá'u'lláh had revealed nineteen years previously on the anniversary of the birth of the Báb.[10] The Manifestation's spirit, Shoghi Effendi writes, had at long last been "released from the toils of a life crowded with tribulations, had winged its flight to His 'other dominions,' dominions 'whereon the eyes of the people of names have never fallen,' and to which the 'Luminous Maid,' 'clad in white,' had bidden Him hasten. . . ." Shoghi Effendi put the time of Bahá'u'lláh's passing "at the hour of dawn" and "eight hours after sunset"—modern calculations placing it between 3:41 am and 5:05 am.[11]

GRIEF

The grief 'Abdu'l-Bahá felt upon the ascension of His Father was intense, overwhelming. He was to describe that event in heart-rending terms such as "the supreme affliction" and "that shattering calamity."[12] Later, when He recalled the ascension in the Tablet of One Thousand Verses, the extent of His grief at the time of that event was made clear. He called the ascension the "most great calamity," and said people in the mansion were distressed and crying. He said He Himself wept night and day.[13] Here is a provisional translation of a verse of a supremely sad poem about His loss that 'Abdu'l-Bahá was to later pen in Persian. The verses are so eloquent that any attempt at translation struggles to convey the full depth of His grief:

See Thou my weeping eyes
See Thou my flaming heart

See Thou my burning sighs
For just one hair of Thine[14]

TELEGRAM

As the oldest son, and the long-time spokesperson and confidant of Bahá'u'lláh, the Master was the de facto leader of the community.[15] It was His role to take care of the funeral arrangements. He rose above His sorrow to do so. He quickly wrote the text of a telegram to communicate the news of Bahá'u'lláh's ascension[16] to Sulṭán 'Abdu'l-Ḥamíd,[17] the tyrannical ruler of the Ottoman Empire, which had governed the Holy Land for more than 365 years.[18] On the Master's orders, a horseman galloped to 'Akká to take the news of the ascension to the muftí there.[19] That rider took the text to the telegraph office in that city.

The telegram began dramatically: "The Sun of Bahá has set." It advised the sultan of "the intention of interring the sacred remains within the precincts of the Mansion." Bahá'u'lláh was still a prisoner of the Ottoman government at the time of His ascension.[20] Via a return telegram, the sultan "readily assented" to the location of the grave.[21]

ROOM

'Abdu'l-Bahá's duty surely included the selection of the burial site.[22] The grave was to be in the northernmost room of "the most northerly of the three houses lying just to the west of the Mansion."[23] At that time, the house—like the two others on the western side—had a flat roof, walls flush on both sides. Its inner courtyard was open to the sky.

Why was that room selected? From this distance in time, we can only attempt an explanation. Two sides of the room were next to a courtyard—an ideal area for pilgrims to pray—and on the other side it had space for extensive gardens. It would not be in the middle of household traffic, as it might have been were it situated elsewhere on the property. The room probably had been graced by the presence of the Manifestation Himself. Bahá'u'lláh's youngest daughter,

Furúghíyyih Khánum, lived in that house with her husband, Ḥájí Siyyid 'Alí Afnán.[24] Staying in that house in the room that was to become the inner shrine, was Furúghíyyih's father-in-law—a brother of the wife of the Báb, Khadíjih-Bagum.[25] This eminent Bahá'í was known as the Great Afnán. A keen astronomer and philosopher, he was much admired by 'Abdu'l-Bahá.[26] It had been in the room selected for the shrine that the Great Afnán had hosted guests,[27] such as Edward Granville Browne. Furúghíyyih Khánum may also have met with Bahá'u'lláh there.

'AKKÁ TO BAHJÍ

The news that had been taken by the horseman to the muftí in 'Akká was soon resounding from the seven minarets of the great mosque.[28] The traditional chant announcing the death of an eminent man was ringing out: "God is great. He giveth life! He taketh it again! He dieth not, but liveth for evermore!"[29]

Although 'Abdu'l-Bahá's family had moved from their home in 'Akká to Bahjí several days before the ascension,[30] there were still Bahá'ís remaining in the town. When they heard the calamitous news, they traveled to Bahjí as fast as possible. Only the wealthy could afford horses. Most walked, rode donkeys or mules, or sat in carts pulled by donkeys. Many years later, Rafí'ih Shahídí, who was a six-year-old girl at the time, remembered with clarity that historic day: "We received the news of Bahá'u'lláh's ascension from my cousin Hayatíyyih Khánum. She came from the blessed Mansion and conveyed with tearful eyes the shocking news. Needless to say how we all felt after hearing what had occurred. Devastated and grief-stricken, all set off for the Mansion of Bahjí. I too went along."[31]

One of those grief-stricken Bahá'ís to hurry from 'Akká to Bahjí, was the seventeen-year-old pilgrim Ṭarázu'lláh Samandarí, who later wrote in his diary:

> Early this morning when the Muslim call to prayer was being said [about 5 am], the news of the Ascension of the Ancient Beauty reached the pilgrim house in 'Akká.[32] Grieved with

> heartache, all the friends including the staff and the visitors went to Bahjí. . . .[33]
>
> Everyone was so sunk in the ocean of grief and sorrow that none could think of anything or anyone else. . . . Mourning and wailing, beating my head and chest, hardly able to walk, I dragged myself to Bahjí and went up to the Mansion. A crowd of people from all walks of life were there, their mourning and crying ascending sky high.
>
> 'Abdu'l-Bahá, the Mystery of God, grief-stricken and sorrowful, was seen going up and down the Mansion, chanting in a murmur the holy verses from Aqdas, and tear drops like pearls were constantly rolling over His blessed face and beard on to the ground.[34]

Young Ṭarázu'lláh approached the room of the Blessed Beauty:

> There I saw The Master who was saying that until this day, we used wisdom to safeguard the Blessed Beauty but of what use is wisdom anymore. Then He asked Agha Mirza Mohamed-i-Kashan to chant one of the Arabic Prayers revealed by Bahá'u'lláh.

Ṭarázu'lláh said he was feeling suicidal and had thought of three ways to end his life. But he noticed that the Master—despite "the storm of grief and the fire of the disastrous event [which] had overtaken Him"—had assigned two men to look after him, to prevent him from inflicting self-harm.[35]

Ṭarázu'lláh described in his diary the arrival of people from all strata of society in 'Akká, Haifa, and the surrounding areas, among them some eminent officials:

> His highness Fariq Pasha [an Ottoman general and public official], the ministers, the muftis, leaders of public affairs, lawyers, Sheikhs, Christians, the prominent dignitaries including members of governmental authorities, leaders of public affairs,

> as well as residents and ordinary public had gathered in Bahjí. Some were seated in a room below in the Mansion and were served tea, coffee, cigarettes and hookahs.[36]

The author Nabíl-i-Aʿẓam was also an eyewitness of that historic day at Bahjí. He wrote: "In the midst of the prevailing confusion a multitude of the inhabitants of ʿAkká and of the neighboring villages, that had thronged the fields surrounding the Mansion, could be seen weeping, beating upon their heads, and crying aloud their grief."[37]

In this excerpt from a poem of lament, the great ʿAndalíb describes the widespread sorrow:

Oh, in life's cup the wine-pourer of the feast of decree
Poured life-ending venom instead of spirit-elating wine.
For every ache there is a remedy, for every trouble a solution,
Oh, for this remediless ache and this balmless trouble.
The eye of creation was stunned, the world's heart darkened,
Heart's orchard was withered, the nightingale of life silenced.
From this loss, the pillars of existence were dismantled,
From this loss, the eternal throne was crushed.
The waves of the surging Sea of Grace were stilled; instead,
Waves of grief's ocean gushed in the hearts and souls of the near ones.
The banner of the Most Excellent Names fell to the dust,
The lamentation of God's Party was raised to the high heavens.
The One by Whose Manifestation the Day of Resurrection dawned upon the world,
By the setting of His sun a commotion made the world to quake.[38]

20

The Establishment of the Shrine of Bahá'u'lláh

A short time after the ascension of Bahá'u'lláh, the inconsolable 'Abdu'l-Bahá began to make the arrangements for the funeral.[1] Although Bahá'í law does not prescribe when a funeral should be held, the tradition in the Middle East was to bury the deceased within twenty-four hours,[2] and the Master now followed this custom. 'Abdu'l-Bahá was totally familiar with all procedures, and the burial laws laid down in the Kitáb-i-Aqdas.[3]

He had experience. With the watchful care of Bahá'u'lláh, the Master had organized the funeral in 1886 for His mother, Ásíyih Khánum (Navváb); most likely in 1887 for His uncle, Mírzá Músá (known as Áqáy-i-Kalím);[4] and for his darling son, Ḥusayn. The laws in the Kitáb-i-Aqdas require that the body be wrapped in shrouds of silk or cotton, and on a finger should be placed a ring bearing the inscription: "I came forth from God, and return unto Him, detached from all save Him, holding fast to His Name, the Merciful, the Compassionate."[5] The coffin should be of crystal, stone, or hard fine wood.[6]

WASHING

There is a Bahá'í requirement for a careful washing of the body, but no direction as to how it should be done. The Islamic tradition, which was likely to have been followed, was to do this as soon as possible after a death. Those involved would wash the body several times using a cloth and warm water, often perfumed for the final time. The body is covered by a sheet at all times during the washing. The washing of the body of Bahá'u'lláh took place on a table in His room.[7]

Ṭarázu'lláh Samandarí wrote in his diary that the Master with His own hands washed and prepared the precious remains with rose water, precisely according to the laws and regulations as revealed in the Kitáb-i-Aqdas.[8] Those assisting 'Abdu'l-Bahá were Dr. Jarráḥ, and Shaykh Maḥmúd-i-Arrabí,[9] a Bahá'í who in 1870 had also washed—in the presence of Bahá'u'lláh—the body of Mírzá Mihdí.[10] The male relatives of Bahá'u'lláh were present but due to customary practice, no women could attend.[11]

It was during the preparations for this process that a disturbing incident took place. In the room were two satchels containing the most precious documents that the Manifestation had entrusted to the Master and said they belonged to Him.[12] Writing about the incident in later days, 'Abdu'l-Bahá described a ruse that occurred before the washing to obtain those satchels, a move orchestrated by his half-brother Mírzá Muḥammad-'Alí.[13]

In His Tablet of One Thousand verses, the Master wrote that together with the other male descendants of Bahá'u'lláh, He entered the room to wash and perfume the body of the Manifestation. At that time, He said, one of the others, later identified as a Covenant-breaker, suggested the Master give him the two satchels to give to Mírzá Badí'u'lláh (also a Covenant-breaker) to keep safely away from all the water. So overwhelmed by the calamity of the ascension, and not expecting the subsequent betrayal, the Master handed over the satchels.[14]

Those who wanted those satchels had imagined that one of them contained Bahá'u'lláh's last Will and Testament, which they knew had been written,[15] but—unknown to them—was in 'Akká. It was clear that they had calculated that if they could obtain that document and prevent it being read, nobody could confirm with any confidence that 'Abdu'l-Bahá had been appointed by Bahá'u'lláh as His successor as Head of the Faith.[16]

SHROUD

After the washing came the time for enshrouding the body of Bahá'u'lláh. The Kitáb-i-Aqdas says: "The Lord hath decreed, moreover, that the deceased should be enfolded in five sheets of silk or cotton. For those whose means are limited a single sheet of either fabric will suffice."[17] There is nothing prescribed in the Bahá'í writings about how the wrapping is to be done.[18] However, after He revealed the Kitáb-i-Aqdas in 1873, Bahá'u'lláh was asked if the "five sheets" mentioned referred to five full-length shrouds wrapped one around the other or "five cloths which were hitherto customarily used" and He responded it was the latter.[19] If Islamic tradition was followed, the final shroud would have covered the body from above the head to below the toes, and the best quality silk would have been used.

As yet, no descriptions of certain other specific matters have been found, so one can only speculate about further details. If the practice for the Master's funeral twenty-nine years later was similar, a mitre (peaked hat), a symbol of authority, could well have been placed upon the head of the Manifestation.[20] Given the provision in the Kitáb-i-Aqdas, the ring prescribed for the deceased would probably have been placed on a finger of Bahá'u'lláh.[21] Again, if the same practice were followed as for the Master in 1921, the body of the Manifestation would have remained on the bed until about an hour before the funeral.

If the prevailing Islamic traditions were followed, male relatives and other men permitted by 'Abdu'l-Bahá would have been permitted to view Bahá'u'lláh's sacred body but the only women permitted to do so would have been close relatives such as His wives and daughters.

COFFIN

The diary of Ṭarázu'lláh Samandarí notes that Bahá'u'lláh's body was "safely and with extreme care and respect put in a strong wooden coffin."[22] Had there not been a coffin available at the mansion, there would have been time to bring one from 'Akká, perhaps one similar to that used for Bahá'u'lláh's first wife, Ásíyih Khánum (Navváb), six years earlier, which can be seen today upstairs in the Mansion of Bahjí.

Details are lacking, but we can look to the descriptions of the Master's coffin three decades later and wonder if similar practices were observed. At that time, the Master's body lay on a silken comforter, the cloth sides draping over the edge of the coffin. His head rested on a silken pillow. The finest quality attar of rose (an essential oil distilled from roses) was sprinkled over Him before the sides of the comforter were drawn up and laid over His body. Then the cover of the casket was closed.[23] Unlike in the West, it was not customary in the Middle East to view the deceased in an open casket.[24]

In the afternoon, shortly after sunset, builders and laborers, "hurriedly and with full force," dug the grave in the room designated for the shrine. The work was challenging. The men needed to remove some of the baked clay bricks that in those days were the likely floor, and then to dig down into the sandy ground, shoring up the sides as they descended.

FUNERAL PROCESSION

The funeral was not to be a public ceremony. It took place "after the dignitaries and leading citizens and vast numbers of ordinary men and women, who were not adherents of His Faith, had paid their last respects to Bahá'u'lláh and gone . . ."[25] Before the procession to the burial site, the Master directed that all the friends, members of the Holy Family, the staff, and the visitors gather together, presumably under the arches adjacent to the ground floor of the mansion. Under the instructions of 'Abdu'l-Bahá, pallbearers, probably including at least two of Bahá'u'lláh's sons, carried the coffin containing the sacred remains of the Manifestation out of His room, through the great hall, and down the stairs.[26]

The stairs are steep and there is a turn high up and a turn to exit through the door on the ground level, so it was a task requiring strength, agility, and great care.[27] The coffin would have reached the ground floor at about sunset or just after. The Bahá'ís, numb with grief, stood back from the coffin, as the Master gave instructions on how the cortege was to move toward the building opposite, and how they were to assemble inside. Eventually it became time for the cortege to begin. A report of the exact route has yet to be uncovered, but the eminent historian Hasan Balyuzi has written that the "the coffin containing the sacred remains was taken from the Mansion to a house a few yards away."[28] That seems to indicate the cortege exited through the most direct, and most easily navigated, route to the room where the interment was to take place. That route was through the gate near the northern end of the wall to the west of the mansion.

We can piece together a description that is likely to be reasonably accurate, but which may be amended in some details in future years.[29]

LAMPS

The funeral of Bahá'u'lláh took place after sunset in the era before electricity arrived at the mansion. Accordingly, as was the practice in processions at night, a solitary individual in front of the cortege carried a lamp to lead the way through the gate and then along the short distance across the lawn to the entrance of the house. Although there is no description of the cortege yet found, we know from descriptions of subsequent holy days commemorating the ascension that the Master organized the friends to walk in an orderly fashion, two abreast, carrying lamps. The Master would walk sometimes in front, sometimes at the side, of this procession.[30]

We can imagine a probable scenario of the coffin of the Manifestation being carried on the shoulders of men, and them being followed by 'Abdu'l-Bahá, wearing His turban and cloak, walking slowly with His characteristic dignity, His appearance distinguished by His strong yet slender stature, his black hair and beard.[31] On the night of the ascension, He was likely to be behind the pallbearers and in front of the procession of male relatives, staff, local Bahá'ís, and pilgrims walking two abreast and carrying lanterns lit by candles and oil. In those days, the usual custom was for women not to participate in a funeral procession.[32]

We can be confident that the lamp-lit procession moved slowly away from the mansion's high wall and into the open air, the great grove of pine trees away and slightly to the right silhouetted under the dark sky. There were very few if any lights in the fields at the northern and western sides of the compound, and the only sounds to be heard were likely the sweet yet sad cries of the nightingales and the chorus of night insects accompanying the sobs of the mourners. The solemnity of the occasion, the spiritually charged atmosphere, and the emotions of overwhelming grief, would all have contributed to the sense of the overall significance and historic importance of this funeral.

They arrived at the entrance, likely to be the place where pilgrims enter today (the northern entrance), except the door then might well have been the original sturdy, black double door which Shoghi Effendi was to replace during his ministry. By being at the head of the procession, 'Abdu'l-Bahá would have been able to position Himself at the door and so been able to carry out His practice of pausing at the entrance, and then anointing with rose water the hands of each person.[33]

As the cortege moved into the house, the men carrying the coffin proceeded into the outer courtyard, which was open to the sky, the floors likely soft with the finest woven carpets from Persia, as were certain floors in the mansion. Wall-mounted oil lamps would have cast their soft light onto the mourners, making their skin glow, their tears glisten. The pallbearers needed to take great care to pass through the narrow doorway into what would be the inner shrine, before lowering the coffin next to the grave site. Only limited numbers of Bahá'ís were able to assemble inside that room around the graveside, the others gathering in the courtyard. Because only Bahá'ís were present, it would have been acceptable for female relatives such as Bahíyyih Khánum, the two widows, and some others to be in the nearby rooms with curtains partially or fully drawn.

INTERMENT SERVICE

It was the practice of 'Abdu'l-Bahá Himself to chant on special occasions. This momentous funeral was surely the supreme occasion for Him to chant the majestic, rhythmic prayer for the dead revealed by Bahá'u'lláh, the prayer recited by one person in the presence of a congregation.[34] On the special occasion of the interment of the Manifestation in 1892, it is probable that 'Abdu'l-Bahá, or a Bahá'í He designated, recited excerpts from the Kitáb-i-Aqdas because it has references to the ascension. He may well have chanted the Tablet of Visitation revealed in 1891 by Bahá'u'lláh for Imám Ḥusayn, which also applies to the Manifestation—being the return of that Figure—and which was the most important Tablet of Visitation that Bahá'u'lláh had revealed during His Ministry.[35] (The text of the Tablet of Visitation that has been recited in the generations since had yet to be selected.)

It was the Master's practice while visiting the holy shrines to direct one or two of the friends with melodious voices to chant, either poems by Bahá'u'lláh or other suitable verses by Bahá'í poets. Ṭarázu'lláh Samandarí later wrote in his diary: "The burial procedures were somewhat delayed until the Greatest Branch, 'Abdu'l-Bahá, with His own blessed hands helped the coffin to be placed in its permanent resting place." Shoghi Effendi wrote that the interment took place "shortly after sunset." On that day the sunset was at 7:41pm.[36]

This historic act established the location of the Qiblih, the point of adoration, the place that Bahá'ís in all parts of the planet now turn to when reciting their obligatory prayers. From that historic moment, the Shrine of Bahá'u'lláh also became a spiritual magnet drawing pilgrims to its threshold.[37]

Today there is an elevation of a rectangular area visible under the carpets but it is not known if that is immediately above where the coffin was interred. We also do not know in which direction the coffin faced. Bahá'ís in the Holy Land during the time of Bahá'u'lláh and the Master followed Islamic practice, and that included in the Haifa

Bahá'í cemetery where the graves were arranged to face Mecca. It was not until the 1920s that the graves faced the Shrine of Bahá'u'lláh.[38] Could it be that they followed that practice with Bahá'u'lláh? If not, what would be more appropriate? In Islamic tradition the deceased was positioned so that the head, looking over the feet, is faced toward Mecca. If that tradition was followed, the direction would be approximately toward the southeast.

After the coffin was lowered to its last resting place, the builders and laborers closed and covered the grave. Ṭarázu'lláh Samandarí observed: "Everything imaginable (was done) to make the grave, the walls and the room strong, safe and protected." Watchmen were posted outside the room to protect the holy shrine, which was on an exposed northerly side of the Bahjí property. Mr. Samandarí takes up the story:

> Once this important procedure and the burial ceremonies were done, 'Abdu'l-Bahá, the one Whom God had purposed came up to the upper floor of the Mansion of Bahjí. As a result of the extreme grief and lamentations of such a tragedy which our beloved Master was going through, His tender and loving heart appeared as though it had stopped functioning. I personally saw and was a witness to His condition as I watched Him from outside the room His Blessed Person was in. Panic and anxiety overtook the friends present. As for me, I was so affected by the anguish of 'Abdu'l-Bahá's state of health that I realized that momentarily I had forgotten that Bahá'u'lláh, The Sun of Truth had set. An unprecedented worry and despondency overtook us all. This lasted almost an hour before our Beloved Master's pure and glorious heart condition returned to normal function. He then bade farewell by honouring everyone with loving words of kindness and left for rest.[39]

Bahíyyih Khánum, The Greatest Holy Leaf.

Bahá'u'lláh's chamber at Bahjí.

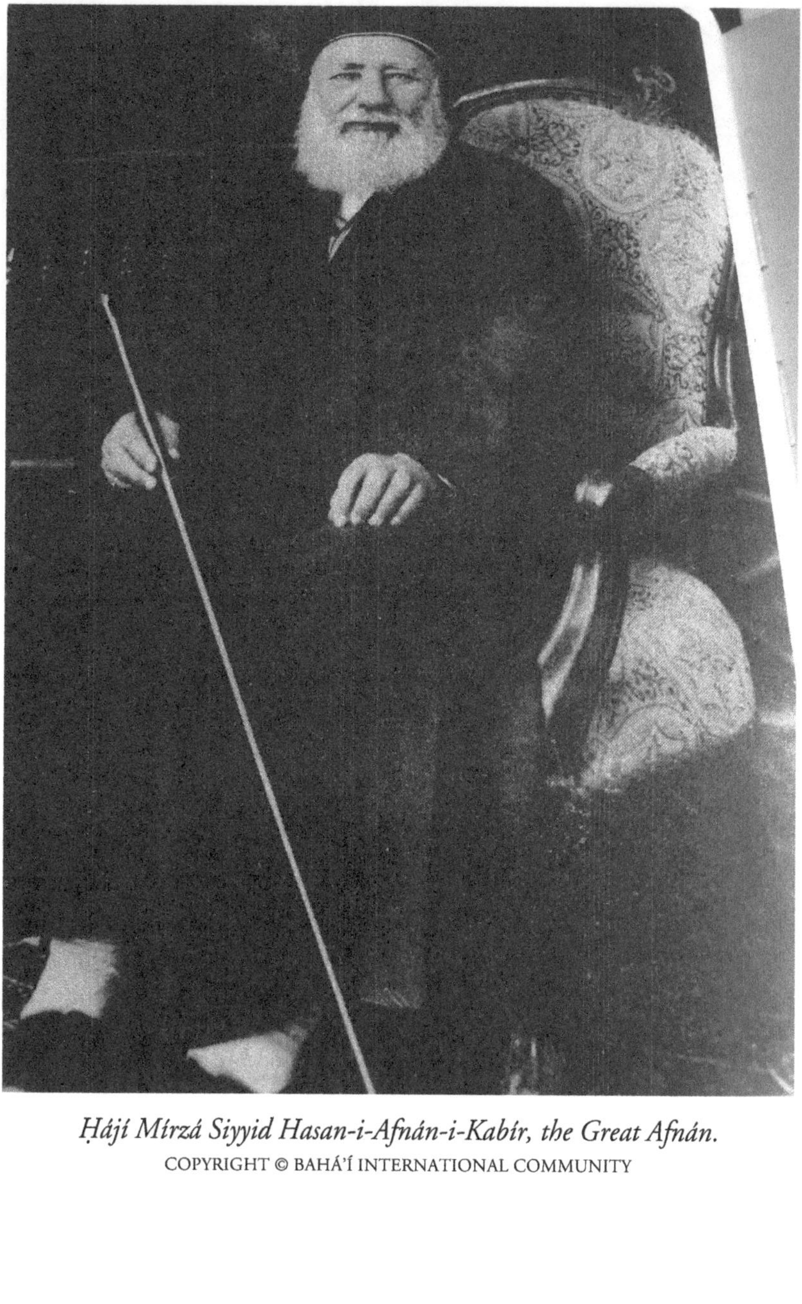

Ḥájí Mírzá Siyyid Hasan-i-Afnán-i-Kabír, the Great Afnán.

Stairway of the Mansion of Bahjí.

Bahá'u'lláh's coffin was carried down this stairway.

21

Days of Mourning

The days of mourning "the supreme affliction" started in spectacular fashion. Just before the dawn that followed the interment of the sacred body of the Manifestation, an Arabian Bahá'í standing on the balcony of the upper floor of the mansion chanted with great musicality the Islamic call to prayer as well as prayers revealed by Bahá'u'lláh.[1] Then the distinguished figure of 'Abdu'l-Bahá, noble in His grief, emerged from the mansion, and—followed respectfully by the Bahá'ís—walked solemnly to the entrance to the shrine, entered, and then approached and crossed the sacred threshold. Within the inner shrine, He chanted Bahá'u'lláh's powerful prayer for the dead, its repetitions resounding through the dawning light. It was also His practice to invite one or two of those who had melodious voices to chant prayers and readings.

During the rest of the day, the area in the precincts of the shrine was one of great activity. Workmen were busily engaged with the task given them by the Master to reinforce and strengthen the outer wall with bricks of Palestinian stone.[2] The northern-most room was the most exposed building and so vulnerable to outsiders, including grave robbers. While the work was going on, Shaykh Maḥmúd-i-Arrabí installed himself as a temporary security guard in a tent next to the wall outside the shrine for the week it took for the work to be complete.[3] There was no indication that the work being done on the outside of the room would lead to the completion of the sepulcher. And in 1952, Shoghi Effendi was to make it quite clear that "a befitting Mausoleum enshrining the precious Dust of the most Great Name" had yet to be built.[4]

For nine days after the ascension, the rich and poor alike crowded into the fields surrounding the mansion and the shrine.[5] More than 500 people camped under the trees, their food—and funds for the poor—provided by 'Abdu'l-Bahá. The Bahá'ís remained stunned in their grief, as Nabíl described: "My inner and outer tongue are powerless to portray the condition we were in. . . ."[6] The other residents of the wider community were also sorrowful because the one they regarded as a saint, the one they saw as bringing blessings to their area, had passed away. Among the mourners were notables of society, including Shí'ahs, Sunnís, Christians, Jews, and Druzes, as well as poets, 'ulamás, and government officials.[7]

Local Shaykhs—the spiritual and political leaders of the district—brought to Bahjí lamb, rice, sugar, and salt to share, traditionally an incentive for those who consumed them to pray for the soul of the deceased.[8] The governor and his officials rode up in style on the finest of horses to pay their respects and offer condolences. Clergy of various religions, some of whom had received the benefit of the insights and inspiration of 'Abdu'l-Bahá, came with their prayers and sympathies. "Among them," wrote historian Hasan Balyuzi, "were the Muftí of Acre and other members of the Islamic tradition.[9] Also there were lavishly gowned Christian priests from both Latin and Greek traditions."[10]

An eyewitness wrote: "White turbaned, bearded leaders of the Druze community and members of their community arrived from Abu-Sinan, and surrounding villages. They had loved Bahá'u'lláh and the Master for years, and treated them with the greatest of respect. Their mourning was genuine and deep."[11] Nevertheless, Shoghi Effendi wrote, their expressions of sorrow and praise, were nothing compared to those of countless thousands of Bahá'ís in Persia, India, Russia, 'Iráq, Turkey, Palestine, Egypt, and Syria.[12]

Inside the mansion there were scenes of anguish. According to an eyewitness, Murassa Rouhaní, who was six years old at the time, the Arab women from the neighborhood and from 'Akká, wearing their burqas and long black gowns, accepted an invitation of 'Abdu'l-Bahá to enter the mansion where they sat cross-legged in a circle on carpets that were laid out for them in the central hall upstairs. "They chanted mourning verses and beat the back of their heads with their palms," Ms. Rouhani recalled. "I was then a child. I sat next to them and did the same."[13]

Outside, the balcony became a platform for the expression of grief and respect, as another eyewitness, Rafí'ih Shahídí, later described: "Bahá'í women occupied the balcony of the Mansion which had been covered with carpets for the occasion. The sound of their wailing and weeping rose sky high. Whatever they did I copied. They hit themselves on the head. I did likewise."[14] During the day, from that balcony (the one facing south),[15] poets chanted songs known as Marthiyah in praise of Bahá'u'lláh. In addition, Muslim leaders chanted prayers and laments. Following them, and standing on those same high balconies, silver-tongued orators wearing robes and turbans delivered—in the most elevated Turkish and Arabic—eulogies, poems, and tributes, some of which had been penned in Damascus, Aleppo, Beirut, and Cairo, and then cabled or otherwise sent to 'Akká. Those panegyrics lamented the loss of the great spiritual figure, Bahá'u'lláh, magnifying His virtues and greatness, and they also often praised the Master.[16]

Among the poets and writers who composed elegies were: Ḥájí Muḥammad Abú'l-Ḥalq (Muslim); Amon Zaydan (a Christian writer); 'Alí Effendi, the Qáḍí (an Islamic judge) of 'Akka; and Ya'qub al-Lubnaní (Lebanese Christian).[17] Ḥájí Muḥammad Abú'l-Ḥalq, a pious Muslim theologian renowned throughout Greater Syria—the area embracing what is now Syria, Lebanon, and the Holy Land—penned this beautiful tribute:

O Thou Who hath soared in knowledge and intellect,
and captivated the sages by the sagacity of Thy mind!

Thy exalted station, a byword among the people, fears no rival
understanding even one lauded and acknowledged by all.

Fear has seized mankind at the loss of Bahá—a fear
so immense, all hearts are shaken by its enormity.

A chief who polarised till His divinity reached above the skies,
unto heaven whence it was returned to its source.

Thus I shed tears of blood over this peerless star,
His like, no age shall ever produce again.

I came, a consoler, offering this elegy of mine;
and a reminder to His kindred, to whom I say:

Be patient in this calamity, even though the
highest unshakeable mountain cannot bear it.

Patience beseemeth the direst adversities—nay it is more
befitting the noble departed and His descendants.

Methinks, this is a day of the most grievous affliction;
a day that pierced noble hearts with its arrows.

May they continue to console and comfort each other,
in the loss of Him for Whom creation came into being.[18]

Then came a masterpiece of ornate prose by the youthful Mr. Jád 'Íd, a renowned literary figure in the Christian community. It was recited in the presence of 'Abdu'l-Bahá at a gathering where many of the notables of 'Akká—such as a judge and an Azharí muftí—were present. A copy of this eulogy was respectfully tendered, addressed to 'Abdu'l-Bahá. Opening with an address to the Master, an excerpt is reproduced here.

> To the ornament of the age and the fount of virtue and beneficence, my lord and master, ruling scholar, His excellency, 'Abbás Effendí—may His might and glory endure.
>
> Deign, my lord—O pride of liberality and prince of noble deeds—to accept from one who is enamoured of your high moral rectitude, these expressions which are as far beneath your most refined essence, as earth is far removed from the luminous sky.

The orator then proclaims his own inadequacies as:

> One who attempted to make mention of but one of the attributes of your venerable Lord, your noble Leader, your lustrous Moon and shining Star. One who essayed to describe a most grievous adversity that has confounded the insights of the wise and perplexed the minds of the learned.

The orator moves on to quote a couplet from a well-known poem suitable on the occasion of the death of a great person:

> An adversity that has been announced unto every region,
> its gravity well–nigh crumbling the loftiest mountains.

He continues referring to himself and his task as:

> One who attempted to describe a calamity that caused the morning sun to be eclipsed, the light of the moon of noble deeds to be dimmed, the trigger of glory to miss its aim, the vastness of heaven to be cleft asunder, and the fair face of determination and resolve to be marred and disfigured.

The climax is remarkable in English as well as in Arabic, a language in which Bahá'u'lláh Himself was a master and had praised for its eloquence. The orator refers to those who supplicated to Bahá'u'lláh:

> He Who loved Him called to Him, and He answered the call, leaving memorable vestiges and far-reaching effects, and after accomplishing His noble mission and engendering into this world a grace and munificence that made it far richer in honour and glory.

The orator addresses 'Abdu'l-Bahá again:

> You, my lord, and your honourable followers, are renewing with the light of your wisdom and knowledge, that which the Star of Bahá now returned to its exalted constellation hath introduced.
>
> If He has saddened you and all of us by His departure, He has assuredly gladdened the angels of paradise His blissful abode. . . .

The orator concludes:

> May God keep and preserve you and your noble brethren, in glory and happiness.[19]

Meanwhile, the Master assigned an important task to the great Bahá'í poet Nabíl.

22

Facets of a Jewel

Shortly after the ascension, the Master—bowed down with grief and multiple responsibilities—asked the literary genius Nabíl to select excerpts from Bahá'u'lláh's writings to form the Tablet of Visitation for the shrine.[1] Before that was ready, the Master is likely to have chanted at the threshold the Tablet of Visitation for the Imám Ḥusayn. That Tablet was the most important and relevant Tablet of Visitation revealed by Bahá'u'lláh. 'Abdul-Bahá's propensity to chant a Tablet of Visitation is shown in many reports. After He had accepted Nabíl's draft, the Master was to chant that magnificent Tablet whenever He visited the Shrine of Bahá'u'lláh.[2]

The Master surely foresaw that generations of pilgrims would recite it for at least one thousand years at the Qiblih.[3] He knew that the magnificent Tablet would also ring out in the Faith's Temples, starting with the one He was to build in 'Is<u>h</u>qábád[4] and then in others to be established throughout the globe long after His ascension. He would have foreseen that its exquisite verses would also resound in Bahá'í homes and centers on all the islands and continents as the believers recited it on holy days, their minds and hearts turning toward the cherished Shrine of Bahá'u'lláh.

The Master had good reason to single out Nabíl for the important commission to collate suitable excerpts for the Tablet. He was the Bahá'í poet laureate and the "immortal chronicler"[5] of the birth of the Faith. The Master called him "the great Nabíl," and said his "native genius was pure inspiration."[6] In Bahá'u'lláh's last days on the planet, He drew Nabíl into His presence almost daily and, on occasions, alone. At those times, Nabíl heard "marvelous things" and was "shown the lights of paradise."[7]

The selection of verses Nabíl made for the Tablet of Visitation lived up to the trust 'Abdu'l-Bahá had placed in Him. Such was Nabíl's spirituality and such was his knowledge of what makes literature great, that he assembled—from diverse sources—paragraphs that fit together seamlessly, like different facets of one exquisite diamond. One special aspect of the Tablet is that the first parts were uplifted from Bahá'u'lláh's Tablets that had been revealed as a gift to those who could not physically attain His presence, but who were spiritually turning toward Him.[8]

SOURCES

The first three paragraphs come from a Tablet to Áqá Bálá, whose full name is Mullá Bábá-i-Sar-Cháh-i-Bírjandí, indicating that he came from Bírjand in the Khurásán province.[9] The next part belongs to a Tablet addressed to a non-identified individual who was lamenting the sufferings of Bahá'u'lláh.[10] The third part is an excerpt—with some minor differences—from a Tablet addressed to the sister of Bahá'u'lláh, called "'Ukht" (sister), referring to Ṣughra Khátún Khánum.[11] Here is that excerpt: "Bless Thou, O Lord my God, the Divine Lote-Tree and its leaves, and its boughs, and its branches, and its stems, and its offshoots, as long as Thy most excellent titles will endure and Thy most august attributes will last. Protect it, then, from the mischief of the aggressor and the hosts of tyranny. Thou art, in truth, the Almighty, the Most Powerful."[12]

The last part of the Tablet calls for the protection of the Faith from "the mischief of the aggressor and the hosts of tyranny."[13] According to the eminent scholar Dr. Vahid Ra'fati, this section is the final part of a short Tablet for protection, probably for the poet Bíbí Rouhaní Bushrú'í.[14] An erudite teacher of the Faith in

Bushrúyih in the Khurásán region, she had visited the mother of the Báb, and chose the surname of "Rouhaní" (meaning "spiritual") to identify her poems.

There are seven paragraphs in the English translation. Four are essentially tributes, initially to the Manifestation, and ultimately to God. Three of the paragraphs contain supplications or requests.

The first paragraph opens with a tribute to the Manifestation. In his translation of the Tablet from the Arabic into English, Shoghi Effendi selected the elevated word "august" to describe Bahá'u'lláh as the Tablet opens in praise of Him. The imagery of praise and glory resting upon the Manifestation seems perfect for a prayer said at the graveside. Those reciting the prayer solemnly testify to their belief in the role of the Manifestations and to the power and historic linkage to other revelations.

The second paragraph attests to the role of the Manifestation through Whom the beauty of God is portrayed to us, and through Whom the difference between the fate of believers and unbelievers is spelled out.

The third paragraph describes the mystical connection between the Manifestation and God. It refers to the bounties bestowed on believers and the woe that descends upon those who dispute and resist the Manifestation (as distinct from mere non-belief).

The fourth paragraph contains the first supplication (or request). It pleads for a wafting of grace from God but not for selfish desires. In fact, the supplication is that we are drawn away from ourselves so that we may enter the courts of nearness to God.

The fifth paragraph resonates with Bahá'ís as we encounter the titles of Bahá'u'lláh ("the Glory" and "Beauty" of God). It is here we acknowledge the great sufferings of the Manifestation for our sake, and His steadfastness through His trials.

The sixth paragraph includes the second supplication. After offering ourselves in recompense for the sufferings of Bahá'u'lláh, we ask God through the Manifestation and His devoted believers to remove the veils between God and His creatures and to supply us with the good of this world and the next.

The seventh and final paragraph is also one of supplication, starting first with a plea for protection of the Faith from aggressors and tyrants. Then we ask for blessings for the believers.

In addition to the Tablet of Visitation, another great Tablet by Bahá'u'lláh will be permanently associated with the Shrine of Bahá'u'lláh, and it is to that Tablet we now turn.

23

The Crimson Book

During His final illness, Bahá'u'lláh had entrusted His Will—written in His own hand and sealed by Him[1]—to 'Abdu'l-Bahá, Who kept it in a locked box in 'Akká. When, nine days after the ascension of Bahá'u'lláh, the Master adjudged the appropriate time to have arrived, arrangements were made for the unsealing and reading of the sacred Tablet at Bahjí.

In the morning, the box had been unlocked and Bahá'u'lláh's wax seals removed in the presence of nine witnesses chosen from amongst Bahá'u'lláh's companions and members of His Family,[2] including the Master's thirty-eight-year-old half-brother Mírzá Muḥammad-'Alí.[3] At the direction of 'Abdu'l-Bahá, Áqá Riḍáy-i-Qannád,[4] a devoted veteran follower of Bahá'u'lláh, read it aloud. Then there was an event at the Shrine of Bahá'u'lláh that—after the interment of the sacred remains of the Manifestation—could surely never be surpassed in importance in that holy place.

The reading of the Kitáb-i-'Ahd,[5] the Book of the Covenant, was before a big group including Bahá'u'lláh's sons and some of the Báb's relatives, as well as some pilgrims and resident Bahá'ís.[6] In attendance on that memorable and historic occasion was the young Ṭarázu'lláh Samandarí, who wrote in his diary about what he witnessed:

When all were gathered, 'Abdu'l-Bahá asked Majdi'd-Dín, son of Músá Kalím,[7] to stand on a chair and in the presence of about two hundred people, The Book of Covenant [Kitáb-i-'Ahd] which was in the original handwriting of Bahá'u'lláh as well signed by His seal, was read by Majdi'd-Dín in their presence.

Once the majority of the people left, the Beloved Master addressed the believers present, and in a clear and distinct voice announced that from this hour onward, no individual has the right to write and send to anyone anything in any form whether it be a word, a sentence or a book unless it is approved and signed by Himself.

He continued on to say that such an action by the friends would inflict untold harm and damage on the Cause of God. He also mentioned that the only thing which would safeguard the Cause was obedience and lack of opposition by the enemies."[8]

In *God Passes By*, Shoghi Effendi said of the Kitáb-i-'Ahd:

> [T]his unique and epoch-making Document, designated by Bahá'u'lláh as His "Most Great Tablet," and alluded to by Him as the "Crimson Book" in His "Epistle to the Son of the Wolf," can find no parallel in the Scriptures of any previous Dispensation, not excluding that of the Báb Himself. For nowhere in the books pertaining to any of the world's religious systems, not even among the writings of the Author of the Bábí Revelation, do we find any single document establishing a Covenant endowed with an authority comparable to the Covenant which Bahá'u'lláh had Himself instituted.

The purpose of the Covenant, as Shoghi Effendi was later to explain, is: "to perpetuate the influence of [the] Faith, insure its integrity, safeguard it from schism, and stimulate its world-wide expansion. . . ."[9]

Among the key provisions of the Kitáb-i-'Ahd is the establishment of the Covenant, which ensured the succession to the Manifestation, thereby avoiding the contention seen in other religious systems. The text also identifies the One who was to be the Covenant's Center.

> The Will of the divine Testator is this: It is incumbent upon the Aghsán, the Afnán[10] and My Kindred to turn, one and all, their faces towards the Most Mighty Branch. Consider that which We have revealed in Our Most Holy Book: "When the ocean of My presence hath ebbed and the Book of My Revelation is ended, turn your faces toward Him Whom God hath purposed, Who hath branched from this Ancient Root." The object of this sacred verse is none other except the Most Mighty Branch ['Abdu'l-Bahá]. Thus have We graciously revealed unto you Our potent Will, and I am verily the Gracious, the All-Powerful.[11]

Shoghi Effendi writes: "And to crown the inestimable honors, privileges and benefits showered upon Him ['Abdu'l-Bahá], in ever increasing abundance, throughout the forty years of His Father's ministry in Baghdád, in Adrianople and in 'Akká, He had been elevated to the high office of Center of Bahá'u'lláh's Covenant, and been made the successor of the Manifestation of God Himself. . . ."[12]

Among the many other provisions of the Kitáb-i-'Ahd,[13] there was one specifically ordaining the station of Mírzá Muhammad-'Alí to be beneath that of his older brother, 'Abdu'l-Bahá, Who alone among Bahá'u'lláh's sons had been accorded the privilege of being called "the Master."[14] Twenty years later in New York City, the Master was quoted as saying:

> As to the most great characteristic of the revelation of Bahá'u'lláh, a specific teaching not given by any of the Prophets of the past: It is the ordination and appointment of the Center of the Covenant. By this appointment and provision He has safeguarded and protected the religion of God against differences and schisms, making it impossible for anyone to create a

> new sect or faction of belief. To ensure unity and agreement He has entered into a Covenant with all the people of the world, including the interpreter and explainer of His teachings, so that no one may interpret or explain the religion of God according to his own view or opinion and thus create a sect founded upon his individual understanding of the divine Words.[15]

On that historic day, there was one more reading necessary. Because the cultural traditions of the day kept some women away from the previous readings, the Kitáb-i-'Ahd was read in the mansion to the women of the Holy Family and other female Bahá'ís.[16] In the story of the Shrine of Bahá'u'lláh, this day was pivotal because, by virtue of the reading of the Kitáb-i-'Ahd to the Bahá'í community in the Holy Land as well as to pilgrims and other visitors, it became absolutely clear to all that as the successor of the Manifestation, 'Abdu'l-Bahá would have complete authority over anything to do with the Faith, and that included over the shrine itself.[17]

It was in those dramatic, momentous, sorrow-drenched days, that 'Abdu'l-Bahá as Head of the Faith sent out a stirring message to the Bahá'ís of the world.

24

A New Ministry

Throughout the wondrous events of the inauguration of the Shrine of Bahá'u'lláh and the proclamation of the Covenant, 'Abdu'l-Bahá was still deeply grieving over the death of one Who was both a Manifestation of God and His beloved Father. The depth of that sorrow is understandable considering the nature of the relationship between the two. 'Abdu'l-Bahá's devotion to His Father was evident in every facet of His behavior, and the high esteem and devotion with which Bahá'u'lláh regarded the Master is apparent throughout His writings.

'Abdu'l-Bahá, when on His way to Bahjí from 'Akká, was known to dismount at a certain point along the way, prostrate Himself, and then walk the remaining distance, thereby showing the greatest respect for His eagerly awaiting Father, Who would ask all those in His presence to go out to meet Him.[1] Bahá'u'lláh had explicitly declared the depth of His affection when, in His own handwriting, He addressed 'Abdu'l-Bahá: "O Thou Who art the apple of Mine eye! My glory, the ocean of my loving-kindness, the sun of My bounty, the heaven of my mercy rest upon thee."[2]

In Adrianople, more than two decades before His ascension, Bahá'u'lláh had declared their mystical closeness in the Súriy-i-Ghuṣn (Tablet of the Branch): "Whoso turneth towards Him hath turned towards God, and whoso turneth away from Him hath turned away from My beauty, hath repudiated My Proof, and transgressed against Me."[3] Ḥájí Mírzá Ḥaydar-'Alí, in his memoirs, wrote that Bahá'u'lláh said it would be seen how 'Abdu'l-Bahá alone would raise the Faith's banner in the world and would gather all of humanity under the Tabernacle of peace and submission.[4]

'Abdu'l-Bahá's grief was made worse by something He had observed on the fourth night after the ascension. He had arisen from His bed and was pacing His room trying to ease His agony when He saw through a nearby window His half-brothers searching through the papers Bahá'u'lláh had entrusted to Him. As was confirmed later, they were searching for a document they could use to undermine the authority 'Abdu'l-Bahá would have when, as those unfaithful siblings expected, the Will and Testament of Bahá'u'lláh appointed the Master as the new Head of the Faith.[5]

Soon after the reading of the Kitáb-i-'Ahd, the Master asked His half-brothers to give Him one of Bahá'u'lláh's seals from the satchels containing the papers of the Manifestation.[6] But to His horror, they denied any knowledge of the satchels, which they had taken during the washing of the body of Bahá'u'lláh. 'Abdu'l-Bahá later described how He began to tremble when He heard that answer from His siblings. He knew that great tests and trials lay ahead.[7] He had already noticed that after the reading of the Kitáb-i-'Ahd in the shrine, the faces of those who were later to explicitly turn against Him were gloomy and despondent. In fact, He said it was at that point that the fire of dissension was lit.[8]

Sorrow was rampant at Bahjí and in 'Akká. Many Bahá'ís who had been in the presence of Bahá'u'lláh were distraught almost to the point of despair at the loss of one "transcendental in His majesty, serene, awe-inspiring, unapproachably glorious."[9] Those who have not experienced being physically in the company of a Manifestation can only approach an understanding of the experience. This can be assisted by contemplating the following words of the Báb:

> There is no paradise more wondrous for any soul than to be exposed to God's Manifestation in His Day, to hear His verses

> and believe in them, to attain His presence which is naught but the presence of God, to sail upon the sea of the heavenly kingdom of His good-pleasure, and to partake of the choice fruits of the paradise of His divine Oneness.[10]

The loss of such an experience must be devastating.

Later, in a Tablet addressed to Mírzá 'Abdu'lláh of Núr, 'Abdu'l-Bahá employed a powerful maritime metaphor to describe the grief of those Bahá'ís who were in Bahjí or 'Akká at the time of the ascension: "Darkness enveloped them from all six sides, the pillars of the world were shaken, the ocean of sedition surged, the gales of severe tests commenced to blow, the most great tempest blew, and the ships of the lives of these unfortunate ones were caught on all sides by waves of agitation. They were thrown into a horrible whirlpool, cutting off the hope of survival, dashing everything to pieces. . . ."[11]

But then something wonderful happened. The Master described in that Tablet how the souls of the Most Glorious and from the Highest Kingdom blessed them, thereby giving the hearts strength and the souls a new life.[12] The Exemplar showed the way by not surrendering to His sorrow. Shortly after the reading of the Will and Testament in the shrine, 'Abdu'l-Bahá exercised His responsibility as the new Head of the Faith, and penned "a stirring proclamation . . . addressed to the rank and file of the followers of His Father."[13] Here is an excerpt:

> The world's great Light, once resplendent upon all mankind has set, to shine everlastingly from the Abhá Horizon, His Kingdom of fadeless glory, shedding splendor upon His loved ones from on high and breathing into their hearts and souls the breath of eternal life. . . .
>
> O ye beloved of the Lord! Beware, beware lest ye hesitate and waver. Let not fear fall upon you, neither be troubled nor dismayed. Take ye good heed lest this calamitous day slacken the flames of your ardor, and quench your tender hopes. Today is the day for steadfastness and constancy. Blessed are they that stand firm and immovable as the rock, and brave the storm and

> stress of this tempestuous hour. They, verily, shall be the recipients of God's grace, shall receive His divine assistance, and shall be truly victorious. . . .
>
> The Sun of Truth, that Most Great Light, hath set upon the horizon of the world to rise with deathless splendor over the Realm of the Limitless. In His Most Holy Book He calleth the firm and steadfast of His friends: 'Be not dismayed, O peoples of the world, when the day-star of My beauty is set, and the heaven of My tabernacle is concealed from your eyes. Arise to further My Cause, and to exalt My Word amongst men.[14]

RESULT

The message had a remarkable result, as Shogi Effendi was later to describe: "The cloud of despondency that had momentarily settled on the disconsolate lovers of the Cause of Bahá'u'lláh was lifted. The continuity of that unerring guidance vouchsafed to it since its birth was assured." Shogi Effendi also explained the new power that had been unleashed:

> [T]he dissolution of the tabernacle wherein the soul of the Manifestation of God had chosen temporarily to abide signalized its release from the restrictions which an earthly life had, of necessity, imposed upon it. Its influence no longer circumscribed by any physical limitations, its radiance no longer beclouded by its human temple, that soul could henceforth energize the whole world to a degree unapproached at any stage in the course of its existence on this planet.[15]

It was clear where pilgrims could best access that radiance, that energy. 'Abdu'l-Bahá Himself had proclaimed that holy places are undoubtedly centers of the outpouring of divine grace.[16] The Guardian was to point out that the spirits of all the Prophets of God, including that of the Báb, revolve around the Shrine of Bahá'u'lláh.[17] And in the Kitáb-i-Aqdas, Bahá'u'lláh declared that His shrine would be "the Point of Adoration for the denizens of the Cities of Eternity."[18]

Soon 'Abdu'l-Bahá, the new Head of the Faith, the Founder of the Shrine of Bahá'u'lláh, would take on the task of establishing lovely gardens around the shrine, honoring the one to be known forever as "the Blessed Beauty."

Notes

Prologue

1. https://www.bahaullah.org/. See also Moojan Momen, *Bahá'u'lláh: A Short Biography.*

2. Bahá'í International Community, *Bahá'u'lláh.* New York, 1991. The Universal House of Justice, ordained by Bahá'u'lláh and inaugurated in 1963, is the Head of the Bahá'í Faith, with its seat in Haifa, Israel.

3. An expanded explanation suggested by the author is: The Bahá'í Faith has the oneness of humanity as its pivotal teaching, and a united world society based on justice and love as its aim. Viewing the founders of the major world religions as the key figures in the ongoing development of religion demonstrates an evolutionary view of what is in essence one religion, with eternal principles underpinning it. The abolition of clergy and the use of a special kind of consensus decision-making process means there is no place for individuals having special authority. Authority rests in elected councils.

4. Bahá'u'lláh, quoted in, Shoghi Effendi, *The World Order of Bahá'u'lláh,* p. 113.

5. Ibid., pp. 113–14. The "Ancient of Days" refers to God, and the "Gems of Holiness" refer to the Prophets of God.

6. Bahá'í International Community, *Bahá'u'lláh,* p. 20.

7. Bahá'u'lláh, quoted in ibid., p. 21; *Gleanings from the Writings of Bahá'u'lláh,* no. 22.2–24.

8. Marzieh Gail, *Dawn over Mount Hira*, p. 178.

9. Shoghi Effendi was the head of the Bahá'í Faith from 1921 until 1957, and was known as the Guardian. He was the great-grandson of Bahá'u'lláh, and the grandson of 'Abdu'l-Bahá (https://www.bahai.org/abdul-baha/). He and 'Abdu'l-Bahá were the only two individuals authorized to interpret the sacred scripture bequeathed to humanity by Bahá'u'lláh (1817–92), the Prophet-Founder of the Bahá'í Faith. https://www.bahai.org/shoghi-effendi/.

10. Shoghi Effendi, *The World Order of Bahá'u'lláh*, p. 97; He notes on page 100 that it is the first obligation of Bahá'ís "to strive to obtain a more adequate understanding of the significance of Bahá'u'lláh's stupendous Revelation."

11. Shoghi Effendi, *God Passes By*, Foreword, p. xiv.

12. The Faith is emerging from obscurity but has yet to be a major player in global discourse. Even now, 130 years on since His ascension, the world struggles to catch up with Bahá'u'lláh's assertion of the vital necessity for a global society to prevent or at least assuage multiple potential threats to the peoples of the earth and to assure progress. Consensus decision-making to find answers to problems and implement them, still comes second to debate with all its flaws. The equal rights of every individual—regardless of race, religion, or gender—are still to be universally recognized.

13. 'Abdu'l-Bahá, *Some Answered Questions,* no. 9.15.

Chapter 1: Attaining the Sacred Threshold

1. Ugo Giachery, *Shoghi Effendi,* p. 122.

2. Edward Granville Browne recorded Bahá'u'lláh saying this to him. See chapter 11.

3. https://Pilgrimage.bwc.org. See also the video on that website.

4. Acre is the English name; Akko is the name used in the Holy Land today.

Chapter 2: Scripture of Supreme Importance to the Shrine

1. Shoghi Effendi writes in *God Passes By,* p. 213, that it was revealed after Bahá'u'lláh had been transferred "to the house of 'Údí

Khammár (circa 1873). . . ." The Universal House of Justice, in its introduction to the English translation, writes that "Bahá'u'lláh revealed the Kitáb-i-Aqdas around 1873." Momen, in *Bahá'u'lláh: A Short Biography*, writes that early in 1873, Bahá'u'lláh completed His most important book the Kitáb-i-Aqdas. Dr. David Ruhe says in *Door of Hope*, p. 42: "The Prophet's last months of 1872 and into 1873 were overwhelmingly significant, for it was then the 'brightest emanation of the Mind of Bahá'u'lláh, the Mother Book of His Dispensation,' The Kitáb-i-Aqdas, was elaborated."

2. Hand of the Cause Abu'l-Qásim Faizi wrote: "There are historical events mentioned in this Book, which when put together and coordinated, indicate that it had not been written in one session. The revelation continued at intervals between 1871 and 1873 when it was completed and concluded." https://bahai-library.com/faizi_kitab_aqdas_commentary. Professor John Walbridge wrote that there is some evidence that at least part of the book may have been written even earlier than 1873. See https://bahai-library.com/walbridge_encyclopedia_kitab_aqdas.

3. Adib Taherzadeh, *The Revelation of Bahá'u'lláh*, vol. 3, p. 393: "There is no doubt that when the station of Bahá'u'lláh is universally recognized, posterity will look at the story of His life with awe and wonder. People in the future will be amazed at the blindness of man in His days, and astonished at the treatment that was meted out to Him. When the glory of His station is unveiled to the eyes of humanity, it will be hard to imagine that the Lord of Hosts was made to live in the most desolate of the cities, the Heavenly Father held as a captive by a perverse generation and the King of Kings confined in a small room unfit to be a dwelling. And yet in that small room devoid of all the luxuries of life and not even properly furnished, *The Kitáb-i-Aqdas* described by Him as His 'weightiest testimony unto all people' was revealed. It is a staggering thought that in such a room, in an obscure corner of a prison city, unknown to the world, such a mighty instrument as *The Kitáb-i-Aqdas*, the great Charter for future world civilization, should have been born."

4. Once named after 'Abbúd and then as Genoa Square.

5. There were also about 750 Greek Catholics, 165 Latins, and 80 Maronite Christians. I am grateful to Dr. Boris Handal for this information, which was sourced from G. Schumacher.

6. In *Some Answered Questions,* no. 9.21, 'Abdu'l-Bahá says: "Bahá'u'lláh never studied Arabic, had a teacher or tutor, or entered a school. Nevertheless His eloquence and fluency in spoken Arabic, as well as in His Arabic Tablets, would astonish the most articulate and accomplished among the Arab men of letters, and all acknowledged that in this His attainments were without peer or equal." Hand of the Cause George Townshend refers to it in an article as "a great poem" (*The Bahá'í World, 1950–54,* p. 865). He also writes in that same article: "The Fire Tablet adds all the poignancy and impassioned power of divine poetry to the story of the boundless suffering He (Bahá'u'lláh) and His beloved followers had to endure (p. 867). Adib Taherzadeh writes that it is in "Arabic rhyming verse" (*The Revelation of Bahá'u'lláh,* vol. 3. p. 226).

7. See *Bahá'í Prayers,* pp. 312–18.

8. The Divine Lote-Tree refers to the Manifestation of God. See "Sadratu'l-Muntahá" in Wendi Momen, *A Bahá'í Dictionary,* p. 200, and Macias, https://bahai-library.com/macias_verse_light; Baharieh Rouhani Ma'ani, *Leaves of the Twin Divine Trees,* pp. xviii–xx.

9. Historian Adib Taherzadeh writes in *The Revelation of Bahá'u'lláh,* vol. 3, pp. 233–34: "Man's ignorance, his cruelty, his ungodliness, his selfishness, his insincerity and all his sins and shortcomings act as tools of torture inflicting painful wounds upon the soul of the Manifestation of God Who has no alternative but to bear them in silence with resignation and submissiveness. . . . He has the sin-covering eye to such an extent that some may think that He does not know."

10. Bahá'u'lláh, in *Bahá'í Prayers,* p. 318.

11. Shoghi Effendi, *God Passes By,* p. 213.

12. The Universal House of Justice has noted: "The Arabic of The Kitáb-i-Aqdas is marked by intense concentration and terseness

of expression." The Universal House of Justice, in The Kitáb-i-Aqdas, "Introduction," p. 10.

13. Ibid., p. 9.

14. Ibid., p. 1. See also "The Kitáb-i-Aqdas: its place in Bahá'í literature," *The Bahá'í World, 1992–1993*. pp. 105–17.

15. "After the revelation came 'Questions and Answers,' a compilation made by Zaynu'l-Muqarrabín, the most eminent of the transcribers of Bahá'u'lláh's Writings. Consisting of answers revealed by Bahá'u'lláh to questions put to Him by various believers, it constitutes an invaluable appendix to the Kitáb-i-Aqdas. In 1978 the most noteworthy of the other Tablets of this nature were published in English as a compilation entitled *Tablets of Bahá'u'lláh Revealed After The Kitáb-i-Aqdas*." The Universal House of Justice, in The Kitáb-i-Aqdas, "Introduction," p. 9.

Chapter 3: Guidelines for the Shrine

1. Bahá'u'lláh, The Kitáb-i-Aqdas, ¶174; See also Note 184, p. 246.

2. Ibid., ¶121.

3. Was the absence of the name of the Master a way of protecting Him from becoming the target of enemies, of the jealousies of His half-siblings? We have no guidance on that, but there may be a precedent. 'Abdu'l-Bahá wrote in his book, *A Traveller's Narrative* that Mírzá Yaḥyá's appointment as leader of the Bábís was a stratagem that Bahá'u'lláh, His brother Mírzá Músá, and Mullá 'Abdu'l-Karím-i-Qazvíní, one of the Báb's secretaries, came up with, with the Báb's approval, to divert attention onto a little-known figurehead and away from Bahá'u'lláh.

4. Shoghi Effendi, *God Passes By*, p. 214.

5. Bahá'u'lláh, The Kitáb-i-Aqdas, ¶137.

6. Shoghi Effendi, quoted in the Universal House of Justice, *Synopsis and Codification of the Kitáb-i-Aqdas*, p. 145.

7. Bahá'u'lláh, The Kitáb-i-Aqdas, ¶6.

8. "Indeed, the laws of God are like unto the ocean and the children of men as fish, did they but know it. However, in observing

them one must exercise tact and wisdom. . . . Since most people are feeble and far-removed from the purpose of God, therefore one must observe tact and prudence under all conditions, so that nothing might happen that could cause disturbance and dissension or raise clamor among the heedless." Bahá'u'lláh, quoted by the Universal House of Justice in its introduction to the English translation of the Kitáb-i-Aqdas, p. 6.

9. Bahá'u'lláh, The Kitáb-i-Aqdas, Notes, no. 7, p. 168: "The concept of Qiblih has existed in previous religions. Jerusalem in the past had been fixed for this purpose. Muḥammad changed the Qiblih to Mecca . . ."

10. The Kitáb-i-Aqdas, Notes, no. 8.

11. For more, see Michael V. Day, *Journey to a Mountain*, pp. 150–56, 230–31.

12. 'Abdu'l-Bahá, quoted in the Universal House of Justice, *Synopsis and Codification of the Kitáb-i-Aqdas,* p. 61.

13. Bahá'u'lláh, The Kitáb-i-Aqdas, ¶32.

14. Bahá'u'lláh, The Kitáb-i-Aqdas, "Questions and Answers," no. 25.

15. Ibid., no. 29.

16. Ibid., p. 191.

17. Shoghi Effendi, *God Passes By*, p. 177; H. M. Balyuzi, *King of Glory*, p. 245; Glenn Cameron and Wendi Momen, *A Basic Bahá'í Chronology*, pp. 76–77.

18. Shoghi Effendi, *God Passes By*, p. 177.

19. Glenn Cameron and Wendi Momen, *A Basic Bahá'í Chronology*, p. 79.

20. Shoghi Effendi, *God Passes By*, p. 177.

21. The author is grateful to John Walbridge for the summary in *Sacred Acts, Sacred Space, Sacred Time*, pp. 113–14.

22. *Muhazirat,* vol. 3, pp. 152–54.

23. Ibid. The father of Shakykh Damarchí was wealthy. He deprived him from among all his brothers of inheritance, but his brothers one by one died. Thus Shakykh Damarchí became the only

recipient of the wealth of his father. This dedicated believer spent everything in the path of the Faith.

24. The house was destroyed in 2013. https://news.bahai.org/story/961/.

25. The author is grateful to John Walbridge for the summary in *Sacred Acts, Sacred Space, Sacred Time*, pp. 113–14.

26. For the complete prayer, see Bahá'u'lláh, *Gleanings from the Writings of Bahá'u'lláh*, no. 57.

27. Shoghi Effendi, *God Passes By*, p. 177. That appointment had been foreshadowed in Adrianople a few years earlier in the Súriy-i-Ghuṣn (Surih of the Branch), bestowed in the Kitáb-i-Aqdas, and confirmed after Bahá'u'lláh's ascension in the Book of His covenant (Kitáb-i-'Ahd).

28. In response to an inquiry as to the date that the Master declared the shrine as a place of pilgrimage and any Tablet to that effect, the Universal House of Justice sent the following memorandum from the Research Department to the author on 21 September 2021: "After the Ascension of Bahá'u'lláh, 'Abdu'l-Bahá designated the Shrine of Bahá'u'lláh as a place of pilgrimage. This is described in an undated Tablet of 'Abdu'l-Bahá addressed to Ethel Rosenberg. Referring to this Tablet of 'Abdu'l-Bahá, note 54 of The Kitáb-i-Aqdas: The Most Holy Book states that "the 'Most Holy Shrine, the Blessed House in Baghdád and the venerated House of the Báb in Shíráz' are 'consecrated to pilgrimage,' and that it is 'obligatory' to visit these places 'if one can afford it and is able to do so, and if no obstacle stands in one's way.'" The authorized translation of a passage from this Tablet of 'Abdu'l-Bahá . . . is published in *A Synopsis and Codification of the Kitáb-i-Aqdas: The Most Holy Book of Bahá'u'lláh* (Haifa: Bahá'í World Centre, 1973), p. 61.

It reads: "You have asked about visiting holy places and the observance of marked reverence toward these resplendent spots. Holy places are undoubtedly centres of the outpouring of Divine grace, because on entering the illumined sites associated with martyrs and holy souls, and by observing reverence, both physical and spiritual, one's heart is moved with great tenderness. But there is no obligation for everyone to visit such places, other than the three, namely: the Most Holy Shrine, the Blessed House in Baghdád and the venerated House of the Báb in Shíráz. To visit these is obligatory if one can afford it and is able to do so, and if no obstacle stands in one's way. Details are given in the Tablets. These three Holy Places are consecrated to pilgrimage. But as to the other resting places of martyrs and holy souls, it is pleasing and acceptable in the sight of God if a person desires to draw nigh unto Him by visiting them; this, however, is not a binding obligation."

29. Bahá'u'lláh, The Kitáb-i-Aqdas, Notes, p. 191. It may strike people today as interesting that Bahá'í pilgrimage does not solely focus on the holy places that are graves but also includes places—and nearby locations—where the Manifestations declared Their Missions.

30. Ibid., p. 192.

31. The Kitáb-i-Aqdas, Notes, no. 8, p. 169.

32. Bahá'u'lláh, The Kitáb-i-Aqdas, ¶38.

33. Ibid., ¶39.

Chapter 4: Two Special Weeks

1. Shoghi Effendi, *God Passes By,* p. 221. The Guardian gives the date as "nineteen years [prior to the ascension of Bahá'u'lláh] on the anniversary of the birth of His Forerunner." Stephen Lambden writes: "In various sources this Tablet is said to date from nineteen years prior to the ascension of Bahá'u'lláh . . . and to the (eve of) the anniversary of the birthday of the Báb in the year 1290 A.H. or March 1st, 1873 CE." https://bahai-library.com/bahaullah_lawh_ruya_lambden.

2. 'Abdu'l-Bahá, *Selections from the Writings of 'Abdu'l-Bahá,* no. 5.2.

3. A commentator has written his opinion that the "Maid" primarily symbolizes the Reality of the Báb: https://bahai-library.com/bahaullah_lawh_ruya_lambden.

4. Shoghi Effendi, *God Passes By,* p. 221.

5. Also known as Khánum Buzurg.

6. For an account of the sisters of Bahá'u'lláh, see Adib Taherzadeh, *The Revelation of Bahá'u'lláh*, vol. 1, pp. 49–51. Other details from *Iqlim-e-Noor* by Malak Khusravi, referred to by Fuad Izadinia in email to the author on 28 July 2021.

7. H. M. Balyuzi, *King of Glory*, pp. 343–44.

8. Munírih Khánum, *Episodes in the Life of Munírih Khánum*, translated by Ahmad Sohrab. https://bahai-library.com/khanum_episodes_life#a22.

9. Ibid. https://bahai-library.com/khanum_episodes_life#a37.

10. Lady Blomfield, *The Chosen Highway*, pp. 87–88.

11. From the memoirs of Munírih Khánum as quoted in, Lady Blomfield, *The Chosen Highway*, p. 88.

12. David S. Ruhe, *Door of Hope*, p. 47.

13. Ibid.

14. Munírih Khánum, *Episodes in the Life of Munírih Khánum*, translated by Ahmad Sohrab. https://bahai-library.com/khanum_episodes_life#a22.

15. Ásíyih Khánum (?–1886) had the same name as the daughter of the Pharaoh who left the royal palace and followed Moses. Bahá'u'lláh's first wife was known for her "rare physical beauty and wonderful spiritual qualities." Baharieh Rouhani Ma'ani, *Leaves of the Twin Divine Trees*, p. 86.

16. Shoghi Effendi, *God Passes By*, p. 347. The Guardian said the Greatest Holy Leaf, Bahíyyih Khánum, was "comparable in rank to those immortal heroines such as Sarah, Ásíyih, the Virgin Mary, Fáṭimih and Ṭáhirih."

17. Baharieh Rouhani Ma'ani, *Leaves of the Twin Divine Trees*, pp. 112, 153.

18. Munírih Khánum, *Memoirs and Letters*, translated by Sammireh Anwar Smith, https://bahai-library.com/munirih_khanum_memoirs_letters.

19. Lady Blomfield, *The Chosen Highway*, p. 88.

20. Two times for the ceremony are cited. The Bride in her memoirs says three hours after sunset. https://bahai-library.com/munirih_khanum_memoirs_letters; also see https://bahai-library.

com/khanum_episodes_life#a37. Historian Hasan Balyuzi also says three hours after sunset in *King of Glory*, p. 348. These weigh against a time given in a description of the wedding by Bahíyyih Khánum as quoted by Myron H. Phelps: "the ceremony was performed by the Blessed Perfection about two pm." Myron H. Phelps, *The Master in 'Akká*, p. 118.

21. Munírih Khánum, *Episodes in the Life of Munírih Khánum,* translated by Ahmad Sohrab. https://bahai-library.com/khanum_episodes_life#a37.

22. A description of 'Abdu'l-Bahá had appeared in a letter by one Thomas Chaplin M.D. to *The Times* of London two years earlier, saying he was "apparently about 30 years of age, and has a fine intellectual countenance, with black hair and beard, and that sallow melancholic look."

23. Lady Blomfield, *The Chosen Highway*, p. 89.

24. Munírih had briefly stayed in that room after she first arrived in 'Akká. Lady Blomfield, *The Chosen Highway*, p. 87.

25. David Ruhe says the couple moved into the room where the Kitáb-i-Aqdas was revealed, and that Navváb moved into a room next to Bahá'u'lláh's. David S. Ruhe, *Door of Hope*, p. 47. Munírih Khánum says she moved into a specially provided room in the House of 'Abbúd. Lady Blomfield, *The Chosen Highway*, p. 87.

26. Lady Blomfield, *The Chosen Highway*, p. 89.

27. During his thirty-six-year ministry (1921–57), Shoghi Effendi expanded the gardens to the extent that as they continue to evolve they could be regarded as a modern-day version of the paradise garden of Cyrus the Great near Shíráz, the Biblical Garden of Eden, and the Jannah of Islam on earth, complete with its mansion. His devotion led to a precious legacy, the continuation of which would be the responsibility of the Universal House of Justice.

Chapter 5: The World of the Soul

1. His confinement in such limited quarters began in late August 1868 and ended in about June 1877. See Glenn Cameron and Wendi Momen, *A Basic Bahá'í Chronology*, pp. 85, 107.

2. Shoghi Effendi, *God Passes By*, p. 193.

3. David S. Ruhe, *Door of Hope*, pp. 47, 72.

4. This Bahá'í was a renowned illuminator of books. See Adib Taherzadeh, *The Revelation of Bahá'u'lláh*, vol. 3. p. 403.

5. Adib Taherzadeh, *The Revelation of Bahá'u'lláh*, vol. 3. p. 404. That author writes: "Bahá'u'lláh states in this Tablet [Ma'idiy-i-Asamani, vol. 1 pp. 59–60] that even those who visit the land in which the throne of the Manifestation of God is established will be bountifully blessed in the world to come, how much more will be the reward of those who actually have attained His presence."

6. Mírzá Ḥaydar-'Alí, *Bahjatu'ṣ-Ṣudúr*, p. 249, as quoted in Adib Taherzadeh, *The Revelation of Bahá'u'lláh*, vol. 3, p. 402.

7. Among them were two survivors of the struggle of Ṭabarsí, the father of Badí', Ḥájí 'Abdu'l-Majíd-i-Níshápúrí, and the devout Mullá Ṣádiq-i-Khurásání. Another survivor of Ṭabarsí, Ḥájí Náṣir (a future martyr) was also a pilgrim to His Lord around that time, together with Shaykh Káẓim-i-Samandar, later designated an Apostle of Bahá'u'lláh. See https://bahai-library.com/rafati_mulla_sadiq_khurasani; H. M. Balyuzi, *Eminent Bahá'ís in the Time of Bahá'u'lláh*, chapter 1 and pp. 201, 205.

8. The Master and Munírih Khánum were to live in that house until 1896—four years after the ascension of Bahá'u'lláh—when they moved to the House of 'Abdu'lláh Páshá. Nine children were born to them there, only four girls surviving to adulthood, one being the mother of Shoghi Effendi. The house became one of the first ports of call for pilgrims, mainly coming from Persia. There the Master would show them the room that Bahá'u'lláh had inhabited, a place kept as it was when He lived there. 'Abdu'l-Bahá would also ensure the comfort of the pilgrims, prepare them for meeting Bahá'u'lláh, even often escorting them into His presence, whether at the Mansion of Mazra'ih or at Bahjí. Bahá'u'lláh would often return to that house where He enjoyed spending time with His grandchildren, treating them—like doting grandparents everywhere—with loving latitude as opposed to the stricter regimes of their parents.

9. Adib Taherzadeh, *The Revelation of Bahá'u'lláh*, vol. 3, p. 400.

10. Shoghi Effendi, *God Passes By*, p. 192. For details, see David S. Ruhe, *Door of Hope*, chapter 21, pp. 122–25.

11. David S. Ruhe, *Door of Hope*, p. 71.

12. Bahá'u'lláh addressed this Tablet to Nabíl-i-Akbar (1829–92), not to be confused with Nabíl-i-A'ẓam, the author of *The Dawn-Breakers*. 'Abdu'l-Bahá was to name this eminent scholar and teacher a Hand of the Cause, and Shoghi Effendi titled him a Disciple of Bahá'u'lláh. Author Marzieh Gail has translated with her trademark consummate skill the sparkling tribute to him by the Master. It appears as the very first biography in *Memorials of the Faithful* by 'Abdu'l-Bahá and includes this about Nabil: "He was a universal man, in himself alone a convincing proof."

13. Adib Taherzadeh, *The Revelation of Bahá'u'lláh*, vol. 1, pp. 40–41. It also includes this: "Thou knowest full well that We perused not the books which men possess and We acquired not the learning current amongst them, and yet whenever We desire to quote the sayings of the learned and of the wise, presently there will appear before the face of thy Lord in the form of a tablet all that which hath appeared in the world and is revealed in the Holy Books and Scriptures. Thus do We set down in writing that which the eye perceiveth. Verily His knowledge encompasseth the earth and the heavens." Bahá'u'lláh, *Tablets of Bahá'u'lláh*, pp. 148–49.

14. Shoghi Effendi, *God Passes By*, p. 216, quoted in, David S. Ruhe, *Door of Hope*, p. 47. The Guardian does not specifically refer to where or when those provisions were revealed, saying only this happened as His mission drew to a close.

15. Shoghi Effendi, *God Passes By*, p. 193; David S. Ruhe, *Door of Hope*, pp. 93–101.The stream had previously been called Belus.

16. Moojan Momen, *Bahá'u'lláh: A Short Biography*, p. 120.

17. David S. Ruhe, *Door of Hope*, p. 45.

18. Nouri Bey, Hakki Bey, and Mahmoud Effendi. *Star of the West*, vol. 8, no. 13, p. 175.

19. Ibid., p. 175; David S. Ruhe, *Door of Hope*, pp. 120, 227.

20. David S. Ruhe, *Door of Hope*, pp. 49–50.

21. For a short but fascinating account of the life of 'Abdu'lláh Pá<u>sh</u>á, see David S. Ruhe, *Door of Hope*, pp. 206–7.

22. Fuad Izadinia, "The Mansion of Mazra'ih." Unpublished manuscript sent to the author on 4 August 2021. The author, Fuad Izadinia, served as custodian of the mansion with his wife, Manijeh <u>Kh</u>ánum. He wrote that in late 2005 officers of the Israeli Department of Agriculture measured the diameter of two giant cypress trees located to the south of the building. They estimated that their age could be more than 300 years, thus helping an estimate of the age of the building for which they were an entry point. Officials from the Department of Antiquities said that carvings on the wall surrounding the courtyard indicated that it was the original wall, built in the early 1700s.

23. Fuad Izadinia, "The Mansion of Mazra'ih," p. 2.

24. Ibid.

25. J. E. Esslemont, *Bahá'u'lláh and the New Era*, pp. 34–35. Dr. Esslemont writes that Shoghi Effendi translated the words of 'Abdu'l-Bahá, and that the text refers to "about five pounds per annum."

26. *Star of the West*, vol. 8, no. 13, p. 175.

27. Ibid.

28. <u>Sh</u>ay<u>kh</u> 'Alíy-i-Mírí.

29. J. E. Esslemont, *Bahá'u'lláh and the New Era*, pp. 34–36, citing Shoghi Effendi's translation of the words of 'Abdu'l-Bahá.

30. It was unlikely to have come from Beirut, which was about 290 kms to the north, but it is a possibility.

31. *Star of the West*, vol. 8, no. 13, p. 175. The words of 'Abdu'l-Bahá may not be exact, but it is likely that His meaning is well conveyed. Recorded by Ahmad Sohrab, a secretary of the Master. He later strayed from fidelity to the Covenant.

32. https://news.bahai.org/story/1547/.

33. It was restored in 2021. https://news.bahai.org/story/1547/. One of Bahá'u'lláh's services to the people of 'Akká during His years there had been to successfully recommend the repair of an aqueduct so that fresh, clean water was readily available.

34. Shoghi Effendi, *God Passes By*, pp. 200, 219.

35. In 1931, Lilian McNeill, a Bahá'í and a friend of Queen Marie of Rumania, leased the house with her husband, a retired British Brigadier-General. See David S. Ruhe, *Door of Hope*, pp. 87–89. In this author's experience, pilgrims to this day often remark upon the pervasive feeling of joy in the Mansion of Mazra'ih.

36. The restoration completed in 2021 uncovered those paintings. https://www.abdul-baha.bahai.org.au/.

37. Baharieh Rouhani Ma'ani, *Leaves of the Twin Divine Trees*, p. 235. Her eldest, Muḥammad-'Alí, born in 1854, was twenty-three, so probably lived elsewhere.

38. Ibid., p. 253.

39. David S. Ruhe, *Door of Hope*, p. 85.

40. Adib Taherzadeh, *The Revelation of Bahá'u'lláh*, vol. 4, pp. 7–8.

41. Áqá Mírzá Maḥmúd of Ká<u>sh</u>án and Áqá Riḍáy-i-Qannád of <u>Sh</u>íráz.

42. Unpublished memoirs of Ḥájí Muḥammad Ṭáhir-i-Málmírí.

43. The Báb, *Selections from the Writings of the Báb*, no. 3.1.2.

44. Ḥájí Mullá Mihdíy-i-'Aṭrí, also known as Ḥájí Mullá Mihdíy-i-Yazdí (c. 1830–c. 1878/79). His third son was the martyr and Hand of the Cause, Mírzá 'Alí-Muḥammad-i-Varqá (1856–96). 'Aṭrí was grandfather of Hand of the Cause Valíyu'lláh (1884–1955), and great grandfather of Dr. 'Alí-Muḥammad Varqá (1912–2007).

45. Varqá was about twenty-three years old at this time. Both brothers stayed in the Holy Land for several months, grieving the loss of their father under the loving care of Bahá'u'lláh, Who was at that time residing between Mazra'ih and 'Akká.

46. 'Abdu'l-Bahá, *Memorials of the Faithful*, p. 86. According to Adib Taherzadeh, 'Aṭrí died sometime between 15 and 26 April 1878.

47. Unpublished memoirs of Ḥájí Muḥammad Ṭáhir-i-Málmírí, as quoted in, Adib Taherzadeh, *The Revelation of Bahá'u'lláh*, vol. 4, pp. 50–51.

48. Ḥájí Mírzá Ḥaydar-'Alí, *Stories from the Delight of Hearts*, p. 71.

Chapter 6: The Lofty Mansion

1. It was common for the owners of such mansions to throw lavish parties indicative of opulent lifestyles.

2. H. M. Balyuzi, *'Abdu'l-Bahá*, p. 42.

3. Ibid., *Bahá'u'lláh: King of Glory*, p. 362.

4. Ibid., p. 362.

5. See nineteenth century map on p. 61.

6. The Jamál brothers were antagonistic to the Bahá'ís, as were the later owners of the southern mansion, the Baydun family. See H. M. Balyuzi, *Bahá'u'lláh: King of Glory*, p. 162. See also David S. Ruhe, *Door of Hope*, pp. 102–3.

7. According to Mírzá Áqá Ján. David S. Ruhe, *Door of Hope*, p. 204.

8. For more information, see Boris Handal, *Mirza Mihdi, The Purest Branch*, chapters 9–10.

9. Ugo Giachery, *Shoghi Effendi*, p. 138.

10. David S. Ruhe, *Door of Hope*, p. 205.

11. Ibid., p. 227.

12. Ibid., 204.

13. Ibid., p. 227.

14. On p. 155 in his book *Thief in the Night*, Hand of the Cause William Sears identified the plague as cholera. Although there were recurrent cholera plagues, mentions by such authors as Dr. David Ruhe, and Dr. Wendi Momen indicate that this time it was bubonic plague. I am grateful to the author Dr. Boris Handal for pointing me to the reference by Mr. Sears.

15. https://en.wikipedia.org/wiki/Bubonic_plague.

16. https://www.sciencedirect.com/science/article/pii S1198743X14608582.

17. The author is grateful to the Universal House of Justice for permission to view the grave, and to a dear Bahá'í for his translation of the inscription.

18. Andravis Khammár married his cousin, the daughter of his uncle Ilyás Khammár and the daughter of 'Abbúd. Both families were wealthy at the time and supported the restorations in the

church of St. George in 'Akká. The square at the back of the House of 'Abbúd was named 'Abbúd Square, though now is it called Genoa Square. David S. Ruhe, *Door Hope,* p. 229.

19. *Star of the West,* vol 8, Issue 13. "Then there was another palace belonging to Abboud and his family. This was the palace of Bahjee. Abboud and his children were sick and went into town. I wanted to rent this palace from him; he wished to present it to me and insisted upon it. Finally I rented it from him at £150 a year, and Baha'o'llah and the members of the holy family moved into it. From that time on he lived in Bahajee and Acca, alternately, till the day of his departure dawned upon us and threw us into the depths of despair and sorrow. ('Abdu'l-Bahá, Diary of Mirza Sohrab, March 23, 1914.)

20. Ugo Giachery, *Shoghi Effendi,* p. 139; David S. Ruhe, *Door of Hope,* p. 205.

21. Shoghi Effendi, *God Passes By,* p, 193; Adib Taherzadeh, *The Revelation of Bahá'u'lláh,* vol. 4, p. 104. On p. 450 the author cites *Athar-i-Qalam-i-A'la,* vol. 5, pp. 456–57.

22. Shoghi Effendi, *God Passes By,* p. 193.

23. Sulṭán 'Abdu'l-'Azíz (1830–76).

24. Adib Taherzadeh, *The Revelation of Bahá'u'lláh,* vol. 4, p. 104.

25. Ibid., p. 106.

26. In Bahá'u'lláh's time, Bahá'í traveling teachers had visited India, Burma (now Myanmar), and the islands of the Dutch East Indies (modern-day Indonesia). There were also Bahá'ís in China. Cambridge academic Edward Granville Browne was that visitor.

27. For an obituary, see *The Bahá'í World,* vol. XII, pp. 692–94.

28. H. M. Balyuzi, *'Abdu'l-Bahá,* p. 43.

29. She was born in 1874. https://bahaipedia.org/. Before her was a boy, Mírzá Mihdí, but he died, aged about three, presumably in 1876.

This list of the children of the Master and Munírih Khánum was compiled by the author after viewing various sources. There are some dates missing, and there may be the need for some adjustment if new information comes to hand.

1. Mírzá Mihdí (1873–76 approximately)
2. Ḍíyá'íyyih (1874–1951)
3. Ṭúbá Khánum (1880–1959)
4. Rúḥá Khánum (non-identical twin of Tuba, 1880–1950 approximately)
5. Ḥusayn (1884–88 approximately)
6. Fu'ádíyyih (born after 1888, died in infancy)
7. Rúḥangíz (died in infancy in 1893)
8. Munavvar (date of birth uncertain, died 1971). See: https://bahaipedia.org.
9. Another daughter.

30. Moojan Momen, *Bahá'u'lláh: A Short Biography,* p. 144.

31. Ḥaydar-'Alí, *Stories from the Delight of Hearts,* pp. 106–7. This may refer to those, such as Muḥammad-'Alí—a half-brother of the Master, and the son of Bahá'u'lláh and His second wife, Fáṭimih Khánum (Mahd-i-'Ulyá)—who was to dispute the appointment by Bahá'u'lláh in His Will and Testament of 'Abdu'l-Bahá as His successor as Head of the Faith. See chapter 20 for an example of that behavior.

32. See tributes to her from Bahá'u'lláh and 'Abdu'l-Bahá in Shoghi Effendi, *This Decisive Hour,* pp. 47–49.

33. The Universal House of Justice, *Messages: 1963 to 1986,* p. 732. "Bahá'u'lláh named her His 'perpetual consort in all the worlds of God.'"

34. Adib Taherzadeh, *The Revelation of Bahá'u'lláh,* vol. 4, p. 113.

35. Bahá'í International Community, *Bahá'í Holy Places in Haifa and the Western Galilee,* p. 27.

36. Ugo Giachery, *Shoghi Effendi,* p. 140.

37. See Diala Khasawneh, *Memoirs Engraved in Stone: Palestinian Urban Mansions.*

38. This description is adapted by the superb writer, Dr. Ugo Giachery in *Shoghi Effendi,* p. 144.

39. Eventually, that grove and the spacious land encircling the mansion were to come into the hands of the Bahá'ís of the world.

40. H. M. Balyuzi, *'Abdul-Bahá,* p. 42; Ugo Giachery, *Shoghi Effendi,* p. 124. Some have said that the building of the great Aswan dam in Egypt in the 1960s has led to higher humidity in Israel. See: https://www.israelweather.co.il/english/page3.

Chapter 7: Lively Scenes

1. See an interesting account by Mírzá Aḥmad Yazdí in, Moojan Momen, *Bahá'u'lláh: A Short Biography,* p. 142.

2. See Baharieh Rouhani Ma'ani, *Leaves of the Twin Divine Trees;* Lady Blomfield, *The Chosen Highway;* 'Abdu'l-Bahá, *Memorials of the Faithful;* Moojan Momen, *The Bábí and Bahá'í Religions.*

3. Here is an incomplete list of those who stayed at the mansion for longer than a few weeks. There are at least fifteen other Bahá'ís named in *Memorials of the Faithful,* by 'Abdu'l-Bahá, who may have stayed in the compound. I am grateful to the author Baharieh Rouhani Ma'ani and my colleague Fuad Izadinia for assisting with this list, but any errors or omissions are this author's. The calculation is also based on a range of factors (housing availability, and the number of relatives):

1. Bahá'u'lláh.
2. Mahd-i-'Ulya (Fáṭimih Khánum), the second wife of Bahá'u'lláh.
3. Gawhar Khánum, the third wife of Bahá'u'lláh.
4. Mírzá Muḥammad-'Alí. The Greater Branch [Ghusn-i-Akbar], son of Bahá'u'lláh and Mahd-i-'Ulya.
5. Laqá'iyyih Khánum, wife of Mírzá Muḥammad-'Alí, and daughter of Áqáy-i-Kalím.
6. Three sons of Mírzá Muḥammad-'Alí and Laqá'iyyih Khánum, including Mírzá Shu'á'u'lláh and one daughter Ṣamadíyyih.

7. Mírzá Badíʻuʼlláh, son of Baháʼuʼlláh and Mahd-i-Ulya.
8. Mírzá Ḍíyáʼuʼlláh and his wife Soraya (<u>Th</u>urayyá).
9. Samadiyyih <u>Kh</u>ánum, daughter of Baháʼuʼlláh and Mahd-i-ʻUlya.
10. Mírzá Majdiʼd-Dín, husband of Samadiyyih, and son of Áqáy-i-Kalím (Mírzá Músá).
11. Furú<u>gh</u>íyyih <u>Kh</u>ánum, daughter of Baháʼuʼlláh and Gawhar <u>Kh</u>ánum.
12. Siyyid ʻAlí Afnán, husband of Furú<u>gh</u>íyyih <u>Kh</u>ánum.
13. Ḥájí Mírzá Siyyid Hasan-i-Afnán-i-Kabír, the Great Afnán, brother of the wife of the Báb, <u>Kh</u>adíjih-Bagum, father of Siyyid ʻAlí Afnán, and father-in-law of Furú<u>gh</u>íyyih <u>Kh</u>ánum.
14. Nabíl-i-Aʻẓam (Nabíl-i-Zarandí), poet and author of *The Dawn-Breakers* (also had a room in ʻAkká).
15. ʻAndalíb (Áqá Mírzá A<u>sh</u>raf-ʻAlí Láhíján), poet. (Likely to have stayed in ʻAkká as well).
17. Áqá Muḥammad-Hasan of the pilgrim house.
18. Mírzá Áqá Ján (<u>Kh</u>ádimuʼlláh), amanuensis of Baháʼuʼlláh.
19. Ustád Muḥammad-ʻAlíy-i-Salmání, the barber to Baháʼuʼlláh, poet.
20. Mi<u>sh</u>kín-Qalam, the calligrapher (may have stayed in ʻAkká as well).
21. Áqá Mírzá Afnán, Núriʼd-Dín (visitor from Egypt, may have stayed for lengthy period). His mother was Zahra Bagum, the sister of the wife of the Báb. His wife was Maryam-Sulṭán Bagum, a daughter of Abuʼl-Qásim, known as Sakka<u>kh</u>ání, one of the two brothers of the wife of the Báb.
22. Ḥájí Mírzá Ḥabíbuʼlláh-i-Afnán, nine months (son of Núriʼd-Dín).
23. Ḥájí Mírzá Buzurg, brother of Ḥájí Mírzá Ḥabíbuʼlláh-i-Afnán.
24. Ḥájí Mírzá Ḍíyá.
25. Zivar-Sulṭán <u>Kh</u>ánum, the mother of the father of Shoghi Effendi (she was the grandmother of 22, 23, 24).
26. Ḥájí Mírzá Ḥaydar-ʻAlí (Angel of Carmel).

27. 'Abdu'l-Ghaffár of Iṣfahán.
28. Áqá Faraj, a servant of Bahá'u'lláh.

Perhaps: Mírzá Javád-i-Qazvíní and his wife, the sister of the wife of 'Abdu'l-Bahá's half-bother, Mírzá Muḥammad-'Alí, and daughter of 'Alí-'Askar-i-Tabrízí. Bahá'u'lláh bestowed the title of Ismu'lláhu'l-Javád on Mírzá Javád-i-Qazvíní. After the ascension of Bahá'u'lláh, he sided with Muḥammad-'Alí and wrote several treatises supporting him. 'Abdu'l-Bahá expelled him from the Bahá'í community. See Moojan Momen, *The Bahá'í Communities of Iran*, vol. 1, p. 478.

4. Baharieh Rouhani Ma'ani, *Leaves of the Twin Divine Trees,* fn 29, p. 383.

5. Muḥammad-'Alí had two wives. Baharieh Rouhani Ma'ani, *Leaves of the Twin Divine Trees,* p. 249.

6. An eighteen-month-old daughter of Bahá'u'lláh and Mahd-i-'Ulya, Samadiyyih, died circa August–November. Her burial site is outside the Adirnih Gate of Istanbul. H. M. Balyuzi, *King of Glory*, p. 203; Glenn Cameron and Wendi Momen, *A Basic Bahá'í Chronology*, p. 72.

7. https://bahai-library.com/uhj_wives_bahaullah.

8. The Bahá'í law is that monogamy alone is permissible.

9. For an extensive look at the lives of women closely related to Bahá'u'lláh and the Báb, see Baharieh Rouhani Ma'ani, *Leaves of the Twin Divine Trees.*

10. See also: https://bahaipedia.org.

11. See Shoghi Effendi, *God Passes By*, chapter 15.

12. Baharieh Rouhani Ma'ani, *Leaves of the Twin Divine Trees,* p. 130. On the following page the author quotes memoirs of an attendant to the Greatest Holy Leaf that give another explanation.

13. Shoghi Effendi, *God Passes By*, chapter 15. Sources differ on the details.

14. Moojan Momen, *Bahá'u'lláh: A Short Biography*, p. 134.

15. David S. Ruhe, *Door of Hope*, p. 103.

16. Ibid., 127.

17. Unlike in 'Akká when Ustád Muḥammad-'Alíy-i-Salmání would carry water in waterskins from a good distance away so that the Holy Family and the companions would not have to drink the dirty, unhealthy water of the city. H. M. Balyuzi, *King of Glory*, p. 483. Bahá'u'lláh successfully recommended the restoration of the aqueduct, and eventually clean water was delivered to the city.

18. Áqá Mírzá Maḥmúd of Káshán and Áqá Riḍáy-i-Qannád of Shíráz were partners in a confectionary shop, and boxes of their product would find their way into the hands of Bahá'u'lláh. See an extremely moving tribute to them by 'Abdu'l-Bahá in *Memorials of the Faithful*, pp. 39–41.

19. Lady Blomfield, *The Chosen Highway*, p. 98.

20. H. M. Balyuzi, *King of Glory*, p. 411. See also Moojan Momen, *Bahá'u'lláh: A Short Biography*, p. 136, regarding Bahá'u'lláh's concern for educating children, especially girls.

21. 'Alí-Akbar Furútan, *Stories of Bahá'u'lláh*, p. 87.

22. For information about horses in Persia, see: https://iranica-online.org/articles/asb-savari-horse-riding.

23. Dr. Youness Afroukhteh, *Memories of Nine Years in 'Akká*, p. 43.

24. https://en.wikipedia.org/wiki/List_of_birds_of_Israel.

Chapter 8: Bahá'u'lláh at Bahjí

1. David S. Ruhe, *Door of Hope*, p. 52: ". . . 'Abdu'l-Bahá undertook many aspects of their care and assistance, overseeing their housing and nourishment and often escorting them Himself to the presence of the Blessed Beauty." For a more extensive description, see Adib Taherzadeh, *The Revelation of Bahá'u'lláh*, vol. 4 p. 2. Here the author says that the Master prepared the pilgrims spiritually: "In some cases, He even inspected their clothes and if they were found to be worn or unsuitable, He would arrange for them to wear new outfits worthy of entering the presence of Bahá'u'lláh."

2. E. G. Browne, Introduction, *A Traveller's Narrative*, pp. 209–10. See also Moojan Momen, *The Bábí and Bahá'í Religions, 1844–1944*, pp. 222, 240.

3. For descriptions by pilgrims of their experiences, see Moojan Momen, *Bahá'u'lláh: A Short Biography,* pp. 141, 142.

4. The Master had blue-grey eyes. For a description of Shoghi Effendi's eyes, which were hazel, see Rúḥíyyih Rabbani, *The Priceless Pearl,* p. 7; Lady Blomfield, *The Chosen Highway,* pp. 105–6; Adib Taherzadeh, *The Revelation of Bahá'u'lláh,* vol. 4, pp. 413–17.

5. In addition to the descriptions by Edward Granville Browne (see chapter 11), there are several references to His clothing. One is by Ṭarázu'lláh Samandarí, later appointed a Hand of the Cause. See 'Alí-Akbar Furútan, *Stories of Bahá'u'lláh,* p. 100.

6. Moojan Momen, *Bahá'u'lláh: A Short Biography,* p. 133.

7. Rúḥíyyih Rabbani, *The Priceless Pearl,* pp. 6–7: "Fine-boned, even as a mature man, shorter than his grandfather had been, Shoghi Effendi was more akin physically to his great-grandfather, Bahá'u'lláh. He told me himself that 'Abdu'l-Bahá's sister, the Greatest Holy Leaf, would sometimes take his hand in hers and [p. 7] say "These are like the hands of my father." The relative height of the beloved Guardian can be observed in a photo in Michael V. Day, *Coronation on Carmel,* plate facing p. 268, and by other photos.

8. David S. Ruhe, *Door of Hope,* p. 104.

9. Bahá'u'lláh was first in Haifa in 1868 before He was known by the locals.

10. David S. Ruhe, *Door of Hope,* pp. 104–5.

11. Bahá'u'lláh, *Epistle to the Son of the World,* p. 135.

12. The Universal House of Justice selected the Garden of Firdaws as the site for the new Shrine of 'Abdu'l-Bahá.

13. The site of the new Shrine of 'Abdu'l-Bahá.

14. David S. Ruhe, *Door of Hope,* pp. 98, 100. See map on p. 99.

15. Ibid., p. 104.

16. Michael V. Day, *Journey to a Mountain,* p. 43.

17. H. M. Balyuzi, *King of Glory,* p. 360.

18. Moojan Momen, *Bahá'u'lláh: A Short Biography,* p. 125, quoting Mírzá Aḥmad Yazdí describing the first days there.

19. J. E. Esslemont, *Bahá'u'lláh and the New Era,* p. 38.

20. Arabic.

21. Moojan Momen, *Bahá'u'lláh: A Short Biography,* p. 127.

22. Bahá'u'lláh, *Tablets of Bahá'u'lláh,* p. 38.

23. Lady Blomfield, *The Chosen Highway,* p. 98.

24. Moojan Momen, *Bahá'u'lláh: A Short Biography,* p. 127.

25. David S. Ruhe, *Door of Hope,* p. 104.

26. H. M. Balyuzi, *King of Glory,* p. 364. The author says that in much later years when the Master was incarcerated in 'Akká, He would wistfully ask those who were able to visit the Shrine of Bahá'u'lláh: "Were red, red flowers blooming on Buq'atu'l-Ḥamrá'?" It is on a hill named Samaríyyih.

27. Ṭarázu'lláh Samandarí, *Moments with Bahá'u'lláh,* pp. 45–48.

28. David S. Ruhe, *Door of Hope,* p. 120. Browne wrote: ". . . one afternoon I saw Beha[sic] walking in one of the gardens which belonged to him. He was surrounded by a little group of his chief followers. How the journey to and from the garden was accomplished I know not: probably under cover of the darkness of night." See also Moojan Momen, *The Bábí and Bahá'í Religions, 1844–1944,* p. 230.

29. The Tablet of the Land of Bá, Lawḥ-i-Arḍ-i-Bá. See Adib Taherzadeh, *The Revelation of Bahá'u'lláh,* vol. 4, pp. 240–1.

30. Bahá'u'lláh, *Tablets of Bahá'u'lláh,* p. 227.

31. Governors of administrative districts in the Ottoman Empire.

32. J. E. Esslemont, *Bahá'u'lláh and the New Era,* p. 37.

33. Ḥájí Mírzá Ḥaydar-'Alí, *Stories from the Delight of Hearts,* p. 106.

34. Shoghi Effendi, *God Passes By,* p. 192. See also H. M. Balyuzi, *King of Glory,* p. 366.

35. J. E. Esslemont, *Bahá'u'lláh and the New Era,* pp. 37–38.

36. Ibid., p. 38. Dr. John Esslemont (1874–1925).

37. Moojan Momen, *Bahá'u'lláh: A Short Biography,* pp. 139–40.

38. Ustád Muḥammad-'Alíy-i-Salmání.

39. Moojan Momen, *Bahá'u'lláh: A Short Biography,* pp. 18–19.

Chapter 9: Three Poets

1. See Rúmí, *The Essential Rúmí.*

2. 'Aṭṭár (twelfth and thirteenth centuries), Saná'í (eleventh and twelfth centuries) and Sa'dí (thirteenth century).

3. Rúmí, quoted in Bahá'u'lláh, The Kitáb-i-Íqán, ¶204: "Flingest thou thy calumnies unto the face of Them Whom the one true God hath made the Trustees of the treasures of His seventh sphere?" Ibid: "All human attainment moveth upon a lame ass, whilst Truth, riding upon the wind, darteth across space."

4. Among other prominent Bahá'í poets was Na'ím. See reference to Mírzá Muḥammad in, H. M. Balyuzi, *Eminent Bahá'ís in the time of Bahá'u'lláh,* p. 366.

5. Hafiz, "The Gift," *Poems by Hafiz, the Great Sufi Master.*

6. Ferdowsi, tenth and eleventh centuries.

7. 'Abdu'l-Bahá, *Memorials of the Faithful,* p. 35.

8. Bahá'u'lláh also called Nabíl "Bulbul" (Nightingale).

9. It comprises four passages from Bahá'u'lláh's writings, and is known as the *Ziárat-Náma.* See Vahid Rafati, "Nabíl-e A'ẓam Zarandí, Mollá Moḥammad," https://www.iranicaonline.org/articles/nabil-zarandi.

10. Shoghi Effendi, *God Passes By,* p. 177.

11. Ibid., p. 177. The two Tablets of the Pilgrimage are called Súriy-i-Ḥajj I and II. See Boris Handal, *A Trilogy of Consecration,* p. 69.

12. The original Persian manuscript of *Matláli'-i-Anwár,* preserved at the International Bahá'í Archives in Haifa, comprises 1,014 pages of 22–24 lines each. For an article by an eminent scholar on Nabíl, see Vahid Rafati, "Nabíl-e A'ẓam Zarandí, Mollá Moḥammad," https://iranicaonline.org/articles/nabil-zarandi.

13. *The Dawn-Breakers* makes for a riveting read. It is packed with excitement and even shocking violence, but the overwhelming themes are of divine inspiration and ultimate sacrifice. Nabíl witnessed many events himself or had direct access to those who were present at them, and he had the complete confidence of Bahá'u'lláh

and 'Abdu'l-Bahá, both of Whom checked and approved part of the manuscript.

14. 'Abdu'l-Bahá, *Memorials of the Faithful*, p. 36.

15. Ibid., p. 33.

16. Ibid., pp. 34–35

17. E. G. Browne, *Materials for the Study of the Bábí Religion*, p. 353.

18. Shoghi Effendi, *God Passes By*, p. 176.

19. Adib Taherzadeh, *The Revelation of Bahá'u'lláh*. vol. 4, p. 330.

20. Boris Handal, *Mírzá Mihdí, The Purest Branch*, pp. 121–22.

21. Ibid., *A Trilogy of Consecration*, p. 80.

22. 'Abdu'l-Bahá, *Memorials of the Faithful*, p. 38.

23. A daughter of 'Abdu'l-Bahá, Ṭúbá Khánum, attributed those words to Bahá'u'lláh in her spoken chronicle, which is recorded in Lady Blomfield, *The Chosen Highway*, p. 106. The words are likely to be approximate.

24. For a whole chapter on 'Andalíb, see H. M. Balyuzi, *Eminent Bahá'ís in the Time of Bahá'u'lláh*.

25. Provisional translation by Fuad Izadinia.

26. E. G. Browne, *A Year Amongst the Persians*, p. 367.

27. Ibid., p. 367.

28. Ibid., p. 397.

29. Ibid., chapter 9.

30. Ibid., p. 399.

31. Ibid., pp. 399–400.

32. See Michael V. Day, *Journey to a Mountain*, p. 86. It was later called the Eastern Pilgrim House.

33. The author appreciates the gracious help given to him by the late Mrs. Nayyereh Shadravan and Ms. Siavash Shadravan concerning their relative, 'Andalíb.

34. Dr. Banani was a Knight of Bahá'u'lláh, a distinguished professor in the United States, and a brother of Violette Nakhjavani. https://www.bahai.us/9/community/news/2013/september-october/

amin-banani-was-an-influential-scholar-and-a-knight-of-bahaullah/. See also a video of a tribute to him at Stanford University: https://www.youtube.com/watch?v=w0cwmoxKV50. See videos of his presentations: https://www.youtube.com/watch?v=sjD-OR178ro.

35. H. M. Balyuzi, *King of Glory*, pp. 325–30.

36. Salmání, *My Memories of Bahá'u'lláh*, pp. 115, 120–21.

37. *Khooshe-ha*, vol. IV, pp. 89–104.

Chapter 10: A Curious Visitor

1. Bahá'u'lláh, in *Bahá'í Prayers*, p. 10.

2. According to Adib Taherzadeh, during the ministry of Bahá'u'lláh, Sulaymán Khán-i-Tunukábání (Jamál Effendi) visited not only India, including the Punjab, but also Ceylon (now Sri Lanka), Burma, Malaya (now Malaysia), Siam (now Thailand), as well as Java, Bali, and the Celebes (now Sulawesi in what is part of Indonesia). "On one of these trips, which lasted one and a half years, he visited Lahore, Punch, Yarkand, Kashmir, Laddakh (Ladakh), Tibet, and Balkh and Bahakshan, both now part of Afghanistan." *The Revelation of Bahá'u'lláh*. vol. 4, pp. 182–83.

3. Shoghi Effendi provided a list of the fifteen countries opened to the Faith by the end of Bahá'u'lláh's ministry in 1892. In the period of the Báb's ministry (1844–53), Iraq and Persia were open. In the time of Bahá'u'lláh (1853–92): Adhirbayján, Armenia, Burma, Egypt, Georgia, India, Israel (known then as part of Syria, the Holy Land, or Palestine), Lebanon, Pakistan, Sudan, Syria, Turkey, Turkmenistan. See Shoghi Effendi, *The Bahá'í Faith 1844–1952, Information Statistical and Comparative*, p. 6.

4. See reference to Mírzá Muḥammad-'Alí, the Afnán, traveling to China in, 'Abdu'l-Bahá, *Memorials of the Faithful*, p.18. He lived in Hong Kong (see Adib Taherzadeh, *The Revelation of Bahá'u'lláh*, vol. 4, p. 248). Jimmy Seow, *The Pure in Heart*, p. 24, refers to Ḥájí Mírzá Muḥammad-'Alí-i-Afnán as the first recorded Bahá'í in China. He was the son of Ḥájí Mírzá Siyyid Muḥammad-i-Afnán, for whom the Kitáb-i-Íqán was revealed.

5. Shoghi Effendi, *God Passes By*, pp. 205–15. There was said to be a faint acknowledgement by Queen Victoria, the sovereign of the most powerful nation on the planet, Great Britain.

6. https://www.britannica.com/place/British-Empire/Dominance-and-dominions.

7. Among the alumni of Cambridge University were Isaac Newton, Charles Darwin, William Wordsworth, and John Milton.

8. E. Denison Ross, *Edward Granville Browne: A Memoir*: "His understanding of spoken Persian when he first came among the people was already of a standard rarely attained by Europeans after years of residence, for he was at once able to discuss metaphysics, and to grasp the full meaning of quoted verses which were new to him." http://bahai-library.com/books/ayatp/ayatp.00.htmlp.

9. He gives tips on how to learn a language in his book, *A Year Among the Persians*. Professor Denis Ross said he had a gift possessed by few orientalists: namely of being able to write letters in the oriental language he professed. Ross, *Both Ends of the Candle*, p. 55. Browne said he learned to speak Persian "pretty fluently" in London, though improved enormously in Persia. Ibid., p. 62.

10. E. Denison Ross, *Edward Granville Browne, A Memoir*: http://bahai-library.com/books/ayatp/ayatp.00.html. This can be tested by reading his accounts of Persian Bahá'ís talking to him in ways that today's Bahá'ís would recognize as being the exact words, or version of them, that a modern Bahá'í would use to explain the Faith. In his book, *Both Ends of the Candle*, p. 70, Ross wrote: "That E. G. B., was a genius, no man could deny."

11. Ross wrote that Browne "devoted precious years to the study of a subject [Babiism] which was not perhaps wholly worthy of so much strenuous labour, especially in view of the later development of Beha'ism and the resultant obscuring of the Bab, 1890." http://bahai-library.com/books/ayatp/ayatp.00.html. Ross himself later met Bahá'ís in Persia, which gave him "the greatest intellectual pleasure." In his book is the text of a broadcast he delivered in 1931 on what he would do with the world. Many of his ideas would seem to

have arisen from his study of the Bahá'í teachings, though this is not mentioned. See E. Denison Ross, *Both Ends of the Candle*, pp. 85, 328–38.

12. Wrote Browne of Ḥájí Mírzá Ḥaydar-'Alí, "His manners were pleasing, and his speech, when he spoke, persuasive. Altogether he was a man whom one would not readily forget, even after a single interview, and on whose memory one dwells with pleasure."

13. H. M. Balyuzi, *Edward Granville Browne and the Bahá'í Faith*, p. 62.

14. E. G. Browne, *A Year Among the Persians*, p. 409.

15. Christopher Buck writes in his paper on Browne: "This marks a lifelong pattern in which Browne characteristically—and perhaps quixotically—consistently favored the underdog, even if undeserving." Browne's colleague and friend Sir E. Denison Ross points it out in his autobiography, *Both Ends of A Candle*, p. 69, and Cambridge University researcher Dr. John Gurney confirmed in correspondence with the author on 11 June 2019 that, referring to favoring an underdog, Browne had an element of this in his attitude.

16. As Professor Ross recalled: "I never heard him discuss either Religion or Art." Ibid., p. 69.

17. E. G. Browne, quoted in, E. Denison Ross, *Both Ends of the Candle*, p. 60.

18. E. Denison Ross, *Edward Granville Browne, A Memoir*, p. xvii. http://bahai-library.com/books/ayatp/ayatp.00.html.

19. *Les religions et les philosophies dans l'Asie Centrale* by Joseph Arthur Comte de Gobineau.

20. H. M. Balyuzi, *Edward Granville Browne and the Bahá'í Faith*, p. 51; E. G. Browne (ed.), *A Traveller's Narrative*, vol. II, p. xxiv.

21. Siyyid 'Alí Afnán was married to Furúghíyyih (daughter to Bahá'u'lláh and Gawhar Khánum).

22. His report is mostly reproduced in his lengthy introduction *to A Traveller's Narrative*, a history written in 1886 by 'Abdu'l-Bahá and translated by Browne, who had it published in 1891. There are also notes in his diaries.

23. Moojan Momen, *The Bábí and Bahá'í Religions, 1844–1944,* p. 228. From E. G. Browne, *A Traveller's Narrative,* Introduction, pp. xxvii–xliii. Among those he first met in 'Akká were Mírzá Asadu'lláh, a brother-in-law of the Master's wife, and one of Bahá'u'lláh's nephews, Mírzá Majdi'd-Dín. Both became Covenant-breakers.

24. Ḍíyá'u'lláh, twenty-six, and Badí'u'lláh, twenty-three. Both were later declared Covenant-breakers. See Adib Taherzadeh, *The Covenant of Bahá'u'lláh,* p. 117.

25. Father-in-law to Bahá'u'lláh's daughter Furúghíyyih. Father of Siyyid 'Alí Afnán.

26. i.e., with the salutation ordinarily used by the Muhammadans, or with that peculiar to the Bábís.

27. From a manuscript of Ustád 'Alí-'Akbar Banná, the architect of the Ishqabád Temple.

28. 'Abdu'l-Bahá, *Memorials of the Faithful,* pp. 21–23.

29. E. G. Browne, *A Traveller's Narrative,* Introduction, pp. xxxviii to xxxix. See: http://bahai-library.com/books/tn/tn.intro.html.

Chapter 11: The Manifestation Grants an Audience

1. Browne is mistaken in his diary, referring to Wednesday, April 15.

2. This makes it clear that it was not 'Abdu'l-Bahá or Muḥammad-'Alí, His half-brother and later a Covenant-breaker, but rather Ḍíyá'u'lláh or Badí'u'lláh.

3. H. M. Balyuzi, *King of Glory,* p. 371. The author says the pen-portrait is the only one of its kind in existence.

4. By 1867, when Bahá'u'lláh was fifty years old, his hair had turned white as He Himself stated. Shoghi Effendi, *God Passes By,* p. 169. It was the custom to have white hair dyed once it turned grey or white.

5. ". . . portion of that epistle (lawh) whereof the translation occupies the last paragraph of p. 70 and the greater part of p. 71 of this book." E. G. Browne, quoted in Moojan Momen, *The Bábí and Bahá'í Religions, 1844–1944,* p. 230, referring to his translation of *A Traveller's Narrative.*

6. Supp. 21 Browne Manuscripts, Cambridge University Library, as cited in a footnote on p. 240 of Moojan Momen, *The Bábí and Bahá'í Religions, 1844–1944,* referring to text on p. 231.

7. See Christopher Buck and Youli Ioannesyan, "Scholar meets Prophet: Edward Granville Browne and Bahá'u'lláh (Acre, 1890)," *Bahá'í Studies Review*, 20, 2014, pp. 21–38.

8. Bahá'u'lláh expressly taught that He was not an incarnation of Divinity. As Drs. Buck and Ioannesyan write: "Browne's letter to Baron Rosen also reveals that the prominent western scholar, despite his deep knowledge and understanding of the Bábí (to a lesser extent Bahá'í) teachings, had some misconceptions about the status of the prophetic credentials of Bahá'u'lláh (who, in Bahá'í terms, was considered to be a 'Manifestation of God') in general and of Bahá'u'lláh's theophanic and messianic claims in particular. In his letter, Browne states that Bahá'u'lláh, contrary to his expectations, was 'like a Master, and a Prophet—but not as an Incarnation of the Divinity' (!). In other words, Browne believed that Bahá'u'lláh had laid claim to being 'an Incarnation of the Divinity.' Whether this misconception came from rival Azali sources—and those Azalis with whom Browne kept up active correspondence—or was merely due to the 'Christian language' that Browne employed in this description (given the fact that Christians represent Jesus Christ in the very same terms) is very much open to speculation. However, even Baron Rosen himself wrote of Bahá'u'lláh in a similar vein, saying that 'even though his identification of himself with the Divinity may appear to us blasphemous, we should not forget that, at least, he [Bahá'u'lláh] has imagined himself not as a scourging divinity . . . but rather a mild, forgiving, loving and peacemaking one.' In the light of this letter, we may assume that Rosen might have been influenced in his personal understanding of Bahá'u'lláh's claim by what Browne had previously written."

9. His hair and beard were dyed, as was the custom.

10. Youli Ioannesyan, *The Development of the Bábí/Bahá'í Communities,* pp. 143–44.

11. Christopher Buck and Youli Ioannesyan, "Scholar meets Prophet: Edward Granville Browne and Bahá'u'lláh (Acre, 1890)," *Bahá'í Studies Review,* 20, 2014, p. 27.

12. Ibid., p. 30.

13. Ibid., p. 30 and fn 48 on p. 39. The authors provide a provisional translation into English by Nahzy Abadi Buck on which they based their view on what Bahá'u'lláh seemed to have meant.

14. Supp. 21 Browne Manuscripts, Cambridge University Library, as cited in a footnote on p. 240 of Moojan Momen, *The Bábí and Bahá'í Religions, 1844–1944,* referring to text on p. 231. Browne provided what Buck and Ioannesyan describe as doubtful dates, and also doubtful quotes by Bahá'u'lláh on the shah and Iran. "Scholar meets Prophet: Edward Granville Browne and Bahá'u'lláh (Acre, 1890)," *Bahá'í Studies Review,* 20, 2014, p. 31.

15. To read about a visit by Bahá'u'lláh to the Junayn garden, see H. M. Balyuzi, *King of Glory,* pp. 415–16.

16. H. M. Balyuzi, *Edward Granville Browne and the Bahá'í Faith,* p. 52. It was addressed to Ḥájí Mírzá Muḥammad Áqá, whose son, the historian Hasan Balyuzi, later appointed a Hand of the Cause, translated and published an excerpt.

17. Moojan Momen, *Browne, Edward Granville,* 1995. https://bahai-library.com/momen_encyclopedia_browne.

18. For an interesting summary and study guide compiled by Brett Zamir, see: https://bahai-library.com/zamir_tn_crossreference.

19. The introduction has errors and fittingly does not accompany the 1980 edition. To read it, visit https://www.h-net.org/~bahai/diglib/books/A-E/B/browne/tn/tnfrnt.htm. The original edition had the introduction by Browne.

20. A plaque at the Art Institute of Chicago is at the entrance to Fullerton Hall. There are two main doors into the Hall and they both have double sets of doors because concerts are given there, so it's more like a vestibule. It is very appropriate that the sign is where it is, but it's the doorway that is only used occasionally, unless there is a large event. (Candace Melville at the House of Worship in Wilmette Facebook site, Bahá'í HOW.)

21. https://en.wikipedia.org/wiki/Henry_Harris_Jessup. The paper introduced the quotation with: "In the palace of Behjeh, or Delight, just outside the fortress of Acre on the Syrian coast, there died a few months since a famous Persian sage—the Babi saint, named Beha Allah, the 'Glory of God'—the head of that vast reform party of Persian Moslems who accept the New Testament as the word of God, and Christ as the deliverer of man; who regard all natives as one, and all men as brothers. Three years ago he was visited by a Cambridge scholar, and gave utterance to sentiments so noble, so Christlike that we repeat them as our closing words." https://bahai-library.com/jessup_neelys_history_religions. This site includes an article by Henry Jessup that was published in *Neely's History of the Parliament of Religions and Religious Congresses of the World's Columbian Exposition*, pp. 637–41. See a shorter version in Shoghi Effendi, *God Passes By*, p. 256.

Chapter 12: Apostle of the Crimson Ark

1. Ṭarázu'lláh Samandarí, *Moments with Bahá'u'lláh*, pp. 20–21 (the translation into English of a talk that Mr. Samandarí delivered on 27 December 1967, at the home of Curtis Kelsey, 3019 Bay Drive, Bradenton, Florida.) A complementary account is by Mihdí Samandarí, a son of the Hand of the Cause, in an *In Memoriam* obituary, *The Bahá'í World*, vol. XV, 1968–73, pp. 411–12. For another biography, see Barron Harper, *Lights of Fortitude*, pp. 229–37. Mr. Samandarí gives his father's birth year as 1874, Mr. Harper as 1875.

2. In Memoriam, *The Bahá'í World*. vol. IX (1968–73), p. 415.

3. Anthony Lee writing in his forward to Ṭarázu'lláh Samandarí, *Moments with Bahá'u'lláh*, pp. xv–xvi.

4. In Memoriam, *The Bahá'í World*. vol. IX (1968–73), p. 415.

Chapter 13: Light and Glory

1. Bahá'u'lláh, The Kitáb-i-Aqdas, ¶173.

2. Adib Taherzadeh, *The Revelation of Bahá'u'lláh*, vol. 4, p. 277.

3. The duties of the Hands of the Cause are stated in the Will and Testament of 'Abdu'l-Bahá. To see relevant excerpts, visit: https://www.bahai.org/abdul-baha/articles-resources/from-will-testament-abdul-baha.

Hands of the Cause continued in these lifetime duties until the last of the fifty Hands of the Cause passed away in 2007, 121 years after the first was appointed. One of their outstanding achievements occurred between 1957 and 1963 when the Hands of the Cause took stewardship of the Faith after the death of Shoghi Effendi and organized the election of the inaugural Universal House of Justice. They disqualified themselves as potential members.

4. Adib Taherzadeh, *The Revelation of Bahá'u'lláh,* vol. 4, p. 286.

5. Ibid., p. 290.

6. *The Bahá'í World,* vol. III (pp. 80–81). The Hands can be found listed under numbers 8, 11, 16, and 19.

7. Adib Taherzadeh, *The Revelation of Bahá'u'lláh,* vol. 4, p. 306.

8. Barron Harper, *Lights of Fortitude,* p. 13.

9. Adib Taherzadeh, *The Revelation of Bahá'u'lláh,* vol. 4, p. 307.

10. Ibid., p. 307.

11. For excellent biographies on the Hands of the Cause, see Barron Harper, *Lights of Fortitude.*

12. Bahá'u'lláh calls upon His amanuensis to beseech "the All-Abiding Lord to confirm the chosen ones, that is those souls who are Hands of the Cause, who are adorned with the robe of teaching, and have arisen to serve the Cause, to be enabled to exalt the World of God." H. M. Balyuzi, *Eminent Bahá'ís,* p. 173.

13. Barron Harper, *Lights of Fortitude,* p. 8.

14. 'Abdu'l-Bahá titled Mullá Ṣádiq Ismu'lláhu'l-Aṣdaq ("the Name of God the most Truthful"). The Master wrote: "He was like a surging sea, a falcon that soared high. His visage shone, his tongue was eloquent, his strength and steadfastness astounding. When he

opened his lips to teach, the proofs would stream out; when he chanted or prayed, his eyes shed tears like a spring cloud. His face was luminous, his life spiritual, his knowledge both acquired and innate; and celestial was his ardor, his detachment from the world, his righteousness, his piety and fear of God." 'Abdu'l-Bahá, *Memorials of the Faithful*, p. 8.

15. Bahá'u'lláh, quoted in Shoghi Effendi, *Advent of Divine Justice*, p. 84.

16. Ibid., pp. 83–84.

17. Barron Harper, *Lights of Fortitude*, p. 16, quoting Ala'i, *Mu'assisiy-i-Ayadiy-i-Amru'llah*, pp. 450–64. Provisional translation provided by the Bahá'í World Center.

18. Adib Taherzadeh, *The Revelation of Bahá'u'lláh*, vol. 4, p. 314.

19. Ḥájí Á<u>kh</u>únd is also known by the name Hájí Mullá 'Alí-Akbar-i-Shahmírzádí.

20. For an account of his activities, see Michael V. Day, *Journey to a Mountain*, pp. 10–12, 15, 63, 187; Adib Taherzadeh, *The Revelation of Bahá'u'lláh*, vol. 4, pp. 294–301; Barron Harper, *Lights of Fortitude*, pp. 3–7.

21 Adib Taherzadeh, *The Revelation of Bahá'u'lláh*, vol. 4, p. 298.

22. Mullá Abu'l-Ḥasan-i-Ardikání, known as Hájí Amín or Amín-i-Iláhí (the Trustee of God). He was one of the prominent Bahá'ís of Iran and was appointed the trustee (amín) of the Ḥuqúqu'lláh as well as acting as a courier for conveying the letters of Bahá'u'lláh. He was posthumously named a Hand of the Cause of God by Shoghi Effendi and was also listed among the Apostles of Bahá'u'lláh.

23. Bahá'u'lláh, Lawḥ-i-Dunyá (Tablet of the World), *Tablets of Bahá'u'lláh*, p. 83.

24. Barron Harper, *Lights of Fortitude*, p. 5.

25. H. M. Balyuzi, *Eminent Bahá'ís*, p. 266.

26. Adib Taherzadeh, *The Revelation of Bahá'u'lláh*, vol. 4, p. 277.

27. 'Abdu'l-Bahá, *Memorials of the Faithful*, p. 11.

28. Ibid., p. 12.

29. Ibid.

Chapter 14: Encountering Revelation

1. (1874–1968) Shoghi Effendi appointed him a Hand of the Cause of God in 1951.

2. Mírzá Badí'u'lláh (1867–1950) was a son of Bahá'u'lláh who later became a Covenant-breaker.

3. Ṭarázu'lláh Samandarí, *Moments with Bahá'u'lláh*, pp. 60–61. From his written memoirs, translated by his son, Dr. Mehdi Samandarí.

4. Ibid., pp. 62–65.

5. A Bahá'í scholar, Dr. John Hatcher, discusses the process of revelation in his book *The Face of God Among Us*. Wilmette, IL: Bahá'í Publishing, 2010.

6. "Kh̲ádim" is Mírzá Áqá Ján.

7. He later rebelled against the Master and so became a Covenant-breaker.

8. Also known as Mullá Zaynu'l-'Ábidín.

9. Adib Taherzadeh, *The Revelation of Bahá'u'lláh*, vol. 1, pp. 24–28. Mis̲h̲kín-Qalam's original name was Mírzá Ḥusayn. For a tribute by the Master, see *Memorials of the Faithful.* pp. 97–101.

10. Circa 1830–1920. The grave of this long-suffering, humorous, detached Bahá'í—so dearly loved by Bahá'u'lláh and the Master—lies next to that of his much younger friend, Hand of the Cause Ṭarázu'lláh Samandarí, in the Bahá'í Cemetery in Haifa, Israel.

11. Ḥájí Mírzá Ḥaydar-'Alí, *Stories from the Delight of Hearts*, pp. 103–4.

12. H. M. Balyuzi, *Bahá'u'lláh: King of Glory*, p. 413.

13. Martha Root, "White Roses of Persia (Part 2)," *Star of the West*, vol. 23, Issue 3, pp 73–74 (anecdote about Hand of the Cause Varqá, p. 74).

14. Adib Taherzadeh, *The Revelation of Bahá'u'lláh*, vol. 1, pp. 35–36. Mr. Taherzadeh explains: "The Persian and Arabic scripts

are commonly written with reed pens. This type of pen often makes a shrieking sound when moved in a certain way. The calligrapher could control this sound to a certain extent. For instance, he could allow the sound to accompany the writing of a particular stroke or curve throughout. This sound not only revealed the extent to which a single letter had been drawn out, but also aroused feelings of excitement in the calligrapher and the onlookers. Bahá'u'lláh has, in many of His Tablets, referred to the Most Exalted Pen, signifying thereby the Manifestation of God and His Revelation. He has also referred to the shrill voice of that same Pen. This expression is symbolic of the proclamation of His Message among the peoples of the world."

15. Ibid.

16. Bahá'u'lláh, *Tablets of Bahá'u'lláh,* pp. 148–49; For a commentary on the whole Tablet, see: Adib Taherzadeh, *The Revelation of Bahá'u'lláh,* vol. 4, pp. 33–49.

17. Ibid., pp. 72–73. This was the description by pilgrim Jináb-i- Ḥájí Muḥammad-'Alíy-i-Áhmadúff-i-Mílání as recorded by his son Aḥmad-i-Asbaqí.

Chapter 15: The Final Tablets

1. Shoghi Effendi, *God Passes By,* p. 216.

2. Adib Taherzadeh, *The Revelation of Bahá'u'lláh,* vol. 4, p. 114.

3. Ibid., p. 216.

4. Looking at it in terms of preparation for the development of the Faith in the years, decades, and centuries after His ascension, the major themes can be viewed as essential for individuals and institutions to ponder, consult upon, and employ in their plans and activities.

5. Shoghi Effendi, *God Passes By,* p. 216.

6. Ibid., p. 217.

7. Regarding infallibility, see letter from the Universal House of Justice, dated 26 November 1986, to a National Assembly: https://www.bahai.org/library/authoritative-texts/the-universal-house-of-justice/messages/19861126_001/19861126_001.pdf.

8. Shoghi Effendi, *God Passes By,* pp. 217–19.

9. For this brief summary of the contents of the Tablets, the author draws on chapters in Adib Taherzadeh, *The Revelation of Bahá'u'lláh,* vol. 4.

10. This Tablet—and others—have concepts that can be traced back to Lawḥ-i-Mánikchí-Ṣáḥib, a Tablet mostly in pure Persian addressed to a Zoroastrian friend of Bahá'u'lláh. It was the first Tablet to state "Ye are the fruits of one tree and the leaves of one branch." Well-known excerpts from the partial translation by Shoghi Effendi include, for example: "Be anxiously concerned with the needs of the age ye live in, and center your deliberations on its exigencies and requirements." Bahá'u'lláh, *Gleanings from the Writings of Bahá'u'lláh,* no. 106.1. See also Adib Taherzadeh, *The Revelation of Bahá'u'lláh,* vol. 3, pp. 270–71.

11. Shaykh Muḥammad Báqir, surnamed "Dhi'b" (Wolf), and Mír Muḥammad-Ḥusayn, the Imám-Jum'ih of Iṣfahán, surnamed *"Raqshá"* (She-serpent).

12. Adib Taherzadeh, *The Covenant of Bahá'u'lláh,* p. 142. The author said it is alluded to in the Epistle to the Son of the Wolf as the "Crimson Book."

13. Shoghi Effendi, *God Passes By,* p. 220.

Chapter 16: The Tablet of Carmel

1. As a contemporary Bahá'í historian, Siyyid Asadu'lláh-i-Qumí wrote about Bahá'u'lláh in Haifa, and said 'Abdu'l-Bahá was present with Him on most occasions. Moojan Momen, *Bahá'u'lláh: A Short Biography,* pp. 128–29, referring in fn on p. 234 to *Hizar Dastan,* pp. 160–61.

2. Ibid., p. 128.

3. Ibid., p. 129.

4. On another occasion, Bahá'u'lláh visited the lower Cave of Elijah, spending three days there. David S. Ruhe, *Door of Hope,* p. 189.

5. Shoghi Effendi, *Citadel of Faith,* p. 96.

6. https://en.wikipedia.org/wiki/Stella_Maris_Monastery. Javidukht Khadem, *Zikrullah Khadem,* p. 180, citing memoirs of Dr. Habib Mu'ayyad.

7. The tent was called "Tabernacle of Glory" by Shoghi Effendi, *God Passes By*, p. 194. "In that same year Bahá'u'lláh's tent, the 'Tabernacle of Glory,' was raised on Mt. Carmel, 'the Hill of God and His Vineyard,' the home of Elijah, extolled by Isaiah as the 'mountain of the Lord,' to which 'all nations shall flow.' Four times He visited Haifa, His last visit being no less than three months long. In the course of one of these visits, when His tent was pitched in the vicinity of the Carmelite Monastery, He, the 'Lord of the Vineyard,' revealed the Tablet of Carmel, remarkable for its allusions and prophecies. On another occasion He pointed out Himself to 'Abdu'l-Bahá, as He stood on the slopes of that mountain, the site which was to serve as the permanent resting-place of the Báb, and on which a befitting mausoleum was later to be erected." See also David S. Ruhe, *Door of Hope*, p. 187; Adib Taherzadeh, *The Revelation of Bahá'u'lláh*, vol. 4, p. 352.

8. Javidukht Khadem, *Zikrullah Khadem*, p. 280, and fn on p. 360 citing memoirs of Dr. Habib Mu'ayyad, pp. 19, 21, 22, 53.

9. Shoghi Effendi, *God Passes By*, p. 194.

10. Isaiah 2:2–4, King James Version.

11. Javidukht Khadem, *Zikrullah Khadem*, p. 292.

12. Shoghi Effendi, *Messages to the Bahá'í World, 1950–1957*, p. 63 According to Hand of the Cause Khadem, Shoghi Effendi said the Tablet was not completed. See Javidukht Khadem, *Zikrullah Khadem*, p. 291.

13. Javidukht Khadem, *Zikrullah Khadem*, p. 293.

14. Shoghi Effendi, *God Passes By*, p. 194.

15. Adib Taherzadeh, *The Revelation of Bahá'u'lláh*, vol. 4, p. 358.

16. Bahá'u'lláh, *Gleanings from the Writings of Bahá'u'lláh*, no. 11.4.

17. Adib Taherzadeh, *The Revelation of Bahá'u'lláh*, vol. 4, p. 358.

18. Bahá'u'lláh, Epistle to the Son of the Wolf, ¶210.

19. Javidukht Khadem, *Zikrullah Khadem*, p. 281, citing "unpublished memoirs," says the revelation of the Tablet of Car-

mel came after Bahá'u'lláh ordained the site for the shrine, but that seems incorrect. Shoghi Effendi does not state any order. See *God Passes By*, p. 194.

20. For an account of this episode and of the revelation of the Tablet of Carmel see Michael V. Day, *Journey to a Mountain*, pp. 87–90.

21. Rúḥíyyih Rabbani, *The Priceless Pearl*, pp. 263, 255.

22. Shoghi Effendi, *Messages to the Bahá'í World, 1950–1957*, p. 8.

23. Rúḥíyyih Rabbani, *The Priceless Pearl*, p. 247.

Chapter 17: Extraordinary Epistle

1. Moojan Momen, *Bahá'u'lláh: A Short Biography*, p. 127.

2. Adib Taherzadeh, *The Revelation of Bahá'u'lláh*, vol. 4, pp. 372–73.

3. Bahá'u'lláh, *Epistle to the Son of the Wolf*, p. 165; Marzieh Gail, *Dawn over Mount Hira*, p. 179.

4. Bahá'u'lláh, *Tablets of Bahá'u'lláh*, pp. 148–49. See Adib Taherzadeh, *The Revelation of Bahá'u'lláh*, vol. 4, pp. 372–73.

5. Shoghi Effendi, *God Passes By*, p. 219. The epistle is challenging for most non-Muslims because, to understand many references it requires knowledge of the holy Qu'rán and Islamic traditions. For study materials, see Lameh Fananapazir, *A Companion to the Study of the Epistle to the Son of the Wolf*. Oxford: George Ronald, 2020. Mr. Hooper Dunbar provides an introduction. There are two chapters in Adib Taherzadeh, *The Revelation of Bahá'u'lláh*, vol. 4, pp. 368–412, and an appendix (pp. 432–40). Marzieh Gail provides an introduction to the epistle as translated by Shoghi Effendi and published by the US Bahá'í Publishing Trust. She also writes a magnificent chapter about it in *Dawn over Mount Hira*, pp. 176–83. Moojan Momen has an insightful summary in *Bahá'u'lláh: A Short Biography*, pp. 190–91. Melanie Smith has provided an online guide: https://bahai-library.com/smith_esw_guide; as has Brent Poirier: http://study-epistle.blogspot.com/.

6. See Bahá'u'lláh, *Epistle to the Son of the Wolf* (translation by Shoghi Effendi) with Marzieh Gail's introduction, p. ix. This

work had been inadequately translated by an American and published in 1928 by the Bahá'ís of the United States. Shoghi Effendi sent his translation with the tentative title "Tablet to the Son of the Wolf" to his editorial colleague, George Townshend, and the work appeared entitled "Epistle to the Son of the Wolf" in 1941. Mr. Townshend was later appointed a Hand of the Cause of God. See: David Hofman, *George Townshend.* Oxford: George Ronald, 1983.

7. Adib Taherzadeh, *The Revelation of Bahá'u'lláh*, vol. 4, pp. 369–72. The epistle strongly condemns religious fanaticism as a "world devouring fire." Bahá'u'lláh, *Epistle to the Son of the Wolf,* p. 13.

8. In 1940, Shoghi Effendi expressed that purpose in this telegram to the US National Spiritual Assembly: "DEVOUTLY HOPE ITS STUDY MAY CONTRIBUTE FURTHER ENLIGHTENMENT, DEEPER UNDERSTANDING VERITIES ON WHICH EFFECTUAL PROSECUTION TEACHING, ADMINISTRATIVE UNDERTAKINGS ULTIMATELY DEPEND." Shoghi Effendi, *This Decisive Hour,* no. 78, quoted by Hooper Dunbar on p. viii of his foreword to *A Companion to the Study of the Epistle to the Son of the Wolf.* See fn 5.

9. The opening passage of the constitution of the Universal House of Justice, adopted and signed in 1972, is the exordium and the second paragraph of Epistle to the Son of the Wolf.

10. He cites this passage twice. See Bahá'u'lláh, *Epistle to the Son of the Wolf,* pp. 11, 39.

11. "O Son of Spirit! My first counsel is this: Possess a pure, kindly and radiant heart, that thine may be a sovereignty ancient, imperishable and everlasting."

12. Bahá'u'lláh, *Epistle to the Son of the Wolf,* pp. 93–94

13. As cited by Hooper Dunbar on p. ix of his foreword to Lameh Fananapazir's *A Companion to the Study of the Epistle to the Son of the Wolf.*

14. Shoghi Effendi, *God Passes By,* p. 220.

15. H. M. Balyuzi, *King of Glory,* p. 384.

16. Marzieh Gail, Introduction, in Bahá'u'lláh, *Epistle to the Son of the Wolf* (translation by Shoghi Effendi), p. ix. This is based on the testimony of 'Abdu'l-Bahá as reported by Shoghi Effendi.

Chapter 18: Final Illness

1. Ṭúbá Khánum, in Lady Blomfield, *The Chosen Highway,* p. 105.

2. Lady Sheil, *Glimpses of Life and Manners in Persia,* p. 146. Lady Sheil describes seeing a lady of rank mounted on a tall horse "which she managed with skill." She said if no Persians were near, the lady of rank and her servants "made little scruple of raising their veils . . ." For information about horses in Persia, see: https://iranicaonline.org/articles/asb-savari-horse-riding.

3. The three were Mírzá 'Abdu'l- Ḥusayn, eldest of the King of the Martyrs. The second was Nabíl ibn Nabíl, Ḥájí Shaykh Muḥammad-'Alíy-i-Qazvíní (a paternal uncle of Ṭarázu'lláh Samandarí), and the third was Khátún Ján, wife of Áqá Hádíy-i-Qazvíní. Ṭarázu'lláh Samandarí, *Moments with Bahá'u'lláh,* pp. 26–27.

4. "'Know thou,' Bahá'u'lláh, wishing to emphasize the criticalness of the first nine years of His banishment to that prison-city, has written, 'that upon Our arrival at this Spot, We chose to designate it as the "Most Great Prison." Though previously subjected in another land (Tihrán) to chains and fetters, We yet refused to call it by that name. Say: Ponder thereon, O ye endued with understanding!'" Shoghi Effendi, *God Passes By,* p. 185.

5. Adib Taherzadeh, *The Revelation of Bahá'u'lláh,* vol. 4, p. 219.

6. Dr. David Ruhe writes: "The nature of Bahá'u'lláh's final sickness was said to be malaria (see Lady Blomfield, *The Chosen Highway,* p. 105); in view of the endemic malaria of the 'Akká district this is possible, but seems unlikely from the descriptions available." David S. Ruhe, *Door of Hope,* p. 226, fn 3.

7. He also had the stress of the deaths of seven of His own children as well as that of beloved grandchildren, and the 1886 passing of His beloved first wife.

8. Adib Taherzadeh, *The Revelation of Bahá'u'lláh,* vol. 4, p. 219.

9. For a chapter entitled "The Wronged One of the World," see *The Revelation of Bahá'u'lláh,* vol. 3, p. 221–52. It includes a description and commentary on the Tablet of Aḥmad.

10. Ruhiyyih Rabbani, *The Priceless Pearl,* p. 162. For a vivid and heartrending description of the attacks on 'Abdu'l-Bahá, see His Will and Testament. https://www.bahai.org/library/authoritative-texts/abdul-baha/will-testament-abdul-baha/4#149802947.

11. Shoghi Effendi, *God Passes By,* p. 221.

12. 'Abdu'l-Ḥusayn-i-Ávárih, *Al-Kavakibu's-Durriyyih fi Ma'athiri'l-Bahiyyih,* vol. 1, p. 513.

13. *Star of the West,* vol. 8, no. 13, 4 Nov. pp. 177–78. (Diary of Mírzá Sohrab, later to be a Covenant-breaker.)

14. The author expresses his gratitude to Mr. David Merrick, for his well-ordered compilation of the chronology of Bahá'u'lláh's illness, and an accompanying essay: http://www.paintdrawer.co.uk/david/folders/Research/Bahai/Baha%27u%27llah/Ascension%20of%20Baha%27u%27llah%20(Sources).rtf.

15. Ṭúbá Khánum, a daughter of the Master, wrote: "As there was no hospital in 'Akká, the Master paid a doctor, Nikolaki Bey, a regular salary to look after the very poor. This doctor was asked not to say who was responsible for this." Lady Blomfield, *The Chosen Highway,* p. 101. Ṭarázu'lláh Samandarí attests there were "doctors" attending Bahá'u'lláh. See Ṭarázu'lláh Samandarí, *Moments with Bahá'u'lláh,* p. 27. Dr. David Ruhe confirms reports from the Jarrah family; see David S. Ruhe, *Door of Hope,* fn, p. 226. Dr. Petro treated 'Abdu'l-Bahá in the prison and later assisted the Bahá'ís by acting as a courier of messages between the believers outside of 'Akká and exiles in the prison. A Greek doctor was one of those attending. See *Star of the West,* vol. 8, no. 13, 4 Nov. pp. 177–78.

16. Ṭarázu'lláh Samandarí, *Moments with Bahá'u'lláh,* p. 29.

17. This is from a "summary translation" of an account by Nabíl-i-A'ẓam in Adib Taherzadeh, *The Revelation of Bahá'u'lláh,* vol. 4, p. 415, sourced to Ishráq Khávarí, *Ayyám-i-Tis'ih,* pp. 399–

406. See also: Nabíl-i-A'ẓam, *Mathai of Nabíl-i-Zarandí,* National Bahá'í Committee (for publishing in Persian and Arabic), p. 72. The author is grateful to Faruq and Fuad Izadinia for providing the excerpts from this volume.

18. Email from translator Fuad Izadinia, 21 September 2020. From the book of *Mushaira* by Ishráq Khávarí. This pilgrim had taught the Faith in Bombay and Rangoon before reaching 'Akká. In a Tablet 'Abdu'l-Bahá addresses him saying that he was present at the most great calamity and saw everything with his own eyes.

19. Bahá'u'lláh bestowed upon him a new name, Shaykh-i-San'an. Bahá'u'lláh said the difference between him as Shaykh-i-San'an and the other Shaykh-i-San'an in the history of Islam was that the Muslim Shaykh-i-San'an was a believer and became an unbeliever whereas he was an unbeliever and became a believer; and also that the Muslim was the shepherd of a Christian girl and he is the shepherd of the Blessed Beauty. These are the approximate words. See Siyyid Asadu'lláh Qumí, article in magazine *Ahang-i Badi,* Year 20, no. 7, p. 391.

20. The lambs were linked by Ṭúbá Khánum to a later event, but there was no cause for celebration at that time. Lady Blomfield, *The Chosen Highway,* p. 106.

21. Mírzá Ḍíyá'u'lláh and Mírzá Badí'u'lláh, both later designated as Covenant-breakers.

22. Not to be confused with Siyyid Asadu'lláh-i-Iṣfahání, Siyyid Asadu'lláh Qumí later accompanied the Master to Egypt, Europe, and North America, and at the age of seventy-six, he went to the Caucasus to teach with the permission of 'Abdu'l-Bahá. Reference to the blind poet: Lady Blomfield, *The Chosen Highway,* p. 105.

23. Bahá'u'lláh, The Kitáb-i-Aqdas ¶53.

24. Ibid., ¶38.

25. Adib Taherzadeh, *The Revelation of Bahá'u'lláh,* vol. 4, p. 419.

26. Ṭarázu'lláh Samandarí, *Moments with Bahá'u'lláh,* p. 32.

27. Ibid., p. 32.

Chapter 19: The Supreme Affliction

1. Shoghi Effendi cites 1892 and the Islamic date, 2nd Dhi'l-Qa'dih 1309 A. H. The author Nabíl gives the date as the 13th of the month of Azamat 49 Bahá'í Era, seventy days after Naw-Rúz. (Nabíl as quoted in Adib Taherzadeh, *The Revelation of Bahá'u'lláh*, vol. 4, p. 417.) He also cites the Islamic calendar, 2nd Dhi'l-Qa'dih 1309 A. H. In *Memorials of the Faithful*, p. 35, 'Abdu'l-Bahá says that Nabíl found significance in that the numerical value of the word "Shidád"—year of stress—was 309.

2. This is where He had met his relatives and followers during His illness. *Ṭaráz-i-Iláhí*, written by Mrs. Parivash Samandarí (Khoshbin), the granddaughter of the brother of Hand of the Cause Mr. Ṭarázu'lláh Samandarí who was called by Bahá'u'lláh, "Ṭaráz-i-Iláhí."

3. In *God Passes By*, chapter 15, published in 1944, Shoghi Effendi was to describe Muḥammad-'Alí as the "Arch-Breaker of the Covenant" (p. 246), Badí'u'lláh as "treacherous" (p. 247), and Ḍíyá'u'lláh as "vacillating" (p. 247).

4. Baharieh Rouhani Ma'ani, *Leaves of the Twin Divine Trees*, p. 253: "She (Gawhar Khánum) was with Bahá'u'lláh at Mazra'ih and Bahjí." Mahd-i-'Ulyá (Fáṭimih Khánum) stayed in Bahjí too. See *Leaves of the Twin Divine Trees*, p. 236, for excerpt from the unpublished memoirs of Rafi'ih Shahídí, who was a young girl at the time: "One day I went in the company of my grandmother to the Mansion of Bahjí. We entered a room which had a window [mistaking a door for a window] opening to Bahá'u'lláh's chamber. It was the living room of the mother of Mírzá Muḥammad-'Alí [Fáṭimih Khánum]. . . . When the women believers went to the Mansion of Bahjí intending to attain Bahá'u'lláh's presence, they gathered in that room and waited until they were summoned by Bahá'u'lláh. On that day, all the women pilgrims were gathered in that room. Suddenly the curtain on the window [the door] was drawn to one side. Bahá'u'lláh walked to the window. We all rose up to our feet. The eye of Bahá'u'lláh's loving kindness was turned towards me. Then, addressing my grandmother, He enquired whether I attended

school." Visitors today can see that the room next to the room of Bahá'u'lláh, on its left side as you face it, has a door which opens into the room of Bahá'u'lláh. There is no window. As you enter the room of Bahá'u'lláh, the door is on the immediate left. It gets covered and not visible as the door of Bahá'u'lláh's room, is wide open. This is the only room which is connected to His room through this door. it is covered by a white thin curtain, normally not visible unless you are inside the room of Bahá'u'lláh and close its door. When you enter the room in question, this connecting door is on the immediate right, now covered by a wall-carpet hung by the beloved Guardian.

5. In an email to the author on 29 April 2020, Bahá'í historian Baharieh Rouhani Ma'ani said that "since the wives lived in the immediate vicinity of the room where the ascension took place, it is quite possible that they visited Him during His illness, including on the very day of His ascension." Those wives later broke the Covenant.

6. Ṣamadíyyih Kh͟ánum's mother was Mahd-i-'Ulyá.

7. David S. Ruhe, *Door of Hope,* p. 226, fn 5 of chapter 18. Dr. Ruhe may have obtained this information from an interview with Dr. Jarráḥ's granddaughter Mrs. Hayat Jarráḥ (see fn 5). There was another doctor attending Bahá'u'lláh during His final illness, a Greek physician. He is unnamed in Moojan Momen, *The Babi and Bahá'í Religions,* p. 235, citing Ahmad Sohrab's Diary, which quotes 'Abdu'l-Bahá; *Star of the West,* vol. VIII, no. 13, 4 Nov. 1917, p. 178, (reprinted in *Star of the West* vol. 5, Oxford, 1978). However, it was likely to have been Dr. Nikolaki Bey, whom the Master had paid a salary to look after the very poor in 'Akká. See Adib Taherzadeh, *The Revelation of Bahá'u'lláh,* vol. 4, p. 4). In the interview referred to above, Mrs. Hayat Jarráḥ also refers to a Greek doctor in 'Akká, whose name the interviewer seems to have phonetically written down as Nilo-lak-i-bik, obviously Dr. Nikolaki Bey. Another Greek doctor, Dr. Petro, treated 'Abdu'l-Bahá in the prison and later assisted the Bahá'ís by acting as a courier of messages between the believers outside the prison and the exiles inside. It is not yet known if he was present during Bahá'u'lláh's last illness.

8. In an interview conducted in 1989, Dr. Jarráḥ's granddaughter related what she had been told, including by her brother, Saláh, a former caretaker of the Shrine of Bahá'u'lláh, about what happened just before the ascension. "He [Dr. Jarráḥ] was taking His [Bahá'u'lláh's] pulse and he wanted to change the medicine and Bahá'u'lláh said (a movement of the eyes) as if, with His eyes as if he wanted to tell him 'There is no use. Don't change the medicine.' He told him 'Hali Effendi, don't change the medicine.'" Excerpt from an interview of Mrs. Hayat Jarráḥ conducted by Lori Ubben and Mark Perry at the Bahá'í World Center in January 1989 and referred to in a letter from the Department of the Secretariat of the Universal House of Justice to the National Spiritual Assembly of the Bahá'ís of the United Kingdom, 19 April 1989, which notes that during the visit to the World Center in January 1989 of Mrs. Hayat Jarráḥ, a sister of a former caretaker of the Shrine of Bahá'u'lláh, Mr. Saláh Jarráḥ, a tape recording was made of her recollections of the principal events of her brother's life. It was made to help prepare an "In Memoriam" obituary. See *The Bahá'í World,* vol. XX (1986–92). A transcript of that interview was provided to the author by a son of Mrs. Jarráḥ, Abdul Jarráḥ, on 22 April, 2020.

9. Shoghi Effendi, *God Passes By,* p. 221.

10. Ibid. p. 221. The Tablet of the Vision is Lawḥ-i-Ru'yá. See chapter 4 of this volume.

11. Internet search of the times of sunset of 28 May and dawn 29 May: https://www.worldweatheronline.com/akka-weather-history/hazafon/il.aspx.

12. For example in 'Abdu'l-Bahá, *Memorials of the Faithful,* p. 35.

13. Summary permitted by the Universal House of Justice, as advised to author on 16 June 2022. See also Adib Taherzadeh, *The Covenant of Bahá'u'lláh,* p. 148, in which the author outlines the Master's description of events immediately before and after the ascension.

14. Provisional translation by Fuad Izadinia approved for use in this volume by the Universal House of Justice on 16 June 2022.

To hear this poem chanted in Persian: https://www.youtube.com/watch?v=OVpahD-OICo.

15. The Will and Testament of Bahá'u'lláh had yet to be opened and read.

16. Shoghi Effendi, *God Passes By*, p. 222. H. M. Balyuzi, *King of Glory*, p. 420, confirms it was the Master Who sent the telegram.

17. Bahá'í historian Hasan Balyuzi said 'Abdu'l-Ḥamíd and Náṣiri'd-Dín Sháh, of Iran, "were jubilant" at the news of the passing of Bahá'u'lláh. H. M. Balyuzi, *King of Glory*, p. 420.

18. The Ottomans took over the Holy Land in 1516, and but for a period between 1831 and 1840 when the Egyptians were in control, had ruled it ever since. The Empire officially ended in 1922.

19. Lady Blomfield, *The Chosen Highway*, p. 105. Because the Master was in charge, only He could direct the horseman. This book includes a report by Ṭúbá Khánum, a daughter of 'Abdu'l-Bahá, who was twelve years old at the time.

20. H. M. Balyuzi, *King of Glory*, p. 425.

21. Shoghi Effendi, *God Passes By*, p. 222. The originals of these telegrams have yet to be located.

22. There is no report yet located that the site for the shrine had been decided prior to the ascension.

23. Shoghi Effendi, *God Passes By*, p. 222.

24. Baharieh Rouhani Ma'ani, *Leaves of the Twin Divine Trees*, p. 256. He was a nephew of the wife of the Báb, Khadíjih-Bagum. It was the first marriage between an Afnán and a member of Bahá'u'lláh's family. Ibid., p. 26. He was to become a Covenant-breaker, to confess and repent, and to become one again. See also Adib Taherzadeh, *The Child of the Covenant*, p. 146. One of his sons was to be the greatest enemy of Shoghi Effendi during his ministry as the Guardian. See ibid., p. 308.

25. H. M. Balyuzi, *'Abdu'l-Bahá*, p. 47.

26. Ḥájí Mírzá Siyyid Ḥasan-i-Afnán-i-Kabír (the Great Afnán) See the eulogy to him by the Master in, 'Abdu'l-Bahá, *Memorials of the Faithful*, pp. 21–23. The house had been the home of the Great Afnán (H. M. Balyuzi, *'Abdu'l-Bahá*, p. 56). Balyuzi also says

that the Great Afnán was dead at the time of the ascension, which appears incorrect. See 'Abdul-Bahá, *Memorials of the Faithful*, p. 23.

27. H. M. Balyuzi, *'Abdu'l-Bahá*, p. 47.

28. The mosque remains there to this day.

29. Lady Blomfield, *The Chosen Highway*, p. 106. This book printed a report by a daughter of the Master, Ṭúbá Kh͟ánum (1880–1959), who was twelve years old at the time. Ṭúbá Kh͟ánum later married Mírzá Muḥsin, who was a son of the Great Afnán. He passed away in 1927 and was lauded by Shoghi Effendi as a "distinguished servant" of the Cause. However, Ṭúbá, along with her three sons and daughter, was named a Covenant-breaker by the Guardian. Ṭúbá Kh͟ánum, as well as other relatives, later allied herself with the Arab population and left for Lebanon during hostilities that broke out after the formation of Israel in 1948. They integrated themselves into Islamic society. See Adib Taherzadeh, *The Child of the Covenant*, pp. 305, 307–8. See also *The Covenant of Bahá'u'lláh*, chapter 32.

30. Lady Blomfield, *The Chosen Highway*, p. 105. Ṭúbá Kh͟ánum described how her Father and her aunt (the Greatest Holy Leaf) went to Bahjí during Bahá'u'lláh's illness, and then a few days later, Munírih Kh͟ánum and the four daughters went there too.

31. Baharieh Rouhani Ma'ani, *Leaves of the Twin Divine Trees*, p. 156.

32. Known as Kh͟án-i-'Avámíd or Kh͟án-i-Juraynī.

33. The new arrivals who had not yet had a chance to attain His presence also went. Those present included 'Andalíb and the blind poet, Baṣṣár (Mírzá Baqir Bihis͟htí). [See Lady Blomfield, *The Chosen Highway*, p. 105, quoting Ṭúbá Kh͟ánum.] Mírzá 'Alí-Asg͟har and his brother and Dr. Ḥájí Mírzá Muḥammad-'Alí Kh͟án of S͟híráz were also there.

34. Parivash Samandarí (Khoshbin), *Ṭaráz-i-Iláhí*, two volumes, a biography on The Hand of The Cause Mr. Ṭarázu'lláh Parivash Samandarí (Khoshbin), *Ṭaráz-i-Iláhí*, vol. I, pp. 101–25, translated by Dr. Rostam Beheshti.

35. Parivash Samandarí (Khoshbin), *Ṭaráz-i-Iláhí*, Vol. I, pp. 119–22. Mr. Samandarí's words translated and/or summarized for the author in 2020 by Dr. Rostam Beheshti, a former custodian of the Shrine of Bahá'u'lláh. Samandarí wrote that he had beaten his head and face so much he could hardly hold his head upright. He was suicidal. "I was so devastated I felt and became determined to end my life by committing suicide. I was planning in my mind one of the three ways of achieving my aim—one was to drown myself in the sea, another to jump off a rooftop or thirdly strangle myself with my waist shawl. I decided to choose the third option because the sea was far away and knew no appropriate rooftop where people would not notice me. So I was searching for a quiet place, away from the crowd to fulfil my intention of strangling myself. The effulgence of the figure of 'Abdu'l-Bahá kept appearing as He was going in or out of a room. On seeing Him, I would calm down and reassure myself but then seeing the depth of His grievances, I would become even more determined. At the same time I noticed that everywhere I went two friends, Mírzá Núru'd-Dín, the son of Zaynu'l-Muqarrabín and Mírzá Ḥabíbu'lláh, son of Áqá Riḍá Qand-i-Shírází, were following me but I didn't realize their purpose." He commented: "It was then that I was told that The Master had arranged that the two men accompanied me wherever I went to make sure I didn't harm myself. Only the people who are just and fair minded will be able to understand how our Beloved Master, the unmatched leader and the shepherd of the flock of the followers of The Blessed Beauty, at that particular moment of time, while the storm of grief and the fire of the disastrous event had overtaken Him, had thought of an unimportant individual and lowly servant like me giving protection under the wings of His mercy and affection."

36. Parivash Samandarí (Khoshbin), *Ṭaráz-i-Iláhí*, vol. I, pp. 119–22. From Mr. Samandarí's diary. Dated, 2nd. of Zi-Qaddeh 1309 Hijrí Qamarí (28 May 1892).

37. Shoghi Effendi, *God Passes By*, p. 222. The Guardian translated an account by Nabíl-i-A'ẓam.

38. Translation by the late Ahang Rabbani. For the complete poem, see: https://bahai-library.com/rabbani_andalib_bahaullahs_ascension.

Chapter 20: The Establishment of the Shrine of Bahá'u'lláh

1. Baharieh Rouhani Ma'ani, *Leaves of the Twin Divine Trees*, p. 157.

2. "The preparation for the body for burial is a careful washing, and placing in a shroud of white cloth, silk preferably. There is nothing in the teachings with regard to turning the body over to scientific institutions for scientific research, and therefore the individual may do as he wishes, until such a time as the Universal House of Justice may legislate on this matter, if they ever do. The practice in the Orient, is to bury the person within 24 hours of the time of death; sometimes even sooner; although there is no provision in the teachings as to the time limit." (From a letter written on behalf of the Guardian to an individual believer, April 2, 1955.)

3. Parivash Samandarí (Khoshbin), *Ṭaráz-i-Iláhí.*

4. An account of his funeral has yet to be located. 'Abdu'l-Bahá wrote a beautiful eulogy to him: *Memorials of the Faithful*, pp. 86–90.

5. "There is no provision in the Kitáb-i-Aqdas determining the finger on which the burial ring should be placed." (From a letter written on behalf of the Universal House of Justice, dated 13 March 1978, to a National Spiritual Assembly, in *Bahá'í Burial.*)

6. See The Kitáb-i-Aqdas, Notes, no. 149.

7. During an interview conducted by the late Lori Ubben at the Seat of the Universal House of Justice on 18 January 1989 with Mrs. Hayat Jarráh, Ms. Ubben, who transcribed the interview on 23 May 1989, told Mrs. Jarráh that Dr. David Ruhe [an esteemed Bahá'í historian, author, and member of the Universal House of Justice 1968–93] had told her he had retrieved from Covenant-breakers the table said by Amín Jarráh [Hayat's maternal grandfather, the mayor of 'Akká] to be the one that Bahá'u'lláh's body was washed on, and that it was now underneath at the Mansion of Bahjí. The transcript

was emailed to the author by her descendant, Abdul Jarráh, on 26 April 2020.

According to information attached to a letter from the Department of the Secretariat at the Bahá'í World Center to the author, dated 13 October 2020: "A table returned by the Covenant-breakers and purported to be the one on which Bahá'u'lláh's body was washed after His Ascension exists at the World Centre. We have not been able to verify whether Bahá'u'lláh's body was in fact washed on this table after His Ascension." A table was also used for the washing of the body of The Purest Branch by Shaykh Maḥmúd in 1870, assisted by Bahá'u'lláh's cousin Mírzá Ḥasan-i-Mázindarání. These details are from a summary of notes of Ḥusayn-i-Áshchí in his unpublished memoirs. Adib Taherzadeh, *The Revelation of Bahá'u'lláh,* vol. 3, p. 209.

8. Parivash Samandarí (Khoshbin), *Ṭaráz-i-Iláhí,* vol. I, pp. 119–22. Mr. Samandarí's words are translated and summarized by Dr. Rostam Beheshti.

9. For information on Shaykh Maḥmúd Arrabí, see David S. Ruhe, *Door of Hope,* pp. 199–203, in which the author draws on accounts in Lady Blomfield, *The Chosen Highway.* See also H. M. Balyuzi, *King of Glory* and *'Abdu'l-Bahá.*

10. David S. Ruhe, *Door of Hope,* p. 203. In a footnote on p. 209 of *The Revelation of Bahá'u'lláh,* vol. 3, Adib Taherzadeh writes: "In Islamic countries the body of the dead is washed before being wrapped in a shroud. There are men in every city whose profession is to wash the dead."

11. Historian Baharieh Rouhani Ma'ani has written concerning the washing of the body of the Purest Branch: "The traditional restrictions on women probably compelled Ásíyih Khánum [his mother] to remain on the upper floor of the barracks, where the family lived, and mourn the loss of her beloved son away from where his body was being washed." *Leaves of the Twin Divine Trees,* pp. 110–11.

12. The Master recounted the time when He entered Bahá'u'lláh's room and saw all His papers were scattered on the ground. The

Master was starting to put them, along with Bahá'u'lláh's several seals, together in two satchels when in walked Mírzá Majdi'd-Dín, a son-in-law and nephew of the Manifestation, who later became, as Shoghi Effendi was to write, the Master's "most redoubtable adversary" and "Arch-Breaker of Bahá'u'lláh's Covenant." Shoghi Effendi, *Messages to the Bahá'í World*, pp. 87–88. The distressed 'Abdu'l-Bahá told Mírzá Majdi'd-Dín to help to put the papers in the satchels. Then Bahá'u'lláh said to the Master: "These belong to you," presumably in front of Mírzá Majdi'd-Dín. The author is grateful to Dr. Steven Phelps for advising that the most appropriate word in English is "satchel."

13. For an account of this incident, see Adib Taherzadeh, *The Covenant of Bahá'u'lláh,* pp. 148–50. See also 'Abdu'l-Bahá, *Selections of the Writings of 'Abdu'l-Bahá,* no. 5. Muḥammad-'Alí (1853–1937), a half-brother of the Master, was the son of Bahá'u'lláh and His second wife, Fáṭimih Khánum (Mahd-i-'Ulyá). He disobeyed the Will of Bahá'u'lláh and opposed 'Abdu'l-Bahá as Head of the Faith. Referring to him, Shoghi Effendi, wrote in *God Passes By,* p. 249: "He it was who, as testified by Mírzá Badí'u'lláh in his confession, written and published on the occasion of his repentance and his short-lived reconciliation with 'Abdu'l-Bahá, had, while Bahá'u'lláh's body was still awaiting interment, carried off, by a ruse, the two satchels containing his Father's most precious documents, entrusted by Him, prior to His ascension, to 'Abdu'l-Bahá."

14. In accordance with guidance from the Universal House of Justice, this is not a direct quote but rather a paraphrase of part of the Tablet as translated for the author by Fuad Izadinia. For an account of this incident, see Adib Taherzadeh, *The Covenant of Bahá'u'lláh,* pp. 148–50.

15. Ṭarázu'lláh Samandarí recounted that Mírzá Ḍíyá'u'lláh, a son of Bahá'u'lláh, had told him that Bahá'u'lláh had informed him (Mírzá Ḍíyá'u'lláh) during the time of His sickness that He had written in His own pen a Tablet and had sealed it and given it to the Most Great Branch ('Abdu'l-Bahá), spelling out in that Tablet every necessary thing that should be done.

16. Baharieh Rouhani Ma'ani, *Leaves of the Twin Divine Trees,* p. 238. During the day some women who were not members of the Bahá'í community visited the Mansion to offer condolences and had asked who the successor to Bahá'u'lláh was. They were told, wrongly, that it was 'Abdu'l-Bahá's half-brother Muḥammad-'Alí. It was clear that already there were some who were trying to undermine the Master. Ibid., pp. 239–40, quoting letter of Ḥájí Muḥammad Ḥusayn-i-Tabrízí to Jináb-i-Áqá Khalíl, p. 5.

17. Bahá'u'lláh, The Kitáb-i-Aqdas, ¶130. This provision continues "For those whose means are limited a single sheet of either fabric will suffice."

18. Ibid., Notes, p. 230. At present Bahá'ís are free to use their judgement in the matter.

19. Ibid., *Questions and Answers,* no. 56, p. 123.

20. Bahá'u'lláh had given the Master that mitre. See Michael V. Day, *Journey to a Mountain,* p. 125. Recollections by John and Louise Bosch in Marzieh Gail, "'Abdu'l-Bahá: Portrayals from East and West" reprinted in Marzieh Gail, *Dawn over Mount Hira,* p. 213.

21. A reference to this has yet to be located, but given the preceding funerals of three family figures, no doubt a suitably engraved burial ring was either available or could have been quickly arranged.

22. Parivash Samandarí (Khoshbin), *Ṭaráz-i-Iláhí.* The wooden coffin of Bahá'u'lláh's first wife, Ásíyih Khánum, which was recovered intact at her exhumation, is present in a small room on the upper floor of the Mansion of Bahjí and may be viewed by pilgrims and visitors.

23. Report of the events in the Master's House after His ascension by John Bosch, a pilgrim who assisted with placing the Master's body in His coffin. His report is in the Bosch Papers, US National Bahá'í Archives. Angelina Diliberto Allen, *John David Bosch: In the Vanguard of Heroes, Martyrs, and Saints.* Wilmette, IL: Bahá'í Publishing, 2019.

24. The author is grateful to Baharieh Rouhani Ma'ani for this information.

25. H. M. Balyuzi, *'Abdu'l-Bahá,* p. 47.

26. Samandarí wrote later in his diary: "I arrived and joined the friends at the time while still the casket was being carried down in the stairway." Parivash Samandarí (Khoshbin), *Ṭaráz-i-Iláhí.*

27. Bahá'u'lláh's coffin would not have been long, given His physical stature (said in Rúḥíyyih Rabbani, *The Priceless Pearl,* pp. 6–7, to be about the same as that of the beloved Guardian).

28. H. M. Balyuzi, *'Abdu'l-Bahá,* p. 47. He does not mention a far longer route, through the main southern gate and then along the space between the mansion and the buildings to its west.

29. The description was based on (i) an eyewitness report of parts of the event by Ṭarázu'lláh Samandarí; (ii) a brief report in Shoghi Effendi's book *God Passes By;* (iii) reports by the Angel of Carmel and Dr. Yúnis Khán on how the Master conducted the observance of the Ascension Holy Day at Bahjí in future years; (iv) an estimation of the buildings and their relation to each other at the time of the ascension (v) taking into account the time of the event (after sunset on the day on which Bahá'u'lláh ascended); (vi) taking into account the lighting technology at the time; (vii) an understanding of the presence of animals and nearby trees; (viii) how the Master's own funeral was conducted; (ix) consultations with contemporary Bahá'ís.

30. Although a description of how the cortege was organized after the ascension of Bahá'u'lláh has not yet been found, we have clues as to a possibility. We are told about the Master's organization of the friends on two holy days commemorating the Ascension of Bahá'u'lláh. The first is by Ḥájí Mírzá Ḥaydar-'Alí in *Stories from the Delight of Hearts,* pp. 146–47: ". . . the Master prepared two hundred lanterns. One of these contained twenty candles, and each of the others two candles. It was about sunset when the same procession of friends, carrying these lanterns, made their way to Bahjí. It happened that we passed a camp of soldiers. The officers stood in their places and paid their respect to the Master. We were all in tears. When we reached the Shrine there were two rows of worshippers: the friends in one row, and the officers and soldiers in the other. Everyone was in tears. When the pilgrimage came to

an end, the officers encircled the Master. They were served tea and refreshments. This was one of the most memorable nights of my life. Every particle in the air and on the earth seemed both to absorb and reflect the glory and majesty of the Kingdom of God...On that evening, 'Abdu'l-Bahá remained awake all night. The friends could not separate themselves from Him and gathered in the Pilgrim House adjacent to the Shrine. Sometimes tea or coffee was served. . . ." Dr. Yúnis Khán also described a later commemoration of the anniversary of the ascension of Bahá'u'lláh when the Master chanted inside the shrine after the friends, two by two, had approached that place "solemnly and with great dignity." Dr. Khán wrote: "As he chanted, as always tears flowed from his eyes. . . . We all wept aloud with Him. . . ." Quoting from Kháṭirat-i-Nuh-Sáliy-i-'Akká in, Adib Taherzadeh, *The Covenant of Bahá'u'lláh*, pp. 186, 189. See also Dr. Youness Afroukhteh, *Memories of Nine Years in 'Akká*, p. 61.

Although the author is confident the description is accurate in general terms, it might be adjusted somewhat if more details come to hand in future years. The author was advised by the Universal House of Justice on 13 October 2020 that ". . . beyond what is generally known and available, any possible additional material that may exist in the Archives at the Bahá'í World Centre about the Shrine of Bahá'u'lláh has not yet been reviewed, a step that, owing to limited resources, can only take place in the future. . . ."

31. In the years that followed, after sustained difficulties caused by internal malicious power-seekers, 'Abdu'l-Bahá's hair and beard were to turn silver, and His health suffered.

32. Islamic and Jewish traditions were similar in that respect. Email to author from Baharieh Rouhani Ma'ani, May 2020.

33. For a description of such practice, see: Adib Taherzadeh, *The Covenant of Bahá'u'lláh*, p. 189. On p. 19 Yúnis Khán reports: "The Tablet of Visitation would be chanted as usual by 'Abdu'l-Bahá."

34. Adib Taherzadeh, *The Revelation of Bahá'u'lláh*, vol. 3, p. 351.

35. The Master used to chant this Tablet on the anniversary of the martyrdom of the Báb. See also *Lights of Guidance*, no. 1665: "Imám

Ḥusayn has, as attested by the Kitáb-i-Íqán been endowed with special grace and power among the Imáms, hence the mystical reference to Bahá'u'lláh as the return of Imám Ḥusayn, meaning the Revelation in Bahá'u'lláh of those attributes with which Imám Ḥusayn had been specifically endowed." (From a letter written on behalf of Shoghi Effendi to an individual believer, July 30, 1941.) See also: https:// bahai-library.com/bahaullah_fananapazir_visitation_husayn.

36. Shoghi Effendi, *God Passes By*, p. 222. In his notes published long after the Guardian wrote *God Passes By*, Mr. Samandarí, an eyewitness, wrote: "However that sorrowful day passed and at sunset, the builders and the laborers got busy digging the ground and preparing the room in which the earthly remains of our Beloved were to be to rest. By about two hours after sunset the place was quickly and with full force made ready for the burial. All the non-Bahá'ís had left by then." Parivash Samandarí (Khoshbin), *Ṭaráz-i-Iláhí.*

37. Pilgrims do not enter the inner shrine. There is no prescribed ritual at the threshold of the shrine, but the custom is to kneel, and then bow low while praying. There is time to gaze with reverence into the precincts of the inner shrine. This is their opportunity to supplicate to and commune with their Creator while they are within but a short distance from the resting place of the Manifestation of God.

When Holy Day observances are held within the precincts of the shrine, Bahá'ís stand and face the shrine when the Tablet of Visitation is being recited. "The pilgrimage to the Shrines of Bahá'u'lláh and the Báb . . . is considered as one of the greatest bounties which the soul may receive on this earth." Adib Taherzadeh, *The Revelation of Bahá'u'lláh,* vol. 4, p. 165.

38. Shoghi Effendi, *God Passes By,* p. 369: "In the Holy Land, where a Bahá'í cemetery had, before these pronouncements, been established during 'Abdu'l-Bahá's ministry, the historic decision to bury the Bahá'í dead facing the Qiblih in 'Akká was taken—a measure whose significance was heightened by the resolution to cease having recourse, as had been previously the case, to any Muḥammadan court in all matters affecting marriage and divorce, and to

carry out, in their entirety and without any concealment whatever, the rites prescribed by Bahá'u'lláh for the preparation and burial of the dead. This was soon after followed by the presentation of a formal petition addressed by the representatives of the local Bahá'í community of Haifa, dated May 4, 1929, to the Palestine Authorities, requesting them that, pending the adoption of a uniform civil law of personal status applicable to all residents of the country irrespective of their religious beliefs, the community be officially recognized by them and be granted "full powers to administer its own affairs now enjoyed by other religious communities in Palestine."

39. Parivash Samandarí (Khoshbin), *Ṭaráz-i-Iláhí*, vol. I, pp. 101–25, translated by Dr. Rostam Beheshti.

Chapter 21: Days of Mourning

1. Lady Blomfield, *The Chosen Highway*, p. 107. The prayers of Bahá'u'lláh were known as "Munáját."

2. David S. Ruhe, *Door of Hope*, p. 203.

3. Ibid., p. 203

4. Shoghi Effendi, *Messages to the Bahá'í World*, p. 46.

5. Ibid., *God Passes By*, p. 222.

6. Ibid.

7. Ibid.

8. The spoken chronicle of Ṭúbá Khánum, in Lady Blomfield, *The Chosen Highway*, p. 106. "This is an Arab custom: the idea is, that as these gifts are distributed to the poor, they will, in return, pray for the soul of the departed."

9. Both Sunní and Shí'ah branches of Islam.

10. Lady Blomfield, *The Chosen Highway*, p. 106.

11. There was deep mutual regard between Bahá'u'lláh and the Druze. Historian Hasan Balyuzi writes: "Bahá'u'lláh had once lived for three months among these friendly people [the Druze] in the foothills of the Galilee. The room in the house of Shaykh Mazruq, which He had occupied, was always left untenanted." H. M. Balyuzi, *'Abdu'l-Bahá*, p. 411. Other historians note the names of the Druze villages He visited—Abu-Sinan and Yerkih. Moojan

Momen, *Bahá'u'lláh: A Short Biography,* p. 127; David S. Ruhe, *Door of Hope,* p. 124.

12. Shoghi Effendi, *God Passes By,* p. 223. The enemies of the Faith were celebrating the demise of One even they called great despite their implacable hatred for Him and His Cause. The Master later wrote: "For, according to what was heard, the enemies in some of the lands, upon receiving the news of the most great disaster, held banquets. They rejoiced and made merry, celebrated festivals, burned incense, served sweets and flowers, lit many a candle, mixed honey and wine, played lutes and harps, spent that evening in cheerfulness and gladness until dawn, and sought delight and pleasure." 'Abdu'l-Bahá, quoted in *Star of the West,* vol. viii, p. 13.

13. Baharieh Rouhani Ma'ani, *Leaves of the Twin Divine Trees,* p. 157. The report was translated from the unpublished memoirs of Mrs. Murassa Rouhani. Ibid., p. 397.

14. Ibid., p. 156. The report was translated from the unpublished memoirs of Mrs Rafí'ih Shahídí, whose family resided in the Holy Land at the time of Bahá'u'lláh's ascension. Ibid., p. 397.

15. This is virtually certain to have been the case. The two other balconies faced buildings—quite close in the case of the northern one—but the southern one looked out over fields where people could gather.

16. Shoghi Effendi, *God Passes By,* p. 223.

17. John Walbridge, *Sacred Acts, Sacred Space, Sacred Time,* p. 243. He notes that Ya'qub al-Lubnani was one of the Bustanis, a famous Christian Lebanese family.

18. Jinab-i-Abu'l-Fada'il, *Al-Fara'id,*.The author is grateful to Muna Waters, a member of the Tasmanian Bahá'í community, for this translation from Arabic into English, 15 May 2020.

19. Jináb-i-Abu'l-Faḍl, *Al-Fara'id.* The author is grateful to Muna Waters, for this translation from Arabic into English, 17 June 2021.

Chapter 22: Facets of a Jewel

1. Shoghi Effendi described the Tablet thus: "The Tablet of Visitation is a compilation of words of Bahá'u'lláh, revealed at dif-

ferent times for those who were far from Him, made by Nabíl, at the Master's instruction, after the Ascension of Bahá'u'lláh. . . ." (From a letter written on behalf of Shoghi Effendi, dated 7 July 1945, in *Unfolding Destiny*, p. 443.)

2. From 1909, the Master also chanted the Tablet of Visitation in the Shrine of the Báb.

3. For more on Tablets of Visitation, pilgrimage, and other visits, see a presentation by the late Ahang Rabbani: https://bahai-library.com/pdf/r/rabbani_pilgrimage_presentation.pdf.

4. Ashgabat ('Is͟hqábád) is the capital of Turkmenistan.

5. Shoghi Effendi, *God Passes By*, p. 3.

6. 'Abdu'l-Bahá, *Memorials of the Faithful*, pp. 35–36.

7. Ibid., p. 36. His original name was Mullá Muḥammad-i-Zarandí (1831–92), and he was also known as Nabíl-i-Zarandí.

8. Nabíl included his completed text in his *Táríkh Ṣu'úd Ḥaḍrat-i-Bahá'u'lláh hamrah ba Mat͟hnaví: Mullá Muḥammad–'Alí Zarandí* [History of the Ascension of Bahá'u'lláh along with Mat͟hnaví styled couplets of Mulla Muḥammad–'Alí Zarandí].

9. *'Andalíb*, no. 7, published in 1983. The origin is mentioned in Is͟hráq K͟hávarí, *Muhazirat*, vol. 3, pp. 348–49.

10. The whole Tablet is available to consult in the book of *Mubin*, vol. 1, p. 447.

11. Baharieh Rouhani Ma'ani, the author of *Leaves of the Twin Divine Trees*, notes on p. 405, fn 17, that this was her formal name according to M. A. Faizi, *Ḥaḍrat-i-Bahá'u'lláh*, p. 9. Author Ma'ani notes on p. 264 that "All the Tablets addressed to 'Uk͟ht (Sister), unless followed by a name identifying another of Bahá'u'lláh's sisters, are believed to have been revealed in honour of Sárih K͟hánum, who was explicitly referred to as 'Uk͟ht." Baharieh Rouhani Ma'ani, citing Arbab, *Akhtaran-i-Taban*, vol. 1, p. 117, notes that there is a reference to Sárih K͟hánum having a Qu'rán purportedly in the name of Imám 'Alí, and therefore precious, which she presented to the Prime Minister of Iran to spare Bahá'u'lláh's life. She notes, p. 260: "Thus Bahá'u'lláh had two sisters with whom He shared both parents and five half-sisters with whom He shared only one parent.

Two of the half-sisters were from His mother's side and three from His father's side." Bahá'u'lláh once said of Sárih's resting place: "He who visiteth 'Ukht and Masih in Rayy, it is as though he hath visited me." Ibid., p. 269. The author refers to a provisional translation approved for her book of Malik-i husrawvi, *Iqlim-I Nur*, p. 151.

12. Baharieh Rouhani Ma'ani, *Leaves of the Twin Divine Trees*, p. 264, and, importantly, fn 7, p. 404.

13. There are other topics of supplication too in that segment. It seems that the statement in *Muhazirat* that it is from the Tablet of Visitation for the Wife of the Báb is not correct (a statement also seen in John Walbridge, *Sacred Acts, Sacred Space, Sacred Time*, p. 122).

14. The Tablet can be found in *'Andalíb*, no. 71, 1999, p. 20, registered in the Persian Archives under no. 9282. Dr. Ahang Rabbani wrote in a presentation that the author Ishráq Khávarí mistakenly thoughts the final extract, paragraph 7, came from Bahá'u'lláh's Tablet of Visitation for Khadíjih-Bagum (the widow of the Báb): https://bahai-library.com/pdf/r/rabbani_pilgrimage_presentation.pdf.

Chapter 23: The Crimson Book

1. Shoghi Effendi, *God Passes By*, p. 238.

2. Ibid., p. 238.

3. Muḥammad-'Alí (1853–1937) was called by Shoghi Effendi "the Arch-Breaker "of the Covenant of Bahá'u'lláh.

4. A candy maker, also known as Áqá Riḍá, who was a devoted servant of Bahá'u'lláh in Baghdád, Adrianople, and Bahjí). See Adib Taherzadeh, *The Revelation of Bahá'u'lláh*, vol. 2, pp. 403–4; vol. 1, pp. 288–89; 'Abdu'l-Bahá, *Memorials of the Faithful*, pp. 39–41.

5. The title Kitáb-i-'Ahd is used in Bahá'u'lláh, *Tablets of Bahá'u'lláh*, p. 217. It was also known as the Kitáb-i-'Ahdí, "the Book of My Covenant."

6. Shoghi Effendi, *God Passes By*, p. 238.

7. Majdi'd-Dín, a cousin of the Master, married Sádhijíyyih, Bahá'u'lláh's daughter. He later became a Covenant-breaker. His

father, Mírzá Músá, surnamed *Áqáy-i-Kalím,* was the only full brother of Bahá'u'lláh. He remained a faithful follower of Bahá'u'lláh and died in 1887.

8. Parivash Samandarí (Khoshbin), *Ṭaráz-i-Iláhí.* Translated by Rostam Beheshti.

9. Shoghi Effendi, *God Passes By,* pp. 244–45. For more, see Paul Lample, *Revelation & Social Reality,* pp. 184–86, and Adib Taherzadeh, *The Covenant of Bahá'u'lláh.*

10. Descendants of Bahá'u'lláh (Ag͟hṣán) and of the Báb (Afnán).

11. Bahá'u'lláh, *Tablets of Bahá'u'lláh,* p. 221.

12. Ibid., pp. 242–43. Shoghi Effendi mentions the many Tablets of Bahá'u'lláh in which He refers glowingly to 'Abdu'l-Bahá, for example: Súriy-i-G͟huṣn; Tablet addressed to Ḥájí Muḥammad Ibráhím-i-Khalíl; Kitáb-i-Aqdas; Tablet to Mírzá Muḥammad Qulíy-i-Sabzivárí.

13. For the text, see *Tablets of Bahá'u'lláh,* pp. 219–23.

14. To read a summary of the provisions, see Shoghi Effendi, *God Passes By,* pp. 239–40.

15. 'Abdu'l-Bahá, *The Promulgation of Universal Peace,* pp. 455–56. Talk at Home of Mr. and Mrs. Edward B. Kinney, 780 West End Avenue, New York, 2 December 1912.

16. Baharieh Rouhani Ma'ani, *Leaves of the Twin Divine Trees,* p. 240.

17. In 2021, the following words of the Master appeared in a newly published collection of His Tablets: "And then the Tablet of the Year of Stress [The Lawḥ-i-Saniy-i-S͟hidád], which is the year of Bahá'u'lláh's ascension, was revealed and distributed in all regions. In it He clearly and unequivocally stated the severity of the tests and the profusion of the trials. Some time thereafter, the Book of the Covenant and Preserved Tablet of the Testament was revealed by the Supreme Pen, wherein all were bidden, by His clear and explicit behest, to turn unto it and to observe, obey, and follow it, so that when the ocean of the tests and trials of the Year of Stress came to surge, no soul would be perplexed, dismayed, or confused; so that the straight path, the undeviating way, and the manifest light would

become evident and clearly known; so that no room would be left for evil whisperings, no differences would arise, and the unity of the Word of God would be safeguarded." 'Abdu'l-Bahá, *Light of the World*, no. 65.

Chapter 24: A New Ministry

1. H. M. Balyuzi, *'Abdu'l-Bahá*, pp. 43–44: "It had rained and the ground was wet, but coming round the bend of the road into full sight of the Mansion, 'Abdu'l-Bahá prostrated Himself and laid His forehead on the sodden earth." In her book "Servant of Glory," Mary Perkins writes on page 89 about 'Abdu'l-Bahá walking to Bahjí on His weekly visits: "When in sight of the Mansion He would prostrate Himself, bending His forehead to the earth in humility."

2. Shoghi Effendi, *The World Order of Bahá'u'lláh*, p. 135.

3. Bahá'u'lláh, *Days of Remembrance*, p. 145.

4. Ḥájí Mírzá Ḥaydar-'Alí, *Stories from the Delight of Hearts*, p. 106.

5. Mírzá Badí'u'lláh, one of the Master's half-brothers who was present, confirmed this in an epistle of repentance: https://bahai-library.com/badiullah_epistle_bahai_world.

6. The seals were used to show the authenticity of a document.

7. Adib Taherzadeh, *The Covenant of Bahá'u'lláh*, p. 150. That author's father attained the presence of both Bahá'u'lláh and 'Abdu'l-Bahá.

8. Ibid., p. 150.

9. Shoghi Effendi, *The World Order of Bahá'u'lláh*, p. 97.

10. The Báb, *Selections from the Writings of the Báb*, no. 3.1.2.

11. Ishráq Khávarí, *Muhazirat*. Provisional translation by Fuad Izadinia approved with amendments. Email to the author from the Department of the Secretariat of the Universal House of Justice, 6 June 2020.

12. Paraphrase by the author of a translation by Fuad Izadinia.

13. Shoghi Efendi, *God Passes By*, p. 245.

14. 'Abdu'l-Bahá, *Selections from the Writings of 'Abdu'l-Bahá*, no. 5.1–4.

15. Shoghi Effendi, *God Passes By,* p. 245.

16. 'Abdu'l-Bahá, quoted in, The Universal House of Justice, *Synopsis and Codification of the Kitáb-i-Aqdas,* p. 61.

17. Hand of the Cause Leroy Ioas said the Guardian had told him this. Anita Ioas Chapman, *Leroy Ioas,* p. 163.

18. Bahá'u'lláh, The Kitáb-i-Aqdas. ¶6.

Bibliography

Works of Bahá'u'lláh

Epistle to the Son of the Wolf. 1st pocket-size ed. Translated by Shoghi Effendi. Wilmette, IL: Bahá'í Publishing Trust, 1988.

Gleanings from the Writings of Bahá'u'lláh. Translated by Shoghi Effendi. Wilmette, IL: Bahá'í Publishing, 2005.

The Hidden Words. Translated by Shoghi Effendi. Wilmette, IL: Bahá'í Publishing, 2002.

The Kitáb-i-Aqdas: The Most Holy Book. 1st pocket-size ed. Wilmette, IL: Bahá'í Publishing Trust, 1993.

The Kitáb-i-Íqán: The Book of Certitude. Translated by Shoghi Effendi. Wilmette, IL: Bahá'í Publishing, 2003.

Prayers and Meditations. Translated by Shoghi Effendi. 1st pocket-size ed. Wilmette, IL: Bahá'í Publishing Trust, 1987.

Tablets of Bahá'u'lláh revealed after the Kitáb-i-Aqdas. Compiled by the Research Department of the Universal House of Justice. Translated by Habib Taherzadeh et al. Wilmette, IL: Bahá'í Publishing Trust, 1988.

Works of the Báb

Selections from the Writings of the Báb. Compiled by the Research Department of the Universal House of Justice. Translated by Habib Taherzadeh et al. 1st pocket-sized ed. Wilmette, IL: Bahá'í Publishing Trust, 2006.

Works of 'Abdu'l-Bahá

Light of the World: Selected Tablets of 'Abdu'l-Bahá. Haifa: Bahá'í World Centre, 2021.

Memorials of the Faithful. Wilmette, IL: Bahá'í Publishing Trust, 1997.

The Promulgation of Universal Peace: Talks Delivered by 'Abdu'l-Bahá during His Visit to the United States and Canada in 1912. Compiled by Howard MacNutt. 2d ed. Wilmette, IL: Bahá'í Publishing, 2012.

Selections from the Writings of 'Abdu'l-Bahá. Compiled by the Research Department of the Universal House of Justice. Translated by a Committee at the Bahá'í World Center and Marzieh Gail. Wilmette, IL: Bahá'í Publishing, 2010.

Some Answered Questions. Haifa: Bahá'í World Centre, 2014.

"Tablet of One Thousand Verses." Provisional translation by Fuad Izadinia.

A Traveller's Narrative: Written to Illustrate the Episode of the Bab. Wilmette, IL: Bahá'í Publishing Trust, 1980.

Will and Testament of 'Abdu'l-Bahá. Wilmette, IL: Bahá'í Publishing Trust, 1944.

Works of Shoghi Effendi

Advent of Divine Justice. 1st pocket-size ed. Wilmette, IL: Bahá'í Publishing Trust, 1990.

The Bahá'í Faith 1844-1952, Information Statistical and Comparative. London: Bahá'í Publishing Trust, 1953.

Citadel of Faith: Messages to America, 1947–1957. Wilmette, IL: Bahá'í Publishing Trust, 1965.

God Passes By. New ed. Wilmette, IL: Bahá'í Publishing Trust, 1974.

Messages to the Bahá'í World, 1950–1957. Wilmette, IL: Bahá'í Publishing Trust, 1971.

The Passing of 'Abdu'l-Bahá. Written with Lady Blomfield. Haifa: Rosenfeld Bros, 1922.

This Decisive Hour: Messages from Shoghi Effendi to the North American Bahá'ís, 1932–1946. Wilmette, IL: Bahá'í Publishing Trust, 2002.

The World Order of Bahá'u'lláh. First pocket-sized edition. Wilmette, IL: Bahá'í Publishing Trust, 1991.

Works of, and on behalf of, the Universal House of Justice

Messages from the Universal House of Justice, 1968–1973. Haifa: Bahá'í World Centre, 1973.

The Ministry of the Custodians: An Account of the Stewardship of the Hands of the Cause. Haifa: Bahá'í World Centre, 1992.

Synopsis and Codification of the Laws and Ordinances of the Kitáb-i-Aqdas. Translated by Shoghi Effendi. Haifa: Bahá'í World Centre, 1973.

Wellspring of Guidance: Messages from the Universal House of Justice. Wilmette, IL: Bahá'í Publishing Trust, 1976.

Compilations of Bahá'í Writings

The Ascension of Bahá'u'lláh, A Compilation. Los Angeles: Kalimat Press, 1991.

Bahá'í Holy Places at the World Centre. Haifa: Bahá'í World Centre, 1968.

Bahá'í Prayers: A Selection of Prayers Revealed by Bahá'u'lláh, the Báb, and 'Abdu'l-Bahá. New ed. Wilmette, IL: Bahá'í Publishing Trust, 2002.

Other Works

'Abdu'l-Ḥusayn-i-Ávárih. *Al-Kavakibu's-Durriyyih fi Ma'athiri'l-Bahiyyih.* vol. 1, Cairo: Matba'atus's-Sa-adah, 1923.

Afroukhteh, Younness. *Memories of Nine Years in 'Akká.* Trans: Riaz Masrour. Oxford: George Ronald, 2003.

Ahang-e Badi, no. 7, p. 39, Year 20.

Allen, Angelina Diliberto. *John David Bosch: In the Vanguard of Heroes, Martyrs, and Saints.* Wilmette, IL: Bahá'í Publishing Trust, 2019.

Allen, Denny and Taherzadeh, Lesley. *Bahá'í Pilgrimage.* Oxford: George Ronald, 2005.

Bahá'í International Community. *Bahá'í Holy Places in Haifa and the Western Galilee.* Bahá'í World Centre, Haifa, 2005.

———. *Bahá'u'lláh.* New York, 1991.

Bahá'í News. Periodical. National Spiritual Assembly of the Bahá'ís of the United States and Canada. 1924.

Bahá'í Studies Review 1, "'Abdu'l-Bahá in Abu-Sinan, September 1914–May 1915," 2005.

The Bahá'í World: An International Record. Wilmette, IL: Bahá'í Publishing Trust, complete volumes.

———. *A compendium of Volumes of the Bahá'í World I–XII 1925–1954.* Compiled by Roger White, 1981.

———. *In Memoriam, 1992–1997.*

Balyuzi, H. M. *'Abdu'l-Bahá.* Oxford: George Ronald, 1971.

———. *The Báb.* Oxford: George Ronald, 1973.

———. *Bahá'u'lláh.* Oxford: George Ronald, 1963.

———. *Bahá'u'lláh: King of Glory.* Oxford: George Ronald, 1980.

———. *Edward Granville Browne and the Bahá'í Faith.* Oxford: George Ronald, 1970.

———. *Eminent Bahá'ís in the Time of Bahá'u'lláh.* Oxford: George Ronald, 1985.

Banná, Ustád 'Alí-'Akbar Unpublished manuscript.

Blainey, Geoffrey. *A Short History of the World.* Viking, 2000.

Blomfield, Lady. *The Chosen Highway.* London: Bahá'í Publishing Trust, 1940. Reprinted, Oxford: George Ronald, 2007.

Browne, Edward Granville. *A Year Amongst the Persians.* Facsimile edition. London: Adam and Charles Black, 1893.

———. *Materials for the Study of the Bábí Religion.* Cambridge University Press, 1918.

———. Introduction to *A Traveller's Narrative.* https://www.h-net.org/~bahai/diglib/books/A-E/B/browne/tn/tnfrnt.htm.

Buck, Christopher. "Edward Granville Browne (1882–1926)," *Bahá'í Studies Review,* vol. 20, 2014 (published 2018) https://bahai-library.com/buck_browne_british_writers.

Buck, Christopher and Ioannesyan, Youli. "Scholar Meets Prophet." https://bahai-library.com/buck_ioannesyan_scholar_prophet.

Cameron, Glenn and Momen, Wendi. *A Basic Bahá'í Chronology*. Oxford: George Ronald, 1996.

Chapman, Anita Ioas. *Leroy Ioas: A Hand of the Cause of God*. Oxford: George Ronald, 1998.

Dante, Alighieri. *The Divine Comedy. Inferno*. Translated by J. G. Nichols. Alma Classics reprint, 2020.

Day, Michael V. *Journey to a Mountain*. Oxford: George Ronald, 2017.

Esslemont, J. E. *Bahá'u'lláh and the New Era*. Wilmette, IL: Bahá'í Publishing, 2010.

Faizi, A. Q. *Milly: A Tribute to The Hand of the Cause of God Amelia E. Collins*. Oxford: George Ronald, 1977.

Faizi-Moore, May. *Faizi*. Oxford: George Ronald, 2013.

Fananapazir, Lameh. *A Companion to the Study of the Epistle to the Son of the Wolf*. Oxford: George Ronald, 2020.

Furútan, 'Alí-Akbar (compiler). *Stories of Bahá'u'lláh*. Oxford: George Ronald, 1986.

Gail, Marzieh. *Arches of the Years*. Oxford: George Ronald, 1991.

———. *Summon Up Remembrance*. Oxford: George Ronald, 1987.

———. *Khánum: The Greatest Holy Leaf*. Oxford: George Ronald, 1981.

———. *Dawn over Mount Hira*. Oxford: George Ronald, 1976.

Garis, M. R. *Martha Root: Lioness at the Threshold*. Wilmette IL: Bahá'í Publishing Trust, 1983.

Giachery, Ugo. *Shoghi Effendi: Recollections*. Oxford: George Ronald, 1973.

Gobineau (Comte de), Joseph Arthur. *Les religions et les philosophies dans l'Asie Centrale*. Forgotten Books, 2017.

Grundy, Julia M. *Ten Days in the Light of 'Akká*. Wilmette, IL: Bahá'í Publishing Trust, 1979.

Hafiz. *The Gift: Poems by Hafiz, the Great Sufi Master*. Renderings by Daniel Ladinsky. Penguin Books, 1999.

Handal, Boris. *Mírzá Mihdí*. Oxford: George Ronald, 2017.

———. *Varqá and Rúhu'lláh: 101 Stories of Bravery on the Move.* Boris Handal, 2020.

———. "The Religion of the Báb." Unpublished manuscript, 2021.

———. *A Trilogy of Consecration: The Courier, the Historian, and The Missionary.* Boris Handal, 2020.

Harari, Yuval Noah. *Homo Deus.* London: Harvell Secker, 2015.

Harper, Barron. *Lights of Fortitude.* Oxford: George Ronald, 2007.

Hassall, Graham. "Ambassador at the Court: The Life and Photography of Effie Baker." 1999: http://bahai-library.com/hassall_ambassador_court_baker&chapter=all.

Hatcher, John. *The Face of God Among Us.* Wilmette, IL: Bahá'í Publishing, 2010.

Ḥaydar-'Alí, Ḥájí Mírzá. *Stories from the Delight of Hearts: The memoirs of Ḥájí Mírzá Ḥaydar-'Alí.* Translated and abridged by A. Q. Faizi. Los Angeles: Kalimat Press, 1980.

Hobhouse, Penelope. *Gardens of Persia.* Glebe, NSW: Florilegium, 2003.

Hofman, David. *George Townshend.* Oxford: George Ronald, 1983.

———. *Bahá'u'lláh: the Prince of Peace.* Oxford: George Ronald, 1992.

Hogenson, Kathryn Jewett. *Lighting the Western Sky: The Hearst Pilgrimage and the Establishment of the Bahá'í Faith in the West.* Oxford: George Ronald, 2010.

Hornby, Helen. *Lights of Guidance.* Wilmette, IL: Bahá'í Publishing Trust, 1988.

Honnold, Annamarie K. *Vignettes from the Life of 'Abdu'l-Bahá.* Oxford: George Ronald, 1982.

Ḥusayn-i-Á<u>sh</u>chí. Unpublished memoirs.

Ioannnesyan, Youli. *The Development of the Bábí /Bahá'í Communities.* London: Routledge, 2017.

Izadinia, Fuad. "The Mansion of Mazra'ih." Unpublished manuscript.

Keith-Roach, Edward. *Pasha of Jerusalem, Memoirs of a District Commissioner under the British Mandate.* Edited by Paul Eedle. The Radcliffe Press, 1994.

Khadem, Javidukht. *Zikrullah Khadem: The Itinerant Hand of the Cause of God.* Wilmette, IL: Bahá'í Publishing Trust, 1990.

Khadem, Riaz. *Prelude to the Guardianship.* Oxford: George Ronald, 2015.

Khan, Janet *A. Prophet's Daughter: The Life and Legacy of Bahíyyih Khánum.* Wilmette, IL: Bahá'í Publishing, 2005.

Khasawneh, Diala. *Memoirs Engraved in Stone: Palestinian Urban Mansions.* Riwaq Centre for Architectural Conservation, 2007.

Kinross, Lord. *The Ottoman Centuries.* New York: Morrow Quill, 1977.

Khoosheh-ha-i Az Kharman-e Adab va Honar (Persian Society of Letters and Art). Khooshe-ha, vol. IV.

Khusravi, Malak. *Iqlim-e-Noor.*

Lample, Paul. *Revelation & Social Reality.* West Palm Beach, Florida: Palabra Publications, 2009.

Latimer, George Orr. *The Light of the World.* http://bahai-library.com/latimer_light_world.

Ma'ani, Baharieh Rouhani. *Leaves of the Twin Divine Trees.* Oxford: George Ronald, 2008.

Marcus, Della. *Her Eternal Crown: Queen Marie and the Bahá'í Faith.* Oxford: George Ronald, 2000.

Maxwell, Mary and Maxwell, May. "Haifa Notes of Shoghi Effendi's Words, 1937." http://bahai-library.com/maxwell_haifa_notes&chapter=1.

McLean, J. A. *A Celestial Burning: A Selective Study of the Writings of Shoghi Effendi.* New Delhi: Bahá'í Publishing Trust, 2012.

McPherson, James. *Abraham Lincoln.* Oxford University Press, 2009.

Merrick, David. "The Ascension of Bahá'u'lláh." https://www.paint-drawer.co.uk/david/folders/spirituality/bahai/Ascension%20of%20Bahaullah.pdf

Momen, Moojan (ed.). *The Bábí and Bahá'í Religions, 1844–1944.* Oxford: George Ronald, 1981.

Momen, Wendi (ed.). *A Basic Bahá'í Dictionary.* Oxford: George Ronald, 1989.

———. *Bahá'u'lláh: A Short Biography*. Oxford: One World, 2007.

———. (ed.) *Selections from the Writings of E. G. Browne on the Bábí and Bahá'í Religions*. Oxford: George Ronald, 1987.

———. "Browne, Edward Granville, 1995." https://bahai-library.com/momen_encyclopedia_browne

———. *The Bahá'í Communities of Iran, 1851–1921, vol. 1, The North of Iran*. Oxford: George Ronald, 2015.

Muhájir, Iran Furútan. *The Mystery of God*. Wilmette, IL: Bahá'í Publishing Trust, 2012.

Muhazirat, vol. 3.

Munírih Khánum. *Episodes in the Life of Munírih Khánum*. Translated by Ahmad Sohrab. Los Angeles: Persian American Publishing Company, 1924.

———. *Memoirs and Letters*. Translated by Sammireh Anwar Smith. Los Angeles: Kalimat Press, 1986. https://bahai-library.com/munirih_khanum_memoirs_letters.

Nabíl-i-A'ẓam. *The Dawn-Breakers: Nabíl's Narrative of the Early Days of the Bahá'í Revelation*. Wilmette, IL: Bahá'í Publishing Trust, 1999.

———. *Mathnaví of Nabíl*. Langenhain: National Committee for Publishing Bahá'í works in Arabic and Persian, 1995.

Nakhjavani, Ali. *Shoghi Effendi: The range and power of His Pen*. Rome: Casa Editrice Bahá'í, 2006.

———. *Shoghi Effendi: Author of Teaching Plans*. Actuo, Casa Editrice Bahá'í, 2007.

———. "World Order of Bahá'u'lláh: Six Talks on the Various Aspects of." https://bahai-library.com/nakhjavani_talks_world_order&chapter=1

Nakhjavani, Violette. *The Maxwells of Montreal, Early Years*. Oxford: George Ronald, 2011.

———. *Middle Years 1923–1937, Late Years 1937–1952*. Oxford: George Ronald, 2011.

Nash, Geoffrey. *From Empire to Orient*. London: I. B. Tauris & Co. Ltd, 2005.

National Bahá'í Education Task Force, US. *The Báb. Central Figures, vol. 3.* Wilmette, IL: Bahá'í Publishing Trust, 2004.

Perkins, Mary. *Servant of the Glory: The Life of 'Abdu'l-Bahá.* Oxford: George Ronald, 1999.

Phelps, Myron H. *The Master in 'Akká.* Los Angeles: Kalimat Press, 1985.

———. *Life and Teachings of Abbas Effendi.* New York and London: G. P. Putnam's Sons. The Knickerbocker Press, 1903. https://bahai-library.com/pdf/p/phelps_life_teachings_abbas_effendi.pdf.

Porter, Yves, *Palaces and gardens of Persia.* Flammarion, 2003.

Rabbani, Ahang. "Pilgrimage in Bahá'u'lláh's Writings." https://bahai-library.com/pdf/r/rabbani_pilgrimage_presentation.pdf

Rabbání, Rúḥíyyih. *The Priceless Pearl.* London: Bahá'í Publishing Trust, 1969.

———. *Poems of the Passing.* Oxford: George Ronald, 1996.

———. *Twenty-Five Years of the Guardianship.* Wilmette, IL. Bahá'í Publishing Committee, 1948. http://bahai ibrary.com/khanum_25_years_guardianship U.S. Originally published in *The Bahá'í World, Volume XI, 1946–1950,* pp. 113–126.

Rafati, Vahid. "Mulla Sadiq-i-Khurasani (Muqaddas)."

Redman, Earl. *Shoghi Effendi Through the Pilgrim's Eye.* Oxford: George Ronald, 2015.

https://bahai-library.com/rafati_mulla_sadiq_khurasani

———. Nabil-e Aẓam Zarandi, Mollá Moḥammad. https://iranicaonline.org/articles/nabil-zarandi

Randall-Winckler, Bahiyyih. *William Henry Randall: Disciple of 'Abdu'l-Bahá.* With M. R. Garis. Oxford: One World, 1996.

Rohani, Aziz. *Sweet and Enchanting Stories.* Incorporating in Section B, Dr. Zia Baghdadi's Memories. Juxta Press., 2005. http://juxta.com/wp-content/uploads/sweet_enchanting_electronic.pdf.

Root, Martha L. "White Roses of Persia, Part 1." *The Bahá'í Magazine,* vol. 23 (1932), pp. 71–74.

Ross, Edward Denison. *Both Ends of the Candle,* Faber & Faber, 1944.

Ruhe, David S. *Door of Hope: The Bahá'í Faith in the Holy Land.* Third revised edition. Oxford: George Ronald, 2015.

———. *Robe of Light.* Oxford: George Ronald, 1994.

Rumi, *The Essential Rumi.* Translated by Coleman Barks with John Moyne. Penguin Books, 1995.

Sachs, Toscanini. *Musician of Conscience.* New York: Liveright, 2017.

Salmání (Ustád Muḥammad-'Alíy-i-Salmání). *My Memories of Bahá'u'lláh.* Translated by Marzieh Gail. Los Angeles: Kalimat Press, 1982.

Samandarí (Khoshbin), Parivash. *Ṭaráz-i-Iláhí.* Two volumes. Biography on The Hand of The Cause, Mr. Ṭarázu'lláh Samandarí.

Samandarí, Ṭarázu'lláh. *Moments with Bahá'u'lláh. Memoirs of the Hand of the Cause of God Ṭarázu'lláh Samandarí.* Los Angeles: Kalimat Press, 1995.

Samuel, Edwin. *A Lifetime in Jerusalem: The Memoirs of the Second Viscount Samuel. Vallentine.* Mitchell, 1970.

Sears, William. *Thief in the Night.* Oxford: George Ronald, 1990.

Seow, Jimmy Ewe Huat. *The Pure in Heart.* Bahá'í Publications Australia, 1991.

Sheil, Mary. *Glimpses of Life and Manners in Persia.* (Facsimile.) London: John Murray, 1856.

Showers, Anita R. *Gardens of the Spirit: The History of the Gardens at the Bahá'í Holy Places in Haifa and 'Akká, Israel.* Bahá'í Publications Australia, 2010.

Sohrab, Ahmad. *Diary of Mirza Sohrab.* https://bahai-library.com/sohrab_diary_letters_1912-1915.

Star of the West, The Bahá'í Magazine, Periodical. 25 vols. 1910–1935. Vols. 1–14. Oxford: George Ronald, 1978. Online: http://bahai.works/Star_of_the_West.

Storrs, Ronald. *The Memoirs of Sir Ronald Storrs.* Arno Press, 1972.

Taherzadeh, Adib. *The Child of the Covenant.* Oxford: George Ronald, 2000.

———. *The Covenant of Bahá'u'lláh.* Oxford: George Ronald, 1995.

———. *The Revelation of Bahá'u'lláh.* Oxford: George Ronald, 1974–1987; vol. 1: Baghdad 1853–1863; vol. 2: Adrianople 1863–1868; vol. 3: 'Akká. The Early Years 1868–1877; vol. 4: Mazra'ih & Bahji 1877–92.

Thomas, James. "An Exposition on the Fire Tablet by Bahá'u'lláh," in *Lights of Irfán.* Wilmette, IL: Irfán Colloquia, 2002.

Tudor Pole, Wellesley. *Writing on the Ground.* London: Neville Spearman, 1968.

Vernon, Kathy. "Bahá'u'lláh's Garden: Jacksonville Florida, 1919–69." Unpublished manuscript. See http://bahai-library.com/vernon_bahaullahs_garden.

Walbridge, John. *Sacred Acts, Sacred Space, Sacred Time.* Oxford: George Ronald, 1996.

Weinberg, Robert. *Ethel Jenner Rosenberg.* Oxford: George Ronald, 1995.

———. *Lady Blomfield: Her Life and Times.* Oxford: George Ronald, 2012.

Wilhelm, Roy; Cobb, Stanwood; Coy, Genevieve. *In His Presence: Visits to 'Abdu'l-Bahá.* Los Angeles: Kalimat Press, 1989.

Wilson, A. N. *Victoria: A Life.* Atlantic Books, 2014.

Winckler, Bahiyyih Randall. *My Pilgrimage to Haifa, November 1919.* Wilmette, IL: Bahá'í Publishing Trust, 1996.

Yazbak, Mahmoud. *Haifa in the late Ottoman period, 1864–1914.* Brill, 1998.

Yazdi, Ali M. *Blessings beyond Measure.* Wilmette, IL: Bahá'í Publishing Trust, 1988.

Zamir, Brett (compiler). "A Traveller's Narrative, a Study Outline and Cross-Reference." See https://bahai-library.com/zamir_tn_crossreference.

Zarqání, Mírzá Maḥmúd. *Maḥmúd's Diary.* Translated by Mohi Sobhani with the assistance of Shirley Macias. Oxford: George Ronald, 1998.

Index

About the Author

Michael V. Day is a former award-winning newspaper journalist, lawyer, and diplomat. He was the editor of the *Bahá'í World News Service* at the Bahá'í World Center in Haifa, Israel (2003–2006).

He is the author of a trilogy telling the story of the Shrine of the Báb. *Journey to a Mountain* (1850–1921) appeared in 2017, *Coronation on Carmel* (1922–1963) in 2018, and *Sacred Stairway* (1963–2001) in 2019. Those books were published by George Ronald Publisher in the UK.

He has also personally published two Bahá'í histories in the form of photo books: *Queen of Carmel* and *Fragrance of Glory*.

Born in New Zealand, where he became a Bahá'í, Michael is now based in Australia, where he is undertaking Bahá'í history projects. www.michaelvday.com.